Sow Justice, Reaping Peace

Sowing Justice, Reaping Peace

Case Studies of Racial, Religious, and Ethnic Healing Around the World

Michael K. Duffey

NDEG
Resource Center

SHEED & WARD

Franklin, Wisconsin
Chicago

As an apostolate of the Priests of the Sacred Heart, a Catholic religious congregation, the mission of Sheed & Ward is to publish books of contemporary impact and enduring merit in Catholic Christian thought and action. The books published, however, reflect the opinion of their authors and are not meant to represent the official position of the Priests of the Sacred Heart.

2001

Sheed & Ward
7373 South Lovers Lane Road
Franklin, Wisconsin 53132
1-800-266-5564

Printed in the United States of America

Cover and interior design: GrafixStudio, Inc.

Library of Congress Cataloging-in-Publication Data

Duffey, Michael K., 1948–

    Sowing justice, reaping peace : case studies of racial, religious, and ethnic healing around the world / Michael K. Duffey.
       p. cm.
    Includes bibliographic references and index.
    ISBN 1-58051-102-3 (pbk.)
       1.Sociology, Christian (Catholic) 2. Christianity and justice—Catholic Church. 3. Peace—Religious aspects—Catholic Church. 4. Catholic Church—Doctrines. I. Title.

BX1753 .D84 2001
261.8—dc21   2001045860

1 2 3 4 5 / 04 03 02 01

Contents

Dedication

To Mary Beth, John, Teresa, Elizabeth, and Daniel

Acknowledgments

The people in this book are a "cloud of witnesses" to the possibility of overcoming injustice through love and forgiveness. Guatemalans, Filipinos, Northern Irish, Germans, Poles, South Africans, African Americans, and many others who have struggled courageously and patiently to heal their own societies have lessons to teach people everywhere. To those admirable citizens of the world, I am grateful.

Two colleagues at Marquette University, Shawn Copeland and Michael Fleet, brought their own expertise to bear on parts of this manuscript. The Department of Theology also supported the project through release time. Kristeen Bruun, my graduate assistant, spent countless hours reading drafts of the entire manuscript, offering a host of corrections and improvements in hot-pink ink. I am grateful for her help and encouragement.

The people of Sheed &Ward have been wonderfully supportive of this project. Jeremy Langford, co-publisher, encouraged me from the beginning, and Kass Dotterweich, managing editor, took the manuscript through its critical, careful editing, making many corrections and suggestions for clearer text. I am very grateful for their teamwork.

My wife, Mary Beth, a part-time professor, knows well the experience of injustice, and has a keen interest in the struggles for justice discussed in this book. Her countless acts of love and care for me, for our children, and for her many students are blessings for which I am deeply grateful. Together we watch our children preparing to venture into the wider world to make their contributions to life.

Introduction

Pope John Paul II described the Church's social teaching as the *"application* of the word of God to people's lives and the life of society, as well as to the earthly realities connected with them" (emphasis added). That body of teaching contains "principles for reflection," "criteria for judgment," and "directives for action."[1] Social teaching encourages Catholics and all Christian churches to analyze and critique every economic, political, and social structure in light of the Gospels. The economic, political, and social systems are human creations that human beings have the duty to continuously reform. Inspired by the gospel and the long tradition of Christian dialogue with many cultures, the Church's social teaching affirms human dignity, the right and duty of individuals to participate in the shaping of the common good, and the designation of material goods for meeting the needs of all.

This book examines the practices of justice, peace, and reconciliation going on around us. It looks particularly at the commitment and struggle of those whose response is connected with their Christian beliefs. Their acts of courage and compassion offer witness to other Christians to respond more fully to what baptism calls us to be and to do. They can inspire other Christians as well as people who do not share their faith.

Each chapter focuses on a regional social conflict involving combinations of violations of human and civil rights, economic exploitation, and violence. All involve suffering human beings seeking remedies for injustice and yearning to bring about peace. How have Christian church leaders and laity—both Catholic and Protestant, often in cooperation with non-Christians—responded to conflict and injustice in Northern Ireland, South Africa, Guatemala and Argentina, Poland, the Philippines, and the United States? How have they responded in nationalist battlegrounds of the former Yugoslavia, to the exploitation of women and children in sweatshops around the world?

Chapters one, two, and three examine the impact and legacy of colonialism on Central America, Northern Ireland, and South Africa. All three regions have struggled to overcome legacies of injustice in societies deeply divided. Chapter four examines successful nonviolent campaigns for democracy in Eastern Europe and in the Philippines. Chapters five and six address the obstacles and prospects for people to live as neighbors in two volatile parts of the world: the Balkans and the Middle East. Chapter seven considers the struggle for racial equality waged in the U.S. in the 1950s and 1960s. What is its legacy for the world? What is its unfinished agenda? Chapter eight reflects on the sources of widespread suffering of women and children on every continent. The powerful witness of women struggling for social justice and peace encourages us to do likewise.

Each chapter offers historical background to help readers understand the shape and intensity of present conflicts. The drama of the present involves those who identify with the oppressed and are struggling for their liberation contending with those whose interests depend on preserving the *status quo*. Readers meet some of the individuals in the forefront of the struggles. Although some of them have been recognized for their work, even receiving the Nobel Peace Prize, none of them stood or acted alone. They represent the many who stood up, stood firm, and sometimes gave their lives for justice and peace.

As U.S. citizens, we need to understand the experiences of our fellow citizens and the experiences of peoples beyond our own borders. Because we are a nation of immigrants, the contemporary struggles of people sometimes touch us closely. We may have relatives in these places. Our parents, grandparents, or great grandparents may have been involved in these struggles. As Christians, we need to "close the gap" that divides us from other people, people who need our solidarity as much as we need theirs.

Regardless of our personal connection, regardless of whether we are affluent or struggling, we all need a basis for hope. We live in a time when many negative forces bear down on us. The people and communities we encounter in these pages have plenty of cause for despair. But they have not permitted their vision to be defeated. They have kept hope alive in their communities. We, too, need to recognize what people are capable of doing even in unpromising situations. We need these witnesses of hope on our own journeys.

To assist in using *Sowing Justice, Reaping Peace* in social studies, history, religion, and ethics courses, an Appendix is provided containing questions, projects, and resources for further exploration.

Twentieth Century Catholic Social Teaching: A Brief History

The publication of "On the Condition of the Working Classes" by Pope Leo XIII in 1891 marked the beginning of the modern Catholic social tradition. In this powerful statement Pope Leo addressed issues of just compensation and dignified working conditions for workers in factories spawned by the Industrial Revolution. Since that time popes and bishops have addressed pressing issues of economic, political, and social development, and the severe problems of our time: poverty, war-making and militarism, violation of human rights, violence against women, exploitation of workers, and abuse of the environment.

By the turn of the twentieth century the Industrial Revolution had spawned impoverished working classes in Europe, Britain, and the U.S. Men, women, and children worked in abysmal conditions and lived in squalid housing. Fearing the loss of Catholics to Marxism, Pope Leo XIII championed workers and demanded just wages for their labors. The Church addressed the role of workers and owners of productive means, the obligation of governments to create a more just society, and the necessity of closing the gap between rich and poor. The Catholic Church took a mediating position in the debate between advocates of communism and capitalism, insisting that governments ought to intervene in the economy for the sake of the common good and yet protect the right of private ownership and freedom of economic initiative.

In 1931 the Church again spoke out on behalf of workers. Pope Pius XI criticized the structures of unrestrained capitalist and communist systems that enslave human beings. In "The Reconstruction of the Social Order," Pius insisted that governments must work for social justice by narrowing the wide gap between wealthy and impoverished social classes. But Pius did not advocate taking decision-making power away from individuals and communities and giving those powers to "big government." Instead, the Pope urged governments to protect the ability of smaller units of government and private enterprise to provide for the common good of their localities. *Subsidium* is the Latin word for "assist," which is why Pius's assertion is referred to as the "principle of subsidiarity."

In the late 1930s, in response to Nazi aggression, Pope Pius XII affirmed the right of nations to their sovereignty and to defend themselves against aggression. During World War II, Pius condemned aggression, calling on nations to renounce "once and for all wars of aggression as legitimate solutions of international disputes and as a means toward realizing national aspirations." The present generation, he said, has "passed through an ocean of blood and tears . . . lived through indescribable atrocities. . . ." In 1945, at the end of World War II, he urged international cooperation to reduce the causes of war, and encouraged statesmen laying the foundation for the United Nations to build an international order "to restore order, peace and prosperity . . . after thirty years of world war, economic crises, and incalculable destitution." The following decade witnessed the expansion of Soviet control in Eastern Europe. Pius XII lamented the use of military force, advocating restraint in its use to those situations meeting the strict conditions of "justifiable war."[2] The Church has more recently condemned in even stronger terms the existence and proliferation of nuclear arsenals, the allocation of ever larger amounts of nations' resources to military spending, and warfare that increasingly targets civilians and the destroys the environment.

In 1961 the Catholic Church widened its gaze beyond industrialized nations to include human conditions around the world. Pope John XXIII and his successor Pope Paul VI wrote extensively about the obligations of rich nations to aid poor nations. The Second Vatican Council (1963–1965) heard from a chorus of bishops from "developing" countries about the impoverishment of their peoples. Authentic progress is to be measured by whether it supports and contributes to the dignity of persons and promotes the common good.

Beginning in Latin America, the traditional identification of the Church with the privileged classes began to change as Catholic clergy and laity became advocates on behalf of the poor and those suffering political repression. In response to growing numbers of wars of national liberation, the Church supported democracy but advocated gradualist political reforms rather than violent revolutionary change.

In 1991, Pope John Paul II marked the 100th anniversary of the Pope Leo's encyclical "On the Condition of the Working Classes," publishing "The Centenary of Pope Leo's Encyclical." The pope criticized luxurious lifestyles and consumerism within developed nations. He criticized their neglect, nay, their exploitation of poor people and poor nations, and the natural environment to uphold their lifestyle. John Paul warned the West of its "moral underdevelopment," recognizable in its insatiable greed. He called on the rich nations to cancel some of the massive burden of debt that leaves poor nations unable to provide even the most basic human and environmental needs of their people.

Catholic social principles are found in several official church documents throughout the past century. These documents are listed in the table below, followed by an outline of the ten principles of Christian social teaching organized in four categories.

Catholic Social Teaching: Key Documents

Pope Leo XIII, "On the Condition of the Working Classes" (*Rerum Novarum,* 1891)

Pope Pius XI, "The Reconstruction of the Social Order" (*Quadragesimo Anno,*1931)

Pius XII, see especially his "Christmas Addresses" of 1944, 1945, and 1956

Pope John XXIII, "Christianity and Social Progress" (*Mater et Magistra,* 1961)

_____, "Peace on Earth (*Pacem in Terris,* 1963)

The Second Vatican Council, "The Church in the Modern World" (*Gaudium et Spes,* 1965)

Pope Paul VI, "The Development of Peoples" (*Popolorum Progressio,* 1967)

_____, "A Call to Action" (*Octogesima Adveniens,* 1971)

World Synod of Catholic Bishops, "Justice in the World" (*Justitia in Mundo,* 1971)

Pope Paul VI, "Evangelization in the Modern World" (*Evangelii Nuntiandi,* 1975)

Pope John Paul II, "On Human Work" (*Laborem Exercens,* 1981)

_____, "On Social Concern" (*Sollicitudo rei Socialis,* 1987)

_____, "The Centenary of Pope Leo's Encyclical" (*Centesimus Annus,* 1991)

Ten Principles of Christian Social Teaching

I. Regard for Persons in Society

1. The sacredness of human life requires that human beings not be harmed but be respected and accorded freedom and equality.

> "The Church affirms clearly and forcefully that every individual—whatever his or her personal convictions—bears the

image of God and therefore deserves respect" (John Paul II, "The Centenary of Pope Leo's Encyclical," 22).

2. The "common good" requires the promoting of social conditions that allow all persons to achieve their fulfillment.

> The common good "embraces the sum total of those conditions of social living, whereby [human beings] are enabled more fully and more readily to achieve their own perfection" (Pope John XXIII, "Christianity and Social Progress," 65).

> "It is the right of public authority to prevent anyone from misusing his private property to the detriment of the common good" (The Second Vatican Council, "The Church in the Modern World," 71).

3. Members of society share responsibility for one another's well being and must work on behalf of the common good (the principle of solidarity).

> "[Solidarity is] a firm and persevering determination to commit oneself to the common good; that is to say, to the good of all and of each individual, because we are all really responsible for all" (John Paul II, "On Social Concern," 8).

II. Justice for Persons and Groups

4. Distributive justice requires that all persons receive a share of the world's goods sufficient to meet their needs and those of their families. Social justice requires that individuals contribute to the well being of society and that society has a duty to enable them to do so.

> "The right to have a share of earthly goods sufficient for oneself and one's family belongs to everyone" (The Second Vatican Council, "The Church in the Modern World," 69).

> "The distribution of created goods must be brought into conformity with the demands of the common good and social justice" (Pope Pius XI, "The Reconstruction of the Social Order," 58).

5. Societies must give first priority to meeting the needs of the poor and vulnerable (preferential option for the poor).

> "Today, this love of preference for the poor, and the decisions which it inspires in us, cannot but embrace the immense multitudes of the hungry, the needy, the homeless, those without medical care and, above all, those without hope of a better future. It is impossible not to take account of these realities. To ignore them would mean becoming like the 'rich man' who pretended not to know the beggar Lazarus lying at his gate (Cf. Luke 16:19–31)" (Pope John Paul II, "On Social Concern," 42; he makes reference to Pope Paul VI, "The Development of Peoples," 47).

6. Persons have a right to join with others to work for their mutual well being.

> Workers have "a right of association, that is to form associations for the purpose of defending the vital interests of those employed in the various professions. These associations are called labor or trade unions (Pope John Paul II, "On Human Work," 20).

7. Persons have a right to participate in the decisions that effect their social, economic, political, and cultural life. The principle of subsidiary requires that social needs and issues should be addressed at the level of social and political organization which will permit maximum participation of citizens in shaping their own societies.

> ". . . It is wrong to withdraw from the individual and commit to the community at large what private enterprise and industry can accomplish, so too, it is an injustice . . . for a larger and higher organization to [take away] functions which can be performed by smaller and lower bodies" (Pope Pius XI, "The Reconstruction of the Social Order," 79).

8. States must seek peace and justice through nonviolent means, resorting to the use of violence only when the criteria of "justifiable war" exist.

"The United Nations has not yet succeeded in establishing, as alternatives to war, effective means for the resolution of international conflicts. This seems to be the most urgent problem which the international community has yet to resolve" (Pope John Paul II, "The Centenary of Pope Leo's Encyclical, 21).

"War is no solution. Another name for peace is development" (Pope John Paul II, "The Centenary of Pope Leo's Encyclical," 52).

III. Respect for the Earth

9. The principle of stewardship requires care for the physical world, in recognition of its intrinsic value as well as our dependence on it for life.

"People think that they can make arbitrary use of the earth, subjecting it without restraint to their wills, as though the earth did not have its own requisites and a prior God-given purpose, which indeed human beings can develop but must not betray" (Pope John Paul II, "The Centenary of Pope Leo's Encyclical," 37).

IV. Religion and Politics

10. Faith ought to be translated into action in the world. Belief in the coming of the Kingdom of God requires that Christians act and advocate on behalf of more just societies. Governments must protect the freedom of persons and groups to express their religious beliefs.

"[The Lord] judged the cause of the poor and the needy. 'Is this not to know me?' says the Lord" (Jeremiah 22:16).

"Action on behalf of justice and participation in the transformation of the world fully appear to us as a constitutive dimension of the preaching of the Gospel, or in other words, of the Church's mission for the redemption of the human race and its liberation from every oppressive situation" (World Synod of Catholic Bishops, "Justice in the World," 6).

These principles have been articulated and applied by popes, synods of bishops, and national conferences of bishops, and by the Second Vatican Council. The upholding of these principles extends beyond the Catholic Church as well. They are professed by other Christians, by Jews, and by people of other faiths. While rooted in Jewish, Christian, and Islamic faith traditions, they also find expression in secular terms as well. For example, the "Universal Declaration of Human Rights," adopted by the UN General Assembly in 1948, asserts several of these principles. The declaration affirms the freedom and dignity of persons (1); the rights of association, political participation, and religious freedom (6, 7, 10); the requirement of distributive justice in the forms of just wage and social security assistance (4), and the notion of the common good (2). In addition, the Universal Declaration asserts several legal rights: the right to own property, the right of privacy, the right to emigrate, the right to fair trial, and the right of protection from inhumane punishment.

Focusing on Catholic Church teaching and activism is not meant to suggest that institutionally the Church has led the way. It is more accurate to say that some Christians responded to the Scriptures and to the Church's teaching and acted upon it, in time bringing more Christians with them, including representatives of the official Church. Nor would we want to give the impression that Christian believers were always in the vanguard of justice. In fact, we have been timid too often. In some instances the commitment of the churches to justice is an admission of its own past failure to respond to injustice and even its complicity. It becomes an act of repentance and resolve to more faithfully represent the gospel of Jesus Christ by commitment to love and justice.

From Principles to Action

The ten social principles are broadly framed guides for action. For example, "love your neighbor as yourself" gives us a general rule of how we should behave toward others, but it does not specify how. *Directives for action* contain more specificity regarding what love requires in specific situation. *Directives*, however, do not reveal precisely what you or I should do in any particular situations. We must determine what we will do. Perhaps the most pressing question is why we fail to do anything. Is it a lack of knowledge or a lack of will? We may be presented with concrete suggestions for action and even be convinced that we should act. However, if we still let the moment pass without action, why?

I teach theology and ethics to university students. Many of my students come from middle and upper-middle class families living in suburbs or small towns. Some are minorities from urban and less affluent areas. Some come from Latin America, the Middle East, Africa, and Asia. Those of us born in the U.S. learned our nation's civic creed as school children:

- *E pluribus Unum* ("one from many")
- equality and equal opportunity
- "liberty and justice for all"
- two centuries of democratic government ever vigilant of its citizens' rights
- freedom of speech, of the press, and of religion

But our civic ideals are in tension with what we see around us: discrimination against women and minorities, violence in many forms, disrespect for one another. "Hate crimes" committed against blacks, Jews, and gays fill the news. The numbers of needy people—poor families, children, the elderly, immigrants, and strangers—seem overwhelming. Civic participation for the sake of the common good falters and our economic, political, and social structures are less responsive to the civic ideals we profess.

My students are Catholic and Protestant, Jewish, Hindu, Muslim, or humanists. They have experienced the freedom of religious expression that our society protects. Many also recognize that the religious beliefs they hold require a moral response. The belief that human beings bear the image and likeness of God requires us to respect and care for all of them. Christian citizen-believers have been baptized in Christ and are called to be doers of justice and people for others.

Many students volunteer in central city schools, tutoring and teaching conflict-resolution skills to adolescents. University students are amazed by the contrasts between their life experiences and those of inner-city youth, many of whom appear to have lost hope and grown cynical about "equal opportunity." These children experience life as passing them by. Yet my students are grateful for the opportunity to be exposed to the larger world. Indeed, that is part of what education is about: empathizing with the experiences of others separated from us in time and space.

The twentieth century has been marked by sharp and tragic contrasts. On the one hand, rapid advances in medicine, communications, transportation, and production provided many in the First World with extraordinary opportunities and comforts. On the other hand, the new technologies were seldom applied to the hunger, poverty, illness, political instability, and lack of opportunities for the majority of humanity living in the Third World. Throughout the century, death, destruction and displacement because of armed conflict, and grinding poverty were the fate of millions of Africans, Latin Americans, Asians, and Eastern Europeans. The number of casualties of twentieth-century wars is staggering: one hundred and thirty million. That number does not include the victims of "low intensity wars" waged throughout the last three decades.

I recall the words of a Latin American to a U.S. audience: "Don't fall asleep in the American Dream." The challenge for us in the twenty-first century is to translate our principles into practices. The movements described in this book give us hope that justice and peace are possible. We will meet many people who have discovered ways to recreate their social, economic, and political worlds. Some of these people are Christians acting out their faith—clergy and religious, lay church workers, teachers, doctors, labor organizers, political activists, peasants, and students. Their actions inspire the rest of us, including those in leadership positions in the churches. Their stories need to become our stories.

1

The Way of the Cross: Central America Past and Present

Christian faith grew strong in Latin America, despite the cruelties inflicted by European conquerors. Those who brought Christianity, as well as their descendants, have been challenged to hear the gospel in a new way. Today its transformative power is seen in the struggle of those who renounce the class structures born in colonial times to work for justice on behalf of the poor and powerless.

In the first three sections of this chapter, we glimpse the beginning of the Spanish discovery and conquest and meet Bartolomé de Las Casas, Columbus's contemporary, whom the King of Spain appointed as "Protector of the Indians." We meet Cortés and recall an event that transformed Christianity in Mexico and Latin America. Three hundred years after Cortés arrived in Mexico, the rule of Spain and other European nations in Latin America came to an end—but the social, political, and economic patterns shaped by three centuries of colonialism were deeply entrenched. Sections four through six examine the struggle for life and dignity in Central America today.

1. Columbus: For Gold and Glory

At dawn on August 3, 1492, three ships sailed from the port city of Palos, near the southern tip of Spain. Christopher Columbus, commanding his crew of ninety men, traveled west-southwest and, on the seventy-first day, sighted land. As he and his official party went ashore on a small island in the Bahamas (a then uncharted stretch of seven hundred islands, extending from about 750 miles southeast of Palm Beach, Florida, to a point off the eastern coast of Cuba), curious islanders came out to see them. The Spaniards called these people *Indios*, thinking they had reached India. Little did the native people realize that the arrival of these three small ships signaled the end of their world.

Two months later Columbus and his crew discovered a much larger island they called *Hispaniola* (now the Caribbean island nations of Haiti and the Dominican Republic). Columbus wrote to King Ferdinand and Queen Isabella of Spain:

> I [have] found very many islands filled with people . . . and have taken possession [of them] for your Highnesses by proclamation and with the royal standard displayed.[1]

He added that among the natives, "nobody objected" when he claimed the islands for Spain. Columbus recorded in his journal that he had placed a large cross in the harbor of Hispaniola to indicate that the King and Queen of Spain possessed the land in order to bring Christianity to its people. The islanders, of course, could not have known what the symbols of Christianity and the Spanish Crown meant. If they heard Columbus's proclamation in Spanish, that, too, would have been incomprehensible to them.

Columbus believed he was a man with a very special destiny. His own name, Christopher ("Christ-bearer"), signified the role he was to play in bringing Christianity to this new world—and he assured King Ferdinand that these good and gentle people "will easily become Christians."[2] He also believed that he was destined to bring glory and riches to Spain, because the gold of the New World would soon fill Spain's treasury. He wrote to Queen Isabella that this new wealth could even finance another crusade to recapture Jerusalem from the Turks. Above all, the star of the Columbus family would shine.

As Columbus prepared to return to Spain in January 1493, his crews were eager for home and his ships were leaking badly. But he now displayed a changed attitude toward the natives of Hispaniola. He had a fort built to hold a contingent of Spanish soldiers who would remain as representatives of Spain. To frighten the natives so that they "might be kept by fear as well as love," Columbus had his soldiers stage a mock battle, a display of Spanish firepower. Columbus boasted that "ten [Spaniards] could put ten thousand of them to flight."[3] However, after the ships departed for Spain and the soldiers who remained took native women by force for their sexual pleasures, the natives fought back, killing all of the soldiers.

In late 1493 Columbus commanded a fleet of seventeen ships and thirteen hundred people—crewmen, colonists, and many soldiers. The purpose of this voyage was to establish a colony on Hispaniola and to explore and claim other islands. Upon arrival, Columbus wasted no time. Spanish soldiers were ordered to exact tribute in gold from every village—every three months. In 1494, not finding large reserves of gold, the Spaniards captured five hundred natives, shackled them in five ships, and transported them to Spain to be sold as slaves.

By 1496, the morale of the colonists was low and Columbus was blamed for mismanagement of the colony. In response, Columbus returned to Spain to defend himself before the Crown, and returned to Hispaniola with a royal offer of large land grants to the colonists. Columbus, however, added a bonus to the king's offer: in addition to receiving land, the colonists would be granted the right to command the native peoples to work the land for them. The colonists' only obligation to the natives under their control was to instruct them about Christianity.

The natives themselves had no rights. Within a short period of time, this practice of granting lands and their inhabitants to Spanish colonists, called *encomienda*, had catastrophic consequences for the native peoples. Healthy natives were taken from their villages and families to do grueling work in fields and mines. Denied sufficient food and rest, many died from exhaustion or, in their weakened condition, from European diseases against which the natives of the Americas had no natural immunity. The young, elderly, and infirm were left behind in villages with no one to care for them.

Under the *encomienda* system, colonists prospered and their towns grew, while native people died in epidemic numbers and their villages fell into ruin. Natives who lived beyond the *encomiendas* suffered a crueler fate, becoming human cargo exported to Spain to be sold as slaves. The natives were ruled and sold, and worked for Spanish profits. By 1515, between eighty and ninety percent of the natives of Hispaniola were dead.[4]

Columbus made a fourth and final expedition in 1502. Still determined to find gold mines, he explored the coast of Central America. At one point he seized a village chief and set fire to his village, frustrated perhaps because he had found no gold. In his journal, Columbus recorded seeing long boats, which might have led him to the wealthy Aztec civilization of Mexico. It would not be long, however, before other Spaniards would make that discovery—and the next chapter of Spanish conquest would begin.

2. Las Casas: Ministering to Christ Suffering in the Americas

Pedro de Las Casas and his two brothers were among those who traveled with Columbus in 1493 and received a large *encomienda* in Hispaniola. Pedro returned to Spain five years later with an unusual gift for his fourteen-year-old son, Bartolomé: a young native to be his son's personal servant. In 1502, when he was eighteen, Bartolomé sailed to Hispaniola to take charge of the family's *encomienda*. Although most Spaniards treated the natives cruelly, Bartolomé treated them kindly, perhaps because he knew the gentleness of these people through his servant. In 1506, Bartolomé went home to study for the priesthood and, after ordination, returned to Santo Domingo in 1510.

The contradiction of being a priest and possessing an *encomienda* began to trouble Bartolomé. When twelve missionaries, members of the Dominican Order, came from Spain in 1511, they were shocked at the cruelty the Spaniards inflicted on the natives. On a Sunday morning in December, Dominican Friar Anton Montesinos confronted the congregation of Spanish colonists and officials in the Cathedral of Santa Domingo, leveling the following accusation against them:

> I have come here in order to declare it unto you, I am the voice of Christ in the desert of this island. Open your hearts and your senses, all of you, for this voice will speak new things harshly, and will be frightening . . . This voice says that you are living in deadly sin for the atrocities you tyrannically impose on these innocent people. Tell me, what right have you to enslave them? What authority did you use to make war against them who lived at peace on their territories, killing them cruelly with methods never before heard of? How can you oppress them and not care to feed or cure them, and work them to death to satisfy your greed? . . . Aren't they human beings? Have they no rational soul? Aren't you obliged to love them as you love yourselves?[5]

The colonists fumed and the Spanish officials demanded a public apology from the missionaries. Not only did the Dominicans refuse, but they repeated their condemnation on the following Sunday. Bartolomé, of course, knew that the accusations of the missionaries were true. Perhaps to evade the issue, he signed on to serve as chaplain to a Spanish expedition to Cuba. When the Crown granted him another *encomienda*, the cruelties of the colonists toward the natives were more than he could stand. He described what he saw and heard:

> Death made speedier ravages among Indians here than in other places, starvation and hard labor helping. Since all able-bodied men and women were away at the mines, only the old and sick stayed in town with no one to look after them. So they died of illness, anguish, and starvation. I was traveling the Cuban roads then and it happened that entering a town I sometimes heard crying in the houses. I would inquire and was greeted with the words "hungry, hungry."[6]

Bartolomé de Las Casas promptly gave up his lands and freed his laborers, demanded the abolition of the *encomienda* system, and urged Spanish colonists to make restitution for all they had taken from the natives. In 1515 he returned to Spain to appeal to the Crown personally to intervene on behalf of the natives. The king was moved by his appeals and appointed Las Casas "Protector of the Indians."

In opposition to Las Casas, other Spaniards justified the conquest, arguing that the natives of the Americas were inferior by nature, fit to be ruled by the naturally superior Spaniards. In *General History of the West Indies*, which describes Spain's colonization of the Caribbean, royal historian Gonzalo Fernandez de Oviedo characterizes the native people as "lazy, idle . . . and vile [for whom] no amount of punishment, reward, or admonition produces results." To prepare for their conversion, the argument continued, the natives must first be forced to submit and obey. Las Casas, however, responded to his fellow Spanish Christians: How can you kill, maim, and work to death the people to whom you say you are bringing Christ? "When the Spaniards devastate and destroy its people," Las Casas wrote, "Jesus Christ, our God, [is] scourged and afflicted and beaten and crucified, not once but thousands of times." The only legitimate way to attract these people to the gospel, he insisted, was through reasoned explanation and gentle persuasion.

Las Casas labored for fifty years, in person and through his writing, to prevent other peoples of the Americas from falling victim to Spanish greed. He crossed the ocean no less than ten times to appeal to the conscience of Spaniards and to recruit colonists to the New World, encouraging them to live in integrated settlements, establish hospitals, and institute humane labor practices. He also sailed to Venezuela and

Guatemala, trekked to Peru, and eventually was appointed by the pope to be bishop of southern Mexico.

Las Casas traveled more widely and experienced more of the Americas than any other European in the sixteenth century, all in an attempt to reach areas before Spanish slave hunters and colonists arrived, and to prevent the continuation of the tragedies that had befallen the native peoples of Hispaniola and Cuba. His one failure—which he sorely regretted—was not to have opposed the importation of African slaves to replace native workers on Spanish *encomiendas* that began around 1510. He later denounced the enslavement of any peoples as equally immoral.

Bartolomé de Las Casas' influence was felt in many ways:

- In 1537 Pope Paul III was moved by Las Casas to affirm the full humanity of the native peoples of the Americas and to condemn the taking of their lives, liberty, and property.

- The Spanish Crown accepted his view that native peoples on lands claimed by Spain were royal subjects entitled to royal protection.

- The Spanish Crown issued the "New Laws" in 1542, abolishing slavery and requiring that *encomiendas* be returned to the Crown upon the death of their holders.

When Las Casas took up his post as bishop of the Chiapas region of southern Mexico in 1544, he faced the full wrath of the Spanish colonists: they refused to comply with the New Laws and eventually drove him out of Chiapas. He returned to Spain in 1550 and remained a vigorous influence on the royal advisors until his death in 1566.

Although the sixteenth century was the beginning of the era of discovery, the explorers, conquerors, and colonists exhibited an unprecedented racism that visited immense suffering and death on millions of people and their cultures. Bartolomé de Las Casas was among the first to raise his voice against genocide and to affirm the universal dignity and rights of all human beings everywhere. He is the father of human rights, and his views are echoed in national constitutions and the UN "Universal Declaration of Human Rights." The struggle he waged to protect human beings and their rights remains as urgent today as it was five hundred years ago.

3. Cortés and Guadalupe: The Birth of a New People of God

In 1519 Hernán Cortés sailed into the Gulf of Mexico and landed at a place he named *Veracruz* (the True Cross). There he learned of the *Aztec*, a people who evidently possessed great wealth and terrorized neighboring peoples. When Cortés marched his troops two hundred miles to "Mexico," the magnificent Aztec capital built on an island in the middle of a lake, he expected to encounter armed opposition. Instead, the Spaniards were surprised by the hospitality they received from the Aztec ruler, Montezuma. The reason for the warm welcome, it turned out, was a stroke of good luck for Cortés. The Aztec priests had predicted the return of the god known as the "plumed serpent," who would secure the future of the Aztec Empire. Montezuma believed Cortés was that god, but soon discovered, however, that he was no benevolent deity but a demon of destruction. Cortés's troops defeated the Aztec warriors, took Montezuma prisoner, and destroyed all Aztec religious structures and symbols. By 1521 the conquest of the Aztecs was accomplished. An Aztec poet lamented, "Oh cry, oh cry, for we have lost the Aztec nation."

The Spanish missionaries who followed the conquistadors proclaimed a compassionate God who, contrary to Aztec beliefs, did not require human sacrifice. The God of the Christians had become a human being and had suffered death at the hands of evil men in order to defeat the power of evil in the world. Sadly, most of the missionaries who preached this Good News of a nonviolent, merciful, loving, and forgiving God treated Aztec culture as an impediment to Christian faith that must be destroyed. The sacrifice of an entire culture was required.

An event occurred in December 1531, however, that affirmed the cultures of Native Americans and profoundly influenced the development of Christianity in Mexico and elsewhere in Latin America. According to legend, a young Christian native named Juan Diego was walking on a hillside in present-day Mexico City when he had a vision of a woman dressed in native clothing, with facial features similar to his own. The Lady addressed Juan Diego in his native language: "Listen, my most abandoned son, dignified Juan. Where are you going?" She then instructed him to go to the Spanish bishop and tell him that "the Mother of the true God through whom one lives" desires a church to be built on the site where she had appeared. It would be a refuge in which she could "communicate all her love, compassion, help, and defense to all the inhabitants of this land . . . [and] hear their lamentations and remedy their miseries, pain, and suffering." But on his way to the bishop,

Juan was detained with the news that his uncle was gravely ill with smallpox, a disease brought from Europe. When Juan returned to the hill, the Lady again appeared to him, assured him that his uncle would recover, and repeated her request that he take her message to the bishop. Juan went twice to the bishop, who didn't believe him. No doubt, many Spaniards would have found the story hard to believe: Why would Mary appear to a mere native? Why would she appear as one of them?

The third time the Lady appeared to Juan, she gave him roses to take to the bishop. Later, when Juan opened his cloak in front of the bishop, the roses spilled out—and on the lining of the cloak was the Lady's image. Now convinced that Juan had indeed been blessed with apparitions of the Virgin Mary, the bishop had a church built on the hill and placed in it Juan Diego's cloak bearing the image of the Virgin of Guadalupe.

This event brought about thousands of native conversions to Christianity, reassuring them of their dignity. They embraced the Lady as their compassionate mother—beside Jesus, their compassionate father. Many of these converts were the first generation of a new race called *mestizo* (mixed race). Born of native mothers and Spanish fathers, these people were the blending of European and Latin American cultures. As a "new creation," the *mestizos* represent a promise of overcoming cultural barriers and renouncing claims of racial or ethnic superiority. It is a promise yet unrealized, however, insofar as the "superiority complex" on the father's side of the family often causes his native children to be treated as inferior offspring.

Our Lady of Guadalupe remains a symbol of hope for all who are part of this new creation. Each year more than a million pilgrims visit her shrine in Mexico City. Her feast day, December 12, is marked with celebration throughout the Americas.

> Come then to the Lord like living stones and let yourself be built into a spiritual house. You are a chosen race, a royal priesthood, a holy nation, God's own people that you may proclaim the mighty acts of God who has called you out of darkness into God's marvelous light (I Peter 2: 4, 5, 9).

4. The Church in the Struggle for Life

Today, a three-tier social order exists in Mexico: the *criollos*, the *mestizos*, and the *indios*. The *criollos* is a small elite group claiming "pure" Spanish descent who assumed control when Spain's rule ended. This upper ten percent prospered from the close business ties they maintained with Spain, and they continue to possess most of the political and economic power. The *mestizos* (descendants of Spanish and indigenous unions) make up sixty percent of the population. While traditionally poor peasants and artisans, Mexican prosperity from the 1920s through the 1950s helped create a small middle class among the *mestizos.* The indigenous peoples, collectively known as *indios* (Indians), make up the lower thirty percent of the population. These people remain subsistence farmers and laborers living in poverty, without land or political power.

The 1960s brought predictions of quickening economic and political advancement in Latin America hastened by foreign aid, technology, and foreign corporate investments. However, while profits from foreign investment and trade raised the standard of living for some, the new prosperity was not well distributed. For example, foreign aid was often spent on strengthening national security forces against internal threats to the elite, rather than being used to develop education and health programs for the masses and appropriate technologies. Governments incurred large foreign indebtedness by building showcase projects that met few essential human needs.

In 1967, Pope Paul VI's encyclical "The Development of Peoples" pointed to the growing gap between rich and poor nations. The pope accused wealthy nations and privileged elites in poor nations of exploiting the poor. In 1968, one hundred and thirty Latin American bishops met in Medellín, Columbia, to reflect on the present mission of the Church. In words as strong as those of Montesinos and Las Casas, the Catholic bishops of Latin America condemned the unjust political and economic systems of the continent as "institutionalized violence" and a "situation of sin." They urged the Church to stand with the poor, to become poor in order to join the poor in struggling against injustice. Brazilian Bishop Helder Camara, characterized the exploitation of landless peasants by large landowners in his country as "national slavery," and spoke of the transformation that was occurring in the churches of Latin America:

> The Spirit of God was with us pushing us to discover, in our
> continent, the most painful of colonialisms: privileged inter-
> nal groups who maintain personal wealth at the expense of
> the misery of their countrymen.[7]

Catholic bishops from around the world gathered in Rome in 1971 to address development and social justice in the Third World. In their conclusions, entitled "Justice in the World" they affirmed the link between the proclamation of the Kingdom of God and commitment to the liberation of peoples from oppressive situations. "The Gospel Message," they wrote, "contains a . . . demand for justice in the world."[8] Working for justice, they asserted, is a "constitutive dimension of the preaching of the Gospel . . . [and] of the Church's mission for the redemption of the human race and its liberation from every oppressive situation."

Samuel Ruiz: Transforming Church and Society

Among the Latin American church leaders and theologians who heard the cries of the poor and began to question the overwhelming poverty in their countries was Mexican bishop Samuel Ruiz. Born near Mexico City in 1924, Ruiz studied for the priesthood in Rome, and was assigned to teach in a Mexican seminary after ordination—as often happened with priests educated in Europe. In 1959 Pope John XXIII made him Bishop of Chiapas, the diocese that Las Casas had served as bishop four hundred years earlier. Ruiz, born into the *mestizo* class, knew very little about the Mayan peoples who had lived for centuries in southern Mexico and across the border in Guatemala, except that they were among the indigenous people who make up a third of the nation's population—and its poorest people. Ruiz was not familiar with any of the Mayan languages spoken by the people he had come to serve, and few of them spoke Spanish.

In 1959 the newly ordained bishop set out to visit every village and town in his diocese, some so remote that he could reach them only by mule. His tour shocked him. Indigenous Mayan peoples labored almost as slaves on large plantations, or lived abandoned in poverty in the highlands. In words that could have been those of Las Casas in Cuba, he wrote, "I traveled through villages where bosses were scourging debt-slaves who did not want to work more than eight hours a day."[9]

The new bishop's first response was to invite missionaries and international aid workers to Chiapas to address basic needs for food, health care, and education. However, this was only the beginning of Bishop Ruiz's deepening conversion as he came to know the people of the ancient Mayan culture. He learned their languages and encouraged other church workers to do the same. The duty of the Church, he said, was first "to discover the riches that the Father gave to his children even before our humble proclamation of the Good News" and then to "clothe the Word of God with the flesh of the [Mayan] culture," as the Guadalupe event had done early in the evangelization of Mexico.[10]

This was a new kind of evangelization. Mexican American theologian Virgil Elizondo warns of "the elite who dominate church and society . . . only taking the gospel to others, not of listening to it and being converted by it anew . . . creating new idols within itself while fanatically trying to destroy what it does not understand and sees as the idols of others."[11] By learning their languages, Ruiz was affirming that the Church must listen to and learn from the Mayan peoples. When the Church listened, it heard the indigenous peoples' suffering and desperation. By the very act of listening, the Church was affirming their dignity.

Bishop Ruiz challenged *criollo* and *mestizo* Christians to welcome their indigenous brothers and sisters as equals and to acknowledge that it was not inferiority but racism and greed that kept the indigenous people at the bottom. But affirming the equality of the Mayan people offended the upper classes, who viewed their wealth as a function of their cultural superiority. When Ruiz toured the diocese, he contributed to this "offense" by accepting the hospitality of the poor rather than lodging in the "big houses" of the wealthy, as was customary. Bishop Ruiz represented the Church's growing awareness of and response to injustice in Latin American societies by encouraging the Mayan peoples to analyze their situation. Why were they excluded from sharing in the resources so abundant in southern Mexico—the farmland, oil, natural gas, hydroelectric power? Why were they hungry and without education and health care? Why were they denied political participation? He also encouraged them to organize for changing their situation.

5. The Mayan Peoples: Struggling for Survival

When Pope John Paul II came to Mexico in 1979 to address the bishops of Latin America, he spoke of the "admirable bishops deeply involved in the valiant defense of the human dignity of those entrusted to them." He urged them to continue to care for the poor, reminding them that:

> When we draw near to the poor in order to accompany them
> and to serve them, we are doing what Christ taught us to do
> when he became our brother, poor like us.[12]

The pope spoke of the churches of Latin America "penetrating culture
with the Gospel . . . transforming hearts, humanizing systems and structures."[13] The pastoral task of the bishop, he said, must include "forming a social conscience at all levels and in all sectors" so that when
"injustices increase and the gap between the rich and the poor widens
distressingly, then the social doctrine of the Church . . . should be a
valuable tool for formation and action."[14]

Pope John Paul II then traveled to a remote village in southern
Mexico to assure indigenous people of the Church's concern for them.
Recalling the visit of his predecessor Pope Paul VI to the Medellín
meeting of Latin American bishops in 1968, he said:

> I wish to reiterate that the pope is with these masses of peo-
> ple who are almost always left behind in an ignoble standard
> of living. . . . Seeing a situation that remains alarming, that
> is seldom better and sometimes even worse, the Pope
> chooses to be your voice, the voice of those who cannot
> speak or who have been silenced. He wishes to be the con-
> science of consciences, an invitation to action, to make up
> for lost time, which has frequently been a time of prolonged
> sufferings and unsatisfied hopes. . . . [Laborers] have a right
> to be respected. They have a right not to be deprived of the
> little they have by maneuvers that sometimes amount to real
> plunder. They have a right not to be blocked in their desire
> to take part in their own advancement. They have the right to
> have the barriers of exploitation removed. . . . They have the
> right to effective help . . . For their sake we must act
> promptly and thoroughly. We must implement bold and thor-
> oughly innovative transformations. . . . To you, responsible
> officials of the people, power-holding classes who some-
> times keep your lands unproductive when they conceal the
> food that so many families are doing without . . . the cry of
> the destitute and above all the voice of God and the Church
> join me in [declaring] to you that it is not just, it is not
> human, it is not Christian to continue certain situations that
> are clearly unjust.[15]

However, the struggle for justice has met strong resistance from the economically and politically powerful. Chiapas and the neighboring states of Tabasco and Oaxaca, for example, resemble colonies in which a few coffee growers and cattle ranchers hold vast tracts of land, control all influential government posts, command the police, and employ the bosses to control their indigenous laborers.

The struggle in southern Mexico is first of all for land. Early in the twentieth century, Emiliano Zapata and Francisco Villa led armies of landless peasants demanding land reform by the Mexican government. The success of their movement is reflected in the Mexican constitution of 1917, which directed the government to break up large landholdings and distribute them to local communities. The land would be communally owned and held in permanent trust. Small farmers could farm the land to feed their families and grow cash crops.

In Chiapas, however, very little of the land reform of 1917 actually occurred. There the trend was to deprive the indigenous people of more of their lands. In the 1980s the Mayan people began to organize themselves to reclaim the land that was key to their personal and cultural survival. But their aspirations ran headlong into the plans of the landowners as well as those of the Mexican government. The landowners saw potential for greater profits from increased food exports to U.S. and Canadian markets, while the Mexican government wanted to increase oil production in the region to sell on the world market. The increased agricultural and oil production that would profit the wealthy would push the indigenous people closer to death.

Preparing to enter into the North American Free Trade Agreement (NAFTA), the Mexican government amended the constitution in 1992 to permit the sale of community-held farmlands to large landowners. In the spirit of Zapata, Mayans in Chiapas, calling themselves "Zapatistas," rebelled on New Years Day 1994, the day that NAFTA became law. With the rallying cry of "land and liberty," they took control of seven town governments and declared them "autonomous regions" whose internal affairs were under indigenous rule. The protest spread to the two neighboring states, Oaxaca and Tabasco, and by the end of 1994, the Zapatistas controlled thirty-eight local areas.

Not only was the Mexican government embarrassed by the press attention generated by the rebellion, but officials in Chiapas were upset with the Catholic Church's role in the indigenous peoples' political awakening. Yet, across Mexico, sympathy for the Zapatistas was widespread. The government declared a unilateral cease-fire twelve days later, and Bishop Ruiz agreed to serve as a mediator between the Mexican government and the Zapatistas. After two years of talks, the government agreed to constitutional reforms to protect indigenous peoples and their cultures. In late 1996, however, with the world press no longer watching, the Mexican government backed away from implementing its pledges.

Mayans then joined the increasing numbers of landless peasants forced to urban areas in search of work. Many have become a cheap source of labor in the factories (known as *maquiladoras*) established by foreign corporations in over two hundred "export processing zones" throughout Latin America. United States and other foreign industries have moved operations to Latin America where local workers assemble and finish textiles, electronics, and small machinery for very low wages. Latin American governments, of course, have welcomed these industries by offering incentives in the form of minimal regulations and low (or no) taxes. *Maquiladoras* in Nicaragua, Honduras, El Salvador, Guatemala, and Mexico produce much of the seventy percent of imported clothing sold in the U.S. Those who make the clothing are extremely poorly paid: Guatemalan workers earn $.36 per hour; Haitians, $.30; and Hondurans, $.31. This means that those who make the clothes earn only one to four percent of the wholesale value of the clothes that eventually are sold in U.S. stores. To date, they employ over a million people.

How well do the *maquiladoras* that stretch along the northern Mexican border from Texas to California and throughout Central America serve local economic needs? While they do create jobs and bring new technologies into the country, workers cannot meet the basic needs of their families with their meager earnings. Mexico is intent on improving and modernizing its economy. It is interested in increasing raw material exports and attracting foreign corporations to establish factories in Mexico. However, its economic advancement must include the production of adequate food and essential goods for its own people, care for their health and safety, and protection of the environment. In 1994–1995 an economic crisis in Mexico caused the *peso* to reach an all-time low value compared to the dollar. The *peso* devaluation increased foreign profits greatly (U.S. companies, for example, sell the goods made in Mexico for dollars while paying wages in *pesos*) while the average hourly wage (equivalent to $1.80) did not provide enough for families to pay rent and buy food.

The impact of the *maquiladoras* extends well beyond the issue of meeting the material needs of workers and their families; the environmental pollution they produce has created a public health disaster. Residents and government officials on both the Mexican and U.S. sides of the border recognize that an environmental and public health crisis exists along the Rio Grande River. For example, a 1995 environmental report estimated that the factories were producing 164 tons of hazardous waste per day, with about forty percent of it leaving the factories untreated. Lacking water treatment facilities, most human and factory wastewater drains directly into the Rio Grande. A recent study reported that the Rio Grande is so contaminated by human fecal matter (230 times over the safe level) in the El Paso [Texas]-Juarez [Mexico] area that even skin contact poses the threat of typhoid, cholera, and hepatitis.[16] Environmental testing along the Rio Grande in Arizona, New Mexico, and California all produced similar results. The entire populations surrounding these industrial areas—in Mexico and the U.S.—face growing risks to their health.

6. The Church: Accompanying the Oppressed

> Around here the sin that is not forgiven is to have approached [the indigenous] and said, "You are children of God, you are citizens, you have rights, you can get organized, God's word invites you to do so." For committing that sin, church workers are paying with their lives (church official in El Salvador).

The loss of land and livelihood, and the force exerted by foreign corporate presence, all serve to undermine the dignity of millions of Latin Americans. In particular, indigenous peoples and their cultures struggle for life. When they attempt to organize and protest political arrangements and economic development that excludes them, they risk death. Their cries for human dignity, for a share of the earth's resources, for a living wage, for humane working conditions and unions, for environmental protection, often fall on deaf ears.

Penny Lernoux, for many years a journalist in Latin America, offered this observation about the role of the Christian Church in Latin America five hundred years after Columbus and Las Casas:

> Unlike Latin America's political parties and labor unions,
> the Church cannot be silenced through persecution. Cross

> and sword colonized Latin America; now they stand in oppo-
> sition. If the Church cannot end repression, neither can the
> military [frighten] the bishops into submission. For all its
> defects and desertions, the Catholic Church is still a power
> to be reckoned with in Latin America. As the only institution
> capable of withstanding the military, the Church has become
> the surrogate for democracy, providing a protective umbrella
> for popular organizations, such as labor unions and peasant
> federations, which otherwise would succumb to repression . . .
> By any historical measure the cost of this commitment has
> been high. Hundreds of [church workers] have suffered
> harassment, arrest, torture, expulsion, and even death.[17]

Indeed, the most urgent and dangerous task in Latin America is to work on behalf of human rights and socioeconomic development. When the poor protest, organize, and resist, they meet violent retaliation. The repression by police, the army, and paramilitary organizations as seen in Chiapas goes on throughout Latin America, primarily because the lives of these indigenous peoples and their cultures get in the way of the increased profits of the prosperous. The time for making reparations to the indigenous peoples who welcomed Columbus is at hand.

When Bishop Ruiz undertook the role of mediator between the Mexican government and the Mayan people in 1994, he had hoped to prevent violence. He realized, however, that state officials were likely to use the army against the Mayan campaign for autonomy. He also knew what had happened to Mayans making similar demands in Guatemala: leaders of the struggle and their relatives were kidnapped and tortured or "disappeared," thousands of villagers were massacred, and four hundred villages were burned—all to eliminate the indigenous people of Guatemala. Thousands of refugees fled across the border into Chiapas. (Among them was Rigoberta Menchu who had fled for her life in the aftermath of the torture and murder of her father, mother, and brother. After Bishop Ruiz and his sister took her in and nursed her back to health, Menchu became a champion of human rights and an advocate for nonviolence in Guatemala, winning the Nobel Peace Prize in 1992.) Ruiz protested vigorously to the Mexican government when the Guatemalan Army crossed the border to seize "political prisoners" in the refugee camps. In 1998, Bishop Juan Gerardi Conedera of Guatemala City was assassinated, two days after the Catholic Church published a report on massive human rights violations in Guatemala.

The Church of Chiapas became a staunch defender of the human rights of the indigenous and those who dared side with them. In 1989 Ruiz established the Fray Bartolomé Las Casas Center for Human Rights to document human rights abuses.

In 1997 the Mexican government backed away from its earlier agreement with the Zapatistas and increased the presence of the army and security forces in Chiapas. Foreign observers were expelled from the region, and paramilitaries were armed and trained for war. A group of U.S. citizens who traveled to Chiapas in April 1997 described a situation of violent repression and terror by means of "low intensity warfare" waged against groups of poor and indigenous people who are struggling to organize to demand land, justice, and democracy.[18]

Finally, in December 1997, the violent reprisal against the Zapatistas came. A paramilitary group massacred forty-five unarmed Mayans, mostly women and children, sympathetic to the Zapatistas. Because of public outrage, the government of Mexico was forced to conduct an investigation that eventually implicated the highest-ranking government officials of Chiapas in the massacre. But the war against the Zapatistas has continued. In June 1998 ten more civilians died at the hands of the army when the government retook by force an area held by the Zapatistas. As Bishop Samuel Ruiz prepared to retire after forty years of service in Chiapas, Mexican government officials and some of the Mexican bishops sought a successor who would be less active on behalf of the indigenous people.

The struggle of indigenous people is no less than the struggle for democracy, liberty, and justice everywhere. José Saramago, a contemporary Portuguese writer, describes what is at stake in Chiapas:

> The indigenous of Chiapas aren't the only humiliated and offended people in this world. In all places and at all times, regardless of race, color, customs, culture, and religious belief, the human creature we are so proud to be has always known how to humiliate and offend those whom, with sad irony, he continues to call his fellow creatures. We have invented things that don't exist in nature: cruelty, torture, and disdain. By a perverse use of race, we've come to divide humanity into irreducible categories: rich and poor, master and slave, powerful and weak, wise and ignorant. And incessantly in each of these divisions we've made subdivisions so as to vary and freely multiply reasons for disdain, humiliation, and offense.

> In recent years Chiapas has been the place where the
> most disdained, most humiliated, and most offended people
> of Mexico were able to recover intact a dignity and an honor
> that had never been completely lost, a place where the heavy
> tombstone of an oppression that has gone on for centuries
> has been shattered to allow the passage of a procession of
> new and different living people ahead of an endless proces-
> sion of murderers. . . . [W]hat is being played out in the Chi-
> apas mountains . . . reaches beyond the borders of Mexico to
> the heart of that portion of humanity that has not renounced
> and never will renounce dreams and hopes, the simple
> imperative of equal justice for all. [19]

Assisting refugees, listening to those denied a voice, and accompa-
nying families seeking justice for the "disappeared" are among the dangerous work of preaching Christianity in Latin America today. Those
who take up this cross offer hope in the promise of the Resurrection.

2

Northern Ireland:
War No More

When English nobles established plantations in Ireland in the sixteenth century, they grew crops for export to England on lands they took from small farmers, impoverishing generations of Irish. In 1847 a blight infested the potato crop, the staple of the Irish peasant diet, destroying the crops for six straight growing seasons and creating a famine that killed one million people. Another million and a half people left the country, the majority emigrating to the U.S., Canada, and Australia. What had been an island of 8,200,000 in 1847, before the famine and the exodus, became an island of 6,600,000.

In the early 1960s, new "troubles" descended on Northern Ireland, the six counties that remained a Britain province when the other twenty-six counties achieved independence and became the Republic of Ireland in 1921. This chapter examines the past three decades of civil strife that erupted from the injustice of Britain's historical domination of Ireland. Like all social conflicts, the violence that escalated in the northern third of Ireland in the 1960s has a history. Section one briefly describes England's colonization and control of Ireland from the seventeenth century until the twentieth century. In 1921, the southern twenty-six counties of Ireland finally achieved republic status. Six northern counties, however, remained a British province because the Protestant majority refused to give up their link to Britain. This partition of Ireland marked the origins of the "troubles" that have plagued

Northern Ireland for thirty years. Sections two and three trace the outbreak and deepening of the struggle that pitted Irish revolutionaries intent on reuniting Ireland against the British Army, the police, and Protestant militias. Sections four through seven tell the stories of the amazing courage and patience of the peacemakers who are building a new future in Ireland.

This is the story of a society's efforts to spare the next generation its pain by resolving conflict and burying old hatreds. We shall see how a society caught in the cycle of violence and counterviolence is finding ways to bring peace. We shall meet the people who contributed to the peace that is finally turning tears to laughter, and keening to singing. Those who planted and tended the peace seeds, especially those Protestant and Catholic politicians, clergy, and "peace people," have much to teach us about courage and vision. No nation, region, or community is immune to the kind of religious, ethnic, or racial conflict that can tear it apart and inflict wounds for generations. We will follow the Irish people on their long road to peace.

1. When England Ruled Ireland

From the sixteenth century through the eighteenth century, Britain's kings fought Irish nobles for control of Ireland. During that time, two developments had a major role in shaping modern English-Irish relations. The first was the religious upheaval that began in England when King Henry VIII denied the pope's authority over the English Church and declared himself head of the Church of England in 1534. In 1541, he also took the title "King of Ireland." When Henry's daughter Mary became queen in 1553, however, her religious loyalty was to her Catholic mother, Catherine, the daughter of the King of Spain, whom Henry had divorced for not producing a male heir. Queen Mary restored papal authority and married a future King of Spain. When Protestant nobles opposed her Spanish alliance, Mary executed many of them and earned the name "Bloody Mary." After Mary died, her half-sister Elizabeth ascended the throne, becoming Elizabeth I. She ruled from 1558 to 1603 and supported the Church of England. In 1588 her naval forces defeated the Spanish Armada, a fleet dispatched by King Philip II of Spain to invade England, thus ending the Spanish Crown's intent to control the English throne for political and religious purposes.

The second development that heavily influenced the shape of modern English-Irish relations was the English monarchy's colonization of

Ireland by King James I after he succeeded Elizabeth I to the throne in 1603. James, who also expanded English rule in North America by establishing a colony in Jamestown, Virginia, established "plantations" of English and Scottish colonists in the north of Ireland. King James offered English nobles large tracts of land confiscated from Irish farmers. London merchants followed the planters, building a walled city with a military garrison near Derry, naming it "Londonderry." The "planting" of English aristocrats and English and Scottish farmers continued to push Irish farmers off the land and expand British control, and English law prohibited landowners from having Irish peasants farm the land as tenants. Thus, in 1641, Irish peasants rebelled, killing an estimated four thousand colonists and suffering as many casualties themselves.

The struggle, however, was only beginning. The warfare between Protestants and Catholics that was breaking out in England would soon spill into Ireland, bringing a religious dimension to the English-Irish hostilities. Lord Oliver Cromwell rose to prominence during the English civil war that deposed the English king in 1648. Cromwell then led forces of the newly established Parliament against the Irish who remained loyal to the king, massacring peasants and clergy, and burning villages, Catholic churches, and monasteries. The Cromwellian decade of terror and fanatical anti-Catholicism left eighty percent of Ireland in the hands of Britain. From that time on, religious identity was grafted to the conflict for political and economic control of Ireland. After Cromwell's death in 1658, the monarchy was restored by King Charles II, who returned a small portion of Irish lands confiscated by Cromwell's forces.

In 1685, Charles's second son became King James II. A convert to Roman Catholicism, James II sought equality for Catholics in England and power sharing among Catholics and Protestants in the government and army of Ireland. Protestant support was not forthcoming, however: Northern Ireland Protestant landholders feared that James would return more lands, and Protestant nobles mistrusted his alliance with Catholic France. When James brought Irish regiments to London, his opponents championed Prince William of Orange, a Dutchman, and rebelled against James. With the arrival of William's forces in England, James fled to France, where he raised an army and sailed to Ireland, hoping to secure a base from which to regain his throne. In 1690 William's troops pursued James to Northern Ireland, defeating his French and Irish troops. Northern Irish Protestants annually commemorate the

Londonderry men who, in 1690, prevented Irish forces from breaching the city walls until King William's "Orangemen" arrived. As the seventeenth century drew to a close, Protestantism was firmly established and Catholicism suppressed in both England and Ireland.

The yearning for independence from English rule grew stronger throughout the eighteenth century. Encouraged by the successful American and French revolutions, an Irish organization developed in 1795 that was committed to establishing an Irish Republic. Known as "United Irishmen," its members included Protestants as well as Catholics. Such revolutionary developments stirred fears among the landowning descendants of the British "planted" in Ireland almost two centuries earlier. The "Orange Order" was founded that same year to maintain England's control of Ireland. In 1798 the British Army crushed the revolutionary movement and executed its leaders. Fearing that Napoleon would actively assist the Irish in their freedom struggle, the English Parliament, supported by pro-union planters, passed the Act of Union, in 1801, annexing Ireland. The newly appointed British governor pledged the use of military force to preserve English—and Protestant—rule.

Two distinct and increasingly opposed Irish political cultures now inhabited the island: "unionist" were committed to maintaining allegiance to England and the Anglican Church, and "republicans" were committed to an independent Irish republic and clamored for "home rule." By 1880 five-sixths of the members of Parliament elected from constituencies in Ireland favored "home rule" for Ireland. British Prime Minister Gladstone introduced a Home Rule Bill in Parliament in 1886 by saying:

> When five-sixths of the lawfully chosen representatives are of one mind on this matter . . . certainly I cannot allow it to be said that a Protestant minority in Ulster, or elsewhere, is to rule the question at large for Ireland (Prime Minister William Gladstone).[1]

But the British Conservative Party supported the Protestant unionists and was able to block Parliament from granting home rule for the next thirty-five years.

As popular pressure for home rule grew in Ireland, so did Protestant determination to protect their interests. In 1912 nearly half a million unionists signed a covenant to block the "conspiracy" to establish home rule. A hundred thousand Protestants enrolled in the Ulster

Volunteer Force (UVF), formed that year to maintain British rule by force if necessary. Those seeking Irish independence formed the Irish Republican Army (IRA) to force the British out. As paramilitaries, both the UVF and the IRA were illegal. The situation exploded in 1916 when republicans stormed and occupied the post office in Dublin. British troops put down the rebellion and executed rebel leaders—giving the republican cause its martyrs. Finally, in 1921 Parliament granted independence to the southern two-thirds of Ireland but retained Northern Ireland as a British province. When the Irish revolutionary government in Dublin accepted those terms, republicans in the north felt betrayed and remained committed to fight on for a united free Irish state. Thus, the partition of Ireland into north and south did not resolve but only served to concentrate the conflict in Northern Ireland.

Readers will recognize similarities between the Irish and the American struggles for independence from England—but there are differences. Just as the U.S. celebrates its independence on July 4 with parades and fireworks, patriotic Northern Irish march on July 12 to commemorate the 1690 victory of Prince William of Orange over King James II that preserved English Protestant rule of Northern Ireland. While in neither Northern Ireland nor the American colonies were the colonists sympathetic to the native peoples, the fates of the native peoples were different. Native Irish were treated as servile; Native Americans were treated much worse. The victorious American colonists turned their guns on Native Americans—some of whom had actually fought for them against the British. The U.S. achievement of "independence" remained deeply flawed by what was done to both Native Americans and African people on this continent.

The following outline briefly identifies the opposing political and paramilitary organizations in contemporary Northern Ireland.

Glossary

Republic of Ireland (RI): achieved independence from Britain in 1921. It consists of twenty-six counties and has a parliamentary government seated in Dublin.

Northern Ireland (NI, also called "Ulster"): consists of six counties and remains part of the United Kingdom of England, Scotland, and Wales. Its Parliament meets in Belfast and enjoyed considerable autonomy until Britain dissolved the government in 1972 and took direct control.

Royal Ulster Constabulary (RUC): the armed police force of NI. Made up almost entirely of Protestants, it also had reserve units formed in the 1920s to combat the IRA. However, because of their excessive use of force and human rights violations, the reserve units were abolished in the 1970s.

Garda Siochana: the unarmed police force of the RI.

Northern Ireland's Two Cultural Identities

Unionists: northern Irish with historical ties to Britain who desire to remain part of the United Kingdom. Their religious identity is Protestant. **Loyalists** are working-class Unionists.

Nationalists: those who desire the reunification of Ireland, and whose religious identity is Roman Catholic.

Republicans: also want a united Ireland and are committed to ending British rule by force.

Northern Ireland's Opposing Political Parties

Ulster Unionist Party (UUP): the largest party in Northern Ireland, drawing its members from the middle and upper classes. The UUP controlled the government for fifty years.

Social Democratic Labor Party(SDLP): founded by nationalists in 1970 to further full civil rights and political participation by Catholics and eventual reunification of Ireland.

Democratic Unionist Party (DUP): committed to Protestant control and is inflammatory in its rhetoric.

Sinn Fein ("Ourselves Alone"): the political party of the Republican movement.

Progressive Unionist Party: founded in 1979 as the political wing of the Ulster Defense Association (see below).

Note: These are the five leading Political parties. The UUP has the largest electoral support, followed by SDLP and Sinn Fein.

Northern Ireland's Paramilitary Organizations

Ulster Volunteer Force (UVF): founded in 1912 to defeat the independence movement; reestablished in 1966

Irish Republican Army (IRA): founded in 1919 to defeat British rule by guerrilla warfare; known as the Provisional IRA (PIRA) since the early 1970s

Ulster Defense Association (UDA): founded in 1971 and became the largest loyalist paramilitary

Irish National Liberation Army (INLA): breakaway from IRA in 1975

Loyalist Volunteer Force: founded in 1995 to derail the peace process

Real IRA: Breakaway group founded in 1996 to derail the peace process

2. Marching Seasons

The annual parades celebrating the British and Protestant victory of 1690 are not limited to July 12, but wind through Catholic neighborhoods throughout the second half of the summer. The "marching season," as it is called, causes tempers to rise and local police departments to worry. After all, Catholic citizens of Northern Ireland do not need to be reminded of the defeat of Catholics three centuries ago—especially since they continued to be treated as a defeated people. For example, while Protestants experienced rising prosperity in the 1950s, Catholics remained shut out of jobs and the university, Catholic women found work in clothing factories or as servants, and Catholic men were generally lucky to learn a trade but often worked as untrained laborers—or were unemployed. When the extensive German bombing of Belfast during World War II created a severe housing shortage, many Catholics waited years to rent a house while Protestant applicants received housing more quickly.

Catholics experienced severe political and economic inequality. Although Catholics represented forty percent of the population of Northern Ireland, the Protestant-controlled government used a variety of means to lessen Catholic political influence. For example, only property owners (rather than all adults) were permitted to vote in elections.

Imagine the effect in the United States if citizens who rent homes or apartments were to be denied voting rights. The boundaries of voting districts were redrawn to create Protestant majorities among the eligible voters in as many districts as possible. As a result, Catholics had little political representation or power.

> Two crude notions of liberty had come into conflict, one defending a heritage of Britishness and of freedom of religion and [the other] moved not by hatred but by the instinct of freedom. . . . Two sets of Irish Christians . . . engag[ed] in a war which would prove once again that one man's terrorist is another man's freedom fighter (Tim Pat Coogan, *The Troubles*).[2]

Finally, in 1964, after watching U.S. blacks marching for their civil rights in the 1950s and 1960s, Catholics in Northern Ireland founded the Northern Ireland Civil Rights Association to protest discrimination in housing, education, and voting. As civil rights marchers faced angry loyalists, incidents of violence from both unionists and republicans occurred. 1966 marked the fiftieth anniversary of the Dublin uprising of Irish patriots against the British colonial government in 1916. The government of Northern Ireland, fearful of Republican agitation, prohibited public gatherings and marches to commemorate the event. St. Patrick's Day parades were also banned.

Three years later, on New Year's Day 1969, a group of Catholic and Protestant students from Queens University in Belfast organized a seventy-three-mile march from Belfast to Derry to protest housing and voting discrimination. As the marchers entered Derry they were attacked by a loyalist mob that included police (RUC) reservists. Although the RUC witnessed the attacks, it did not intervene. Several months later, when the government banned all civil rights activities in Derry in April, tempers flared on all sides, and that summer the Protestant Marching Season was the spark that ignited a civil war.

On August 12, 1969, Republican militants in Belfast set up barricades to prevent Orangemen from marching through their neighborhoods. They also threatened to burn down an RUC police station. Coogan, author and historian, called it "the hour of widow-making."[3]

On the night of August 14, gangs of Protestants attacked Catholic neighborhoods with bricks and gasoline-filled bottles, driving Catholics out and burning their homes and businesses. A Catholic monastery and adjacent school were attacked and the school set afire. Calls to the RUC went unheeded and British soldiers were finally dispatched to the scene to quell the violence. In the weeks that followed, however, whole neighborhoods were torched and an estimated fifteen hundred Catholic families and three hundred Protestant families were forced to flee their homes.

There were those who tried in vain to calm both sides. For example, one of the priests whose monastery had been attacked told a Catholic audience that "the vast majority of the Protestants are thoroughly ashamed of what has happened [and] we mustn't let hate spring into our hearts for our Protestant brethren."[4] But fear and terrorism spread through the communities as citizens patrolled neighborhood boundaries and Catholics barricaded their neighborhoods to protect themselves and to block the entry of police or military vehicles. The sense of defenselessness that Belfast Catholics experienced in the summer of 1969 helps to explain the rebirth of the Irish Republican Army (IRA) that year.

What brought the conflict between these two major communities of Northern Ireland to the explosion point? At least three reasons seem apparent. First, these two communities lived, worked, socialized, and worshiped separately. Catholics were excluded from education and politics and from many work opportunities. As a result of not knowing or trusting one another, each community feared the other. The lower socioeconomic classes of both sides were most threatened and aggrieved; their neighborhoods were the sites of civil disturbances, and they were the ones who were either jobless or feared losing economic ground if the other community surpassed them. It was the lower socio-economic communities that supplied paramilitary recruits—and sustained the majority of the casualties.

Second, colonial rule left a legacy of violence. Subjugated people are viewed as inherently inferior and dangerous elements who must be "kept in their place." Many in the government of Northern Ireland, in the RUC, and in the British Army bore these attitudes toward the Catholic population. Unable to depend on the government for protection, the Catholic minority responded to mistreatment and injustices by organizing their own means of defense. Coogan described the IRA as "the most ruthlessly efficient guerrilla force to appear in Western Europe since the end of World War II," whose violent methods were "in flagrant disregard of church teaching."[5] The government of Northern Ireland reacted with repressive measures and loyalist paramilitary activity increased.

> A strain ran through [British] military thinking that Northern Ireland and its people were the equivalent of the restless natives encountered in far-flung places of the British Empire—a view that was reflected in the range of military techniques used by the army on the streets of Belfast during the period 1970–71.[6]

Third, and most obvious, was the glaring contradiction between the ideals of democratic government that guarantee equal protection under the law and the realities of life in Northern Ireland. For example, in the 1950s the government passed the Special Powers Act, designed to abridge the civil rights of Catholic dissidents. While the government did little to moderate the Protestant "marching season," it banned Catholic commemorative and protest marches.

3. A Bloody Decade

In the summer of 1969, British troops were dispatched to Northern Ireland to keep the peace. Although Catholic neighborhoods in Belfast initially welcomed the troops as peacekeepers, the British Army's role changed almost overnight when the IRA began to shoot British soldiers. Now the army's task was to put down a Catholic rebellion led by the IRA. In 1971, Northern Ireland's prime minister declared: "Northern Ireland is at war with the Irish Republican Army Provisionals." A curfew was imposed in Catholic neighborhoods and house searches for people suspected of IRA links began. In 1971, the British Army entered and searched more than seventeen thousand houses. That summer, the army began the practice of "internment," the arrest and imprisonment, without trial, of suspected IRA members. On one night in August, 346 men were arrested; none was Protestant. Many were mistakenly arrested because they had the same last name of a person being sought.

The lists from which arrests were made even included people no longer living. The evidence of torture while in police custody that eventually came to light were blatant violations of civil and human rights and glaring contradictions to British ideals of "equal protection under the law." Clearly, the Catholic population was now alienated from the very army that had come to protect them.

Overall, 1971 was a very bad year. Republicans seethed and unionists feared for their security. Another unionist paramilitary unit, the Ulster Defense Association (UDA), sprang up. In the first eight months, 34 people died in the civil conflict. After internment began in August, 140 people were killed, 2,400 people were injured, and 15,000 British troops were on duty in Northern Ireland.

In 1972 Northern Ireland was plunged into deeper destruction and despair. On January 30, British soldiers fired on a group of Catholic civil rights marchers in Derry, killing 14 unarmed people. Known as "Bloody Sunday," the shootings intensified the cycle of retaliations that would produce many more bloody days. In March, the British government dissolved the Northern Ireland government and assumed direct rule of the province. Determined to defeat the IRA, the British government continued to impose curfews and conduct house searches in Catholic neighborhoods. IRA members were subjected to trials without juries, and suspected IRA terrorists were subject to a "shoot to kill" policy. The violations of civil rights, however, only strengthened the will of the IRA and intensified the violent retaliation. (The European Court of Human Rights later ruled that internment constituted "inhuman and degrading treatment" prohibited by the 1948 Universal Declaration on Human Rights.) The year 1972 was the bloodiest time of the Troubles, marked by 467 deaths, 10,600 injuries, and 1,900 bombings. Truly, the entire citizenry of Northern Ireland was now a prisoner of the war between the British Army and the IRA. Time would reveal that the army could neither defeat the IRA nor control the loyalist paramilitary units. Lawlessness and violence reigned.

Although the British government recognized the urgent need to reduce voting and housing discrimination against Catholics and to reform the RUC, the barricades separating Protestant and Catholic neighborhoods of Derry and Belfast reflected the psychological walls between the groups—and with each new act of terrorism, the walls rose higher. As paramilitary units continued to shoot and bomb, moderate nationalists struggled to find peaceful solutions. The largest nationalist party, the Social Democratic Labor Party (SDLP), founded in 1970 by Derry civil rights activist John Hume, had as its platform greater distribution of wealth, civil rights for all, Catholic-Protestant friendship, and cooperation between Northern Ireland and the Republic of Ireland. Although the SDLP was firmly committed to nonviolent change, even moderate unionists resisted any change in Northern Ireland's power structure or relations with Britain. Many Protestants and Catholics desired peace, but all roads to it appeared blocked.

In 1973 the British government proposed a broader power-sharing

John Hume was born in 1937 in Derry and was one of the first Catholics in twentieth-century Northern Ireland to receive a public school education. After attending university, he returned to his poor Derry neighborhood in 1960 where he taught school and helped establish a credit union and a housing association. Hume was inspired by the 1960s civil rights campaigns of the U.S. and by Martin Luther King, Jr. Six months after King's assassination, Hume became involved in the Northern Ireland civil rights struggle. Hume involved himself in politics and won a seat in the Northern Ireland Parliament in 1969. The following year he helped found the SDLP, which reflected his commitment to civil rights for all and to remedying injustices only through nonviolent means. John Hume has pursued his vision for thirty years, saying "I am absolutely certain that agreement will eventually emerge . . . The twenty-first century will be a post-nationalist and interdependent world. . . . Catholic, Protestant, and Dissenter will come together on our small island and at last the gun will have no role in the politics of our land."[7]

structure of government for Northern Ireland. Unionists and nationalists would rule jointly and new forms of cooperation between Northern Ireland and the Republic of Ireland would be created. Although Hume and the SDLP agreed, the plan collapsed after a few months when

Unionists repudiated the new government and staged massive work stoppages. As a result, London was forced to resume direct rule.

By 1974, over two thousand suspected IRA members were in Belfast and British prisons, serving long sentences and frequently subjected to cruel treatment. At first, their status was that of "political prisoners," but in 1976 the British government declared that they were to be regarded no differently than other convicted criminals. Protests by prisoners began.

Although talks among the various political parties, paramilitary organizations, and governments in London and Dublin were desperately needed, beginning a dialogue among the many hostile and distrustful parties would be difficult. Political initiatives were dangerous—if politicians made overtures they risked being accused of making concessions. Political leaders needed sufficient constituent support to prevent differences from leading to division. Political groups associated with paramilitaries (such as Sinn Fein with the IRA) were seen as fronts for terrorists and murderers, and were barred from any peace talks. As long as the paramilitaries were convinced that their goals could not be achieved through political means, they remained committed to physical force. This situation left the entire society trapped in the perception that self-defense was the only option as political goals receded. It would take courageous efforts by many people over several years to stop the violence and dismantle the walls.

4. The Search for Peace

Two events served as catalysts in the movement toward peacemaking that began in the early 1980s. The first involved a trip to Ireland in 1979 by the newly elected pope, Pope John Paul II. The second involved protest in a British prison that ended with the death of ten Irish Republican prisoners.

Pope John Paul II went to Ireland to plead for peace two months after his trip to Mexico. The militant loyalists denounced his visit and the militant republicans rejected his call for an end to violence. While his words angered republicans, they proved to be a catalyst for dialogue to begin.

A Summary of Pope John Paul II, "A Plea for Peace," September 1979

This struggle is not about religion. In fact, many Catholic and Protestant Christians, inspired by their shared faith and Gospel, desire and struggle for peace and unity.

Christians are called to resist unjust situations and to create social orders that respect the dignity and equality of all; governments may not violate human rights or allow inequalities among citizens on grounds of "state security."

The commandment "Thou shalt not kill" is binding on the conscience of all. Violence is evil and unworthy of human beings. Violence destroys what it claims to defend: human dignity, freedom, and life itself.

Justice is not obtained by murder and terrorism. War-making does not resolve conflict. Peacemaking is "the only way to justice . . . [and] is itself the work of justice."

Forgiveness must "be part of the vocabulary of every Christian." Admiration belongs to those who try to walk the path of reconciliation and peace, who offer forgiveness to those who have caused them great harm and suffering. The youth of Northern Ireland must resist joining violent organizations. Their parents must model peace by creating peace and reconciliation opportunities within neighborhoods.

Political leaders on all sides must "prove those wrong who say that political action cannot achieve justice" and must "be leaders in the cause of peace, reconciliation, and justice."

Sinn Fein responded by challenging Catholic Church leaders to assist in finding political solutions to injustices rather than merely condemning the violent alternatives to which republicans had resorted. They declared that the primary violence in Northern Ireland was the political and police systems themselves.

The second event that indirectly aided the peace process underscored the great sadness that afflicted many Northern Irish Catholic families—the imprisonment of over two thousand husbands, fathers, and sons in British and Ulster prisons. In 1981, ten of these Irish prisoners pledged to fast to death unless their political-prisoner status was restored. The British government adamantly refused, despite the appeal of the pope and several governments.

The first prisoner to die was Bobby Sands, a hero for the Irish republican cause who had even won a seat in the British Parliament representing his family's district. The outpouring of sympathy furthered the cause of the IRA and helped make Sinn Fein a political force that would have a key role in reaching any peace settlement. Gerry Adams, who had been a fellow inmate of Sands from 1972–1977, led Sinn Fein in intensive organizing of its popular base.

Gerry Adams was born in 1948 in West Belfast to Catholic parents. The oldest of ten children, he grew up seeing the economic hardship and social discrimination facing Catholics. At seventeen, Adams left the local Christian Brothers school to go to work to supplement his father's income as a laborer and his mother's work as a domestic. Gerry's family and neighbors had strong republican roots, and he soon was involved in the Northern Ireland Civil Rights Association. In August 1969, not yet twenty-one years old, Adams saw his neighborhood attacked by Protestant mobs, friends killed or wounded, and his home bombed. Throughout 1970 and 1971, he saw and eventually experienced the routine brutality used by the British Army against suspected IRA members and sympathizers. He was arrested and imprisoned for five years and was involved in the prison protests described above.

Despite the degrading treatment Adams and other republicans experienced in British prisons, Adams did not emerge hardened or hate-filled. Rather, he turned his energies to political organizing within Sinn Fein, becoming a tireless advocate of democratic reforms in Northern Ireland. He is determined that the past not be repeated. "We cannot be deflected from the task of building peace on this island. History has placed a challenge at our doors. The people of Ireland, from every corner of our country and from throughout the Irish diaspora across the world, have expressed their yearning for a lasting peace settlement and a new democracy. Building a new accord may be a daunting challenge, but it is the challenge facing everyone in political leadership on these islands. If this challenge is to be translated into reality, then we must all respond to it with courage and imagination . . . Let us ignore the naysayers and the begrudgers. Let us confound the skeptics and cynics."[8]

Father Alec Reid, a Catholic priest whose monastery of Clonard had been attacked ten years earlier, responded to Adams's challenge. Years later, John Hume paid tribute to the "patience, skill, and determination" of Fr. Reid, whose "work of reconciliation has been nothing less than indispensable in bringing about the peace we now enjoy." Reid met with Sinn Fein leaders who 1) reiterated its interest in the Church's involvement in a peace process; 2) insisted that the British and Republic of Ireland governments were morally obligated to correct the social injustices that contributed to violence; and 3) endorsed a nonviolent approach only if a strategy for peace was backed by a political coalition that could successfully achieve it. Father Reid communicated Sinn Fein's position to church leaders and began to mediate between republicans, Catholic Church leaders, and politicians in the Irish Republic.

Adams labored to achieve a consensus within the republican community to pursue a negotiated settlement rather than a victory through violence. Father Reid labored intensively as a mediator between Adams, Catholic Church officials, and government officials in the Irish Republic. Talking with Sinn Fein rather than demonizing it was an important step.

5. Talk-Talk Not Shoot-Shoot

> It must be said that an armed people are by no means a sure guarantee to liberation. Our guns may kill our enemies but unless we direct them with the politics of a revolutionary people they will eventually kill ourselves. Guns don't win wars; guns and bombs may kill a man but they cannot lead a man (Bobby Sands, from prison).[9]

What would the talks focus on? If nationalists and unionists were to reach agreement, each needed to distinguish between what they *wanted* and what they *needed*. *Needs* represent what is essential and cannot be given up. *Wants* are subject to negotiation and compromise. While unionists *wanted* the assurance that Britain would never sever its ties with Northern Ireland, what they *needed* were political structures that protect them if they should ever be outnumbered by nationalists. While nationalists *wanted* the reunification of all Ireland into one republic, free of British ties, what they *needed* was assurance that they would be participants in the governing process and would have their cultural links to the Irish Republic preserved and honored. Communal self-understanding and cross-community dialogue took time. The social, political, and economic sources of conflict were not improving quickly. The following timeline outlines the progress toward peace.

1985: "Anglo-Irish Agreement"
The British government in cooperation with the Republic of Ireland recognized the unionists need for the principle of majority consent and the nationalists need for including the Republic of Ireland in the affairs of Northern Ireland. However, Sinn Fein's demand to be included in the peace negotiations was rejected.

1987: "A Scenario for Peace"
Sinn Fein published this statement calling for an end to British rule in Northern Ireland, and proposing a framework and timetable for an "inclusive negotiated democratic settlement." Adams and Hume began talks and issued (at the suggestion of Fr. Reid) "a statement of principles to govern a peaceful settlement" to be jointly considered by the governments in London and Dublin. Adams later described his meeting with Hume as "the beginning of the most significant discussion in formulating a new peace initiative in the north of Ireland." Momentum was building for pursuing political reform through ballots rather than bullets and bombs.

1990: Secret talks between British government and Sinn Fein
The parties who had been at war with each other now explored solutions together. Adams declared that his objective was "a non-armed political movement working for self-determination in Ireland" and recognized as essential the creation of a dialogue with mainstream unionists. But the gulf between republicans and unionists remained wide. Getting unionists to compromise would not be easy. Indeed, the hopes for peace were periodically dashed by atrocities and retaliations committed by paramilitaries on both sides.

1992: Sinn Fein published a framework for settlement

Sinn Fein declared that there were not two but several peoples who shared an Irish identity and called on the British government to recognize the right to self-determination for all Irish people. Sovereignty, Sinn Fein insisted, must rest with an all-Ireland government selected by democratic process. Sinn Fein urged the British government to exert its influence on unionists to accept a democratic political process. It also appealed to the government of the Republic of Ireland to take a leading role in promoting negotiation between all parties. The new Ireland required structures to overcome divisions, achieve national reconciliation, and assure "the cultural integrity and civil rights of all sections of the Irish population."[10]

1993: The "Irish Peace Initiative"

Published jointly by the SDLP and Sinn Fein, this consensus statement called for :
- national reconciliation
- the right of national self-determination
- involvement of the Republic of Ireland in resolving the conflict in Northern Ireland
- a peaceful and democratic accord respecting different traditions and providing means of national reconciliation

British Prime Minister John Majors and Irish Prime Minister Albert Reynolds responded with the **"Downing Street Declaration."** Majors tried to reassure unionists that Britain was not about to desert them. He also said that both governments had agreed to the principles of "democracy, the absence of coercion—in other words consent, no outside interference, and an end to violence."

1994: Paramilitary Cease-fires

In August, the IRA took a momentous step toward peace by announcing a cease-fire: "Recognizing the potential of the current situation and in order to enhance the democratic peace process . . . there will be a complete cessation of military operations . . . We believe that an opportunity to craft a just and lasting settlement has been created." Loyalist paramilitaries jointly announced a cease-fire in October.

> **1995: "Framework Document"**
> In the window of opportunity created by the cease-fires, Dublin and London affirmed the principles of democratic consent for a possible unification of Ireland and an all-Ireland settlement. Could the cease-fires hold while unionists and nationalists worked out a plan? Could Northern Ireland begin to heal itself?

6. Peace People

The peacemakers in Ireland include many people besides political and religious leaders, people who, by their acts of courage, helped create the changes of mind and heart necessary to bring peace. In some cases the people who experienced the trauma of having loved ones killed or maimed became advocates for peace. In other cases, the people responsible for the violence asked forgiveness and worked for reconciliation.

Among the three thousand Catholic and Protestant families whose loved ones were victims of the violence were the Maguires, the Wilsons, the Armstrongs, the Hills, and the McGoldricks. Each in their own way did something extraordinary in their time of grieving—by extending their forgiveness to the persons who had killed their loved ones and by committing themselves to working for peace and reconciliation.

Anne Maguire took her three young sons, the youngest a six-month-old infant, for a walk in Belfast one summer morning in August 1976. A stolen car driven by an IRA member suddenly rounded the corner fleeing a British Army vehicle. When the soldiers shot and killed the driver, the car sped out of control and killed all three children. Betty Williams, a witness to the tragedy, met Mairead Corrigan, Anne Maguire's sister, at the children's funeral. "We reached a point, I think, when we could no longer remain passive, when we felt that we must do something," said Williams, who eventually went door to door collecting signatures on a petition pleading for an end to the violence. Paramilitary organizations were only deepening the conflict, turning young men and boys "violent, aggressive, almost murderers, and . . . the heroes of the community."[11] Within a few weeks, thirty thousand Catholic and Protestant women were marching together for peace through the streets of Belfast—and they did so weekly for months. Although Williams and Corrigan were accused of collaborating with the enemy and their lives were threatened, they were awarded the Nobel Peace Prize in 1977. The "Peace People" organization they helped found continues to educate youth—in Northern Ireland and beyond—in nonviolence and tolerance.

Gordon Wilson and his twenty-year-old daughter *Marie*, a nurse, attended the annual Veterans Day observance in Enniskillen, Northern Ireland in November 1987. So did *Bert Armstrong's* brother and sister-in-law, and Noreen Hill's husband, a school principal. A powerful bomb planted by the IRA in the World War I Monument exploded during the ceremony, killing Marie Wilson, Bert Armstrong's brother and his sister-in-law, and nine other people. Noreen Hill's husband suffered severe and permanent injuries. The Wilson family was devastated by Marie's death, but people were awestruck when her father told the media that he had no desire for revenge: "I bear no ill will, I bear no grudge."[12] In Marie's memory, Gordon Wilson dedicated himself to the cause of peace. Six years later, he arranged to meet personally with IRA officials to urge them to put down their weapons. "They listened," he said afterward, "but they made no change in their position. Perhaps it was naive of me to imagine that because it was me they would. I went in innocence to search for what my heart told me might be a way forward. I got nothing." Within a year, however, the IRA did declare a cease-fire, and Wilson was asked to join the Forum for Peace and Reconciliation that the Dublin government established in 1994.

In time, Bert Armstrong and Noreen Hill came to the Center for Christian Renewal run by Rev. Cecil Kerr, an Anglican priest who works for reconciliation among Christians in Ireland. Bert Armstrong, a retired Protestant minister, remembers that when he got the awful news of the deaths at Enniskillen, he sat before the cross and realized that he had to pray the Christian prayer of forgiveness. "I knew that if I did not do that, I could not stand in the pulpit and preach again." Noreen Hill, who daily cares for her husband, tells church groups, "If only we would pray more for the people of violence." Reverend Kerr refers to these families' "amazing grace of forgiveness" from which peace will flower. Kerr himself speaks to mixed groups of Catholics and Protestants, asking forgiveness for the sins that his own Anglican Church—the Church of the British conquerors—committed against other Irish Christians.

Michael McGoldrick, Jr., was walking home from work one day in 1996 when he was abducted by members of a loyalist paramilitary founded that year to derail the peace process. The gang killed

McGoldrick, leaving his parents suicidal with grief. His father, Michael, Sr., recalled leaving the house late that night and walking about in the dark. When he decided to say a Catholic prayer of repentance, he suddenly felt new life. At his son's funeral he told the television interviewer, "As I stand here the person who killed my son may be watching . . . and I want to say to him now that I forgive him and my wife forgives him. I don't want this to ever happen again. Please, for the sake of the community of Northern Ireland, bury your pride, bury your pride with my son in the grave."[13]

Other centers of reconciliation bring together Protestants and Catholics to pray, to assist the families of victims, and to work for peace. Anglican pastor Kenneth Clarke noted that he and many other Christians are coming to realize that they have grown up confusing cultural identity with Christian identity, and that worshiping "God and country" is simply idolatry. He called on Protestant and Catholic churches to become "down and out churches"—recognizing that their roots go deep into Christ and that they are "meant to be reaching out with the arms of compassion."

Since the early 1990s evangelical organizations of Catholics and Protestants have worked together. In 1996 a National Day of Repentance was supported by 130 Protestant and Catholic church leaders. Churches from other parts of the world have sent monetary aid to their counterparts in Northern Ireland to aid the peace and development work.

> Yes, we do need to pray, but we also need to commit ourselves against sectarianism, and that will take hard political work. There is a feeling [among Protestants]: "We never did anything wrong." There is a lack of a sense of corporate sin and structural sin. When the churches call for repentance, the people don't know what to do with it. We're so anti-Catholic here that we have denied our people the mechanism of repentance, confession, and restitution (Rev. David Porter).

Not only the church leaders and victims of violence have become advocates for peace, however. Some of those who joined paramilitary organizations and used violence to achieve their objectives have experienced dramatic changes of heart: Gusty Spence, Billy Hutchinson, and Joseph Patrick Doherty for example.

Gusty Spence helped to reactivate the Ulster Volunteer Force in 1966 and was charged that year with participating in the murder of three Catholics in Belfast. Although Spence went to prison for eighteen years, he shocked his UVF comrades when he appealed from jail for them and the IRA to put down their weapons. This "tough guy" now talked about the need for reconciliation and integrated schools. It was Gusty who was chosen by the unionist paramilitaries to announce their cease-fire on October 13, 1994. Spence said, "Let us firmly resolve never again to permit our political circumstances to degenerate into bloody warfare."[14] He also expressed "to the loved ones of all innocent victims over the past twenty-five years abject and true remorse."

Billy Hutchinson joined the UVF in 1974 and drove the getaway car for gunmen who murdered two Catholics. After serving fifteen years of a life sentence, Hutchinson was released, went to work in community development, and became profoundly anti-violence and pro-peace. Knowing well the grave wrongs committed by both sides, he did not want to see another generation recruited to continue a war that made Northern Ireland the loser. In the critical months of 1998, Hutchinson led the Progressive Unionist Party and urged unionists to keep the accord they signed by allowing Sinn Fein to take its rightful place in the new government of Northern Ireland, rather than use the IRA's refusal to disarm as an excuse to retreat. With others, Hutchinson established a new political tone, saying "We're still learning how to put ourselves in someone else's shoes, whether they're the British government or Sinn Fein."[15]

Joseph Patrick Doherty, a seventeen-year-old Catholic, was arrested and interned by the British in 1972. When the Doherty home was bombed in 1974, he joined the IRA. In 1980 he was charged with the murder of a British soldier and sentenced to life in prison. Doherty later escaped from the Belfast prison and fled to the U.S., where he lived and worked under an assumed name until he was arrested and returned to Britain as a fugitive.

Back in the Belfast prison to serve out his sentence, Joe Doherty began to speak of the need for republicans to be able to change and be part of the give-and-take negotiation process. He reflected that "when I was younger I really thought we were going to push the Brits into the sea, raise the tricolor, and have a democratic, peaceful Ireland for all. But it's just not as easy as that."[16]

People who were closest to the violence, those who buried family members and friends, those who fired the weapons and planted the bombs, those who have spent half of their lives in prison: many of these people, recognizing that hate could not solve their communities' problems, have dedicated themselves to telling the politicians to let go of old grudges and wrongs and to lead the way to reconciliation.

> Repentance and forgiveness are two sides of one coin. Repentance means to change your mind. I believe that is the greatest need in the country at the moment . . . unless there's a change of heart, there won't be a true peace (Rev. Cecil Kerr).

7. Peace at Last?

After the cease-fires, the momentum for reaching political agreement slowed but did not stop. The Irish Republic established a Forum for Peace and Reconciliation in Dublin and invited representatives from all political parties, north and south, to speak their views. While some unionist views were heard, the official unionist parties refused to participate.

At the request of Britain and the Republic of Ireland, President Bill Clinton sent former U.S. Senator George Mitchell to head a commission to determine how all paramilitaries could be disarmed. When the Ulster Unionist Party insisted that the IRA give up its weapons before talks could begin, and the IRA refused, the UUP in turn refused to enter into any talks with Sinn Fein about political power sharing until the IRA disarmed. In 1996 the IRA suspended its cease-fire, but reinstated it seventeen months later. Meanwhile, British Prime Minister Tony Blair, Irish Prime Minister Bertie Ahern, President Clinton, and many people in the Irish-American community encouraged the negotiation process. Blair offered assurances to unionists that they would not be deserted by Britain; Ahern pledged to remove from his nation's constitution its claim to the six Northern Irish counties; and Clinton offered economic aid.

Fortunately, George Mitchell, the chief mediator, would not allow the IRA's refusal to disarm to stop the peace process. He kept the sides talking, he listened, and in April 1998, he presented a settlement draft for their consideration. David Trimble, UUP leader, took the greatest political risk of his life when he put his name to the settlement agreement three days later. The accord gave practical expression to the principles of consent (the majority of the people would be required to vote to join the Irish Republic before that would ever happen), the principle of participation, and the recognition of the natural and historical connection between north and south peoples of Ireland. The parties agreed to a new Assembly in Belfast with safeguards built in to protect the nationalist minority from being overridden. They agreed to formal cooperation between Northern Ireland and the Irish Republic, and to a timetable for the release of IRA and loyalist prisoners and the disarming of paramilitaries. They established a commission to protect civil rights and to reform the RUC. In May, voters in both Northern Ireland and the Irish Republic gave electoral approval to the plan and the new Legislative Assembly was elected in June.

The crucial phase of creating the power-sharing executive branch had now been reached. But in August 1998 a powerful bomb destroyed the marketplace in the town of Omagh, taking the largest death toll in the thirty years of the Troubles and threatening the peace process. Those responsible, calling themselves the "Real IRA," had broken off from the IRA over the peace talks. They expressed regret over the death of so many civilians, saying it was not intended. But their terrorism was met with revulsion. As Ireland and the world mourned the 29 people killed and 330 injured, the gathering of twenty thousand people—Catholics, Anglicans, Presbyterians, Methodists, unionist and nationalists—in Omagh's marketplace symbolized the people of Northern Ireland's unbroken will for peace. One week later the Irish National Liberation Army, another republican paramilitary, joined the cease-fire, declaring "armed struggle can never be the only option for revolutionaries."[17] In September, David Trimble and SDLP leader John Hume received the Nobel Peace Prize.

In December 1998, Trimble and Hume shook hands on an agreement that the ten departments of the new government would be led equally by unionists and nationalists, six cross-border committees would be established, and unionists and nationalists would each have five cabinet posts. That same day the Loyalist Volunteer Force, established two years earlier to derail the peace process, handed over its arsenal to authorities. Michael McGoldrick had been its first murder victim in 1996—and now his father watched on television as the guns were cut into scrap metal. Through his tears he told a reporter, "I never thought I'd see the day. One of those weapons could very well have been used to kill my boy. I'm just so, so glad they'll no longer be used to kill anyone else."[18]

There is much tragedy in Ireland's past that cannot be forgotten. As the Irish starved in 1847, over ten thousand ships laden with food left Irish ports for England. In 1997 British Prime Minister Blair acknowledged England's responsibility: "Those who governed in London at the time failed their people through standing by while a crop failure turned into a massive human tragedy. We must not forget such a dreadful event." But acknowledging wrongs and offering forgiveness can prevent the past from determining the future.

Today, a peaceful future has begun. Mairead Corrigan continues to educate young people in nonviolence. Churches help Protestants and Catholics get to know one another. Schools build cultural bridges where there were once barricades. Irish emigrants dispersed around the world "give back" to Ireland with economic aid and investment projects that bring jobs and peace to war-torn neighborhoods. The next generation is not being recruited for war but is entrusted with building the peace that has at last come to Ireland.

". . . peace comes dropping slow,
dropping from the veils of the morning
to where the cricket sings" (W. B. Yeats).

3

South Africa's
Stain of Apartheid

The nineteenth century witnessed the struggles for democracy in Europe and the widespread greed and racism in the colonies of European nations. The twentieth century witnessed the struggle of Asians, Africans, and Latin Americans for independence and construction of just societies. The story of South Africa introduces elements that are familiar and all too distinctly twentieth-century developments. At the beginning of the century, the British Army used slash-and-burn tactics against Dutch farming communities in Britain's campaign to control Southern Africa, introducing concentration camps for the thousands of civilians they left homeless. When the descendents of the Dutch regained political control of South Africa in 1910, their governments employed widespread torture as a means of maintaining the "national security state" that was in place by the 1960s. Parallel developments in Africa, Asia, and Latin America were numerous.

In the wake of government-sanctioned violence against its "enemies," an urgent moral task throughout the world is the recognition and protection of human rights, and the dismantling of national security states and their replacement with civilian rule of law. "Never again" has become the chorus of those in South Africa, Guatemala, Chile, Argentina, and many other nations who have uncovered the truth of the crimes committed against enemies—people of color, the poor, the indigenous, and those who joined them in their struggle for life. The movement toward national reconciliation and unity has only begun.

The story of modern South Africa contains all of these elements, including the story of churches as bystanders and then as participants in the struggles against colonialism, racism, and greed. It is also the story of the emerging affirmation of "blackness" and the liberating intent of the Gospels, to which the churches must respond if they are to be true to their purposes for existing.

The first section of this chapter provides historical background for understanding twentieth-century South African society and political arrangements. The second section describes the development of a racially segregated and white-ruled society in its most extreme historical form, the only parallel being the racial segregation in the United States from the end of the Civil War until the passage of federal civil rights legislation in the 1960s. Sections three and four document three decades of black south Africans' struggle to create a democratic nation, an aspiration that frequently made them victims of state ruthlessness. Sections five and six document the last stand and final fall of apartheid (1980–1994), when the churches took their most activist role. Section seven describes the role of the Truth and Reconciliation Commission, South Africa's ambitious attempt to begin the journey toward national reconciliation. The eighth section suggests the challenges facing South Africa in the twenty-first century.

1. Dutch Settlers or British Colonials: Who Will Rule the Africans?

Dutch navigators from the East India Company established a fort on the Cape of Good Hope, in southwestern South Africa, in 1652. Although Dutch farmers, called *Boers* (Dutch for "farmers"), gained control of the land in the Cape region and prospered, British colonists and British military forces took control of the Cape region in 1806, supported by tribal groups who resented the Boers' power.

Resenting British economic and political control, many Boers left the Cape Colony en masse in 1835 and trekked deeper into the interior. Referring to the British Parliament's abolition of slavery throughout the empire in 1830, one departing Boer wrote that as a member of the Dutch Reformed Church (DRC), it was her duty to resist "placing Africans on the same footing as Christians, [which] is contrary to the laws of God."

The leadership of the DRC was not enthusiastic about the departure of scores of its members and refused to allow ministers to accompany them on their migration several hundred miles north and northwest. As a result, the transplanted Boers ordained their own DRC clergy who shared their determination to maintain racial separation and white domination in the two independent states they created (the Orange Free State and the Transvaal Republic). The constitution of the Transvaal Republic declared that the state would "permit no equality between colored people and the white inhabitants of the country, either in church or state."

The abolition of slavery in the Cape Colony, however, did not mean racial equality and integration in the colony. European attitudes toward natives were similar, whether in Boer states or British colonies. The natives were essential to the colonial economy; they served as irreplaceable laborers on farms, in mines, and in industry. The Indian immigrant population were useful as tradesmen and shopkeepers, and were a buffer between whites and natives. A three-tier social system existed: whites (the British and the Boers), natives, and Indians. Non-whites (natives and Indians) were viewed as potential challengers to both British and Afrikaner dominion. White missionaries converted natives and established native churches for them since they were not welcomed into white congregations.

In 1879 British forces battled Zulu warriors, defeating the powerful Zulu kingdom along the Indian Ocean and bringing it under British control. When gold was discovered in the Transvaal in the 1880s, London, of course, grew to covet the Boer Republics, and on the pretext of defending its subjects and interests, waged war against the Boers. The Boer War (1897–1901) incurred seventy thousand casualties, destruction of hundreds of Boer farms, and a military innovation of the British: confinement of displaced Boer civilians into concentration camps. Although the British victory gave natives hope that British rule in the Boer Republics would secure their rights, within a few years the British had closed ranks with the Boers. In fact, the constitution of the Union of South Africa established by Britain in 1910 gave disproportionate electoral power to rural districts with Boer majorities. Although they had lost the war, the Boers' National Party won political control of the Union Parliament and the presidency in 1910—rekindling the dream of Afrikanerdom.

What's in a Name: A South African Lexicon

The history of racial conflict in South Africa is reflected in the names used to designate, classify, and dominate other peoples.

Afrikaners: South African descendents of Dutch colonists (originally called *Boers*, the Dutch word for "farmer"). Their language, derived from the Dutch, is called *Afrikaans*. In the twentieth century, Afrikaners used the term to refer to all whites in South Africa in order to suggest a united front among whites. South Africans of British descent, however, do not wish to be identified as Afrikaners.

Apartheid: means "separateness" in Afrikaans, and refers to the policy of extreme racial separation. The architects and enforcers of apartheid divided South Africans into four racial categories:

1. **Bantu:** native African tribal groups of Central and Southern Africa who are linguistically related. During the apartheid era, the government used the word *Bantu* rather than *African*. All blacks were designated as members of one of eight Bantu groups. In 1954 legislation was passed forcing their removal to "Bantustans," territories specifically created by the government for the majority black population.

2. **Colored:** the classification for persons of mixed race.

3. **Indian (or "Asiatic"):** the classification for descendants of Indians brought to South Africa in the nineteenth century by British colonials as indentured servants who eventually earned their freedom.

4. **Whites:** encompassed all people of European origins. In contrast to the many distinctions the government observed among nonwhites, no differences were acknowledged among whites (e.g., language, culture, religion, and history).

In 1906 Afrikaner politicians called the Indian population the "Asiatic cancer" and pledged to drive them out of South Africa within four years. When the government passed the Asiatic Registration Act (1907) requiring all Indians in the Transvaal over the age of eight to register and be fingerprinted by the government, it met the determined resistance of a newly arrived lawyer, Mohandas Gandhi. It was in South Africa of this period that modern nonviolent resistance was devised and successfully employed.

In 1908, Gandhi and those he called his small "peace army," wielding only spiritual force, committed civil disobedience by burning the registration certificates. For the next four years he and his disciples were in and out of jail for violating the law prohibiting Indians from crossing the state border between Natal and the Transvaal (the Boer-dominated state to its west), culminating in a march of twenty-two hundred, mostly indentured Indian laborers. Finally, after lengthy negotiations with Gandhi, the Union government relented. The Indian Relief Act (1914) removed several restrictions and taxes that had been leveled on the Indian community. The campaign was a milestone of modern nonviolent social struggle, although the victory it won was short-lived as new waves of racially discriminatory legislation were soon on the horizon.

The Afrikaner strategy to maintain South Africa as "a white man's country" depended on preventing all other racial groups from forming a united opposition to them. Thus, racial classification became a primary tool for "dividing and conquering."

2. From Afrikanerdom to Apartheid: 1910–1960

Arguments in support of segregation and white supremacy repeated three themes. First, they denied that the various racial groups in South Africa could ever be united in a single social and political system. Second, they asserted that South African prosperity historically was the result of the white minority, and that the white minority could not (and should not have to) compete on an equal footing with the nonwhite majority. Third, Afrikaners maintained that blacks naturally belonged in rural areas where tribal customs and authority could regulate their lives, whereas urban life would corrupt tribal peoples and destroy their way of life. (What they didn't acknowledge was the fact that the small amount of land "reserved" for Africans was woefully unfit to support the African population, and would turn Africans into migrant workers for use in white industries and farming.) On the basis of these specious claims, Afrikaner-controlled governments made and enforced social, political, and economic policy for eighty years, with the first wave of segregation laws beginning in 1911.

1911   **Mines and Work Act:** barred native Africans from working in the professions, education, business, and the civil service

1913   **Native (Bantu) Land Act:** barred blacks from purchasing property outside areas reserved for them by the government (amounting to thirteen percent of the country).

1923   **Bantu Act:** barred Africans from urban areas designated "white areas" unless deemed necessary by white employers.

1936   Africans denied the vote in Cape Province, the only place in South Africa where any blacks had been eligible to vote.

1937   **Urban Areas Act:** required all black males sixteen years of age and older to carry identification papers. In order to be in a white area, black males required government permission indicated by an official stamp on their "pass book."

White rule met its greatest challenge in 1946, when seventy thousand black miners went on strike. Although the strike was broken by the South African Armed Forces, the tide of freedom was rising. When India gained independence from Britain in 1947, Africans began demanding that South Africa be ruled by Africans.

The National Party appealed to Afrikaner fears in the 1948 elections, pledging permanent racial separation and thus winning a landslide victory. The new prime minister, Daniel Malan (who was also ordained in the DRC), proclaimed triumphantly, "South Africa is ours again." Malan and the four National Party prime ministers who succeeded him pursued a program that segregated, subordinated, and stripped blacks of their birthright, creating a tidal wave of apartheid legislation that battered South African blacks.

1950 **Prohibition of Mixed Marriages Act:** outlawed inter-racial marriage.

1950 **Immorality Act:** prohibited interracial sexual contact.

1950 **Population Registration Act:** required classification and registration by race (white, Bantu, colored, or Indian).

1950 **Group Areas Act:** authorized government relocation of Bantu, Indian, and colored populations away from urban areas.

1951 **Separate Representation of Voters Act:** excluded coloreds from voting in national elections.

1951 **Separate Amenities Act:** designated public facilities exclusively for whites and "nonwhites."

1953 **Bantu Authority Act:** designated tribal chiefs to rule reserves under government trusteeship.

1953 **Bantu Education Act:** declared that Africans would receive vocational training only, in a separate national system of education.

1954 **Bantu Self-Government Act:** established eight such homelands (Bantustans) for different black tribal groups. In 1970 the South African citizenship of blacks was transferred to the Bantustans.

Between the mid 1950s and the 1980s, four million Africans were removed from their towns, villages, homes, farms, and businesses. (Those who resisted were arrested and charged with trespassing.) Transported in flatbed trucks with the few belongings they could carry, they were dumped on arid, rocky, wastelands designated as "ancestral" homelands (Bantustans), in "temporary" tent cities lacking drinking water, electricity, public sanitation, health facilities, or schools.

For three decades Africans were refugees in their own country. With few economic resources available in the homelands, working-age Africans were forced to migrate to white areas to find work in low-paying industrial jobs, in the mines, on white farms, or as domestics in white homes.

The architects of apartheid made no secret of their intentions. Hendrik Verwoerd, Minister of Education and later prime minister, said that the government's vocational training for blacks recognized that "the Bantu should not use his education to slip out of the company of his fellow Bantu and try to go among the white man."

Enforcing Apartheid

1950   **Suppression of Communism Act:** outlawed Communism defined very broadly and empowered government to ban* organizations and individuals it determined to be "Communist."

1953   **Public Safety Act:** authorized government to declare states of emergency with extensive police powers.

1953   **Criminal Law Act:** amended to make protest of government policy illegal.

1060   **Unlawful Organizations Act:** made membership in such organizations a criminal act, punishable by fines and imprisonment.

*Banned persons were prohibited from meeting in groups larger than two persons, from traveling outside a stipulated area, from having any contacts with persons outside the country, and from publishing, teaching, and public speaking. Banned persons were subjected to continuous monitoring by security agents. The penalty for the "crime" of violating the terms of the ban was a prison term.

Most Afrikaners were shocked to learn of the extensive use of illegal tactics (torture, assassination, poisoning) by the intelligence, police, and security forces against apartheid's enemies, both at home and abroad, in the 1970s and 1980s.

How did the churches respond to the erection of apartheid? In 1950 the DRC officially endorsed "territorial apartheid," opening the way for the Group Areas Act, which displaced and impoverished several million South Africans. For two decades the DRC officially approved of the policy that sustained white rule. In fact, the apartheid agenda was often expressed in religious terms. For example, the Boers' survival on the Great Trek (1835 to 1840) from the Cape Colony to what is now the northern part of South Africa, and the establishment of "Afrikanerdom" were hailed by Prime Minister Malan as a "miracle . . . [part of a] divine plan."

The English-speaking white Protestant churches, however, did not speak of white dominance as divine destiny. In fact, from the beginning of Union in 1910, Anglicans, Presbyterians, and Methodists were on record opposing racial legislation. Periodically they issued statements such as, "God created all in his image and beyond all differences remains an essential unity." They called for the extension of the vote, education, and economic opportunities to all races. Likewise, the Southern African Catholic Bishops Conference (SACBC), comprised of all the Roman Catholic bishops of Botswana, South Africa, and Swaziland, objected to apartheid: "We cannot remain silent and passive in the face of injustices inflicted on members of the underprivileged racial classes." But their indignation was not matched by strategies of resistance; rank and file members of Protestant and Catholic churches alike closed their ears to the cries of the oppressed and closed their eyes to the catastrophic effects of apartheid.

Beginning in the 1950s and continuing into the 1980s, the government, with little organized resistance from South African churches, relocated entire black and colored communities further away from white urban areas. In 1956 it declared Sophiatown (a large suburb of Johannesburg, longtime home to middle-class Africans and a center of African music) to be a slum, forcibly removing its residents and bulldozing every structure in the area. The government moved the inhabitants to a new slum it created thirteen miles away, called Soweto. (*Soweto* is not a poetic African word; rather, it is the shortened form of the sterile name given by the government to the site of relocation: "Southwestern Township.")

A few white clergy did become active in opposing apartheid practices. Father Trevor Huddleston, an Anglican priest who had come from England, attempted to assist black families who lost everything when Sophiatown was razed by the government. Father Huddleston not only spoke out, but gave a detailed account of what had happened to Sophiatown and its inhabitants in a book read throughout the world (*Naught for Your Comfort*)—except in South Africa, where it was banned. Lamenting the churches' ineffective voices, he wrote: "The Church sleeps on—though it occasionally talks in its sleep and expects (or does it?) the government to listen."[1] Recalling the official silence of the Anglican Church when one his parishioners in Sophiatown, Oliver Tambo, was banned for his work in the African National Congress, he recalled that "the Church's silence, indifference and submission were deafening."[2]

3. *Cry, the Beloved Country:* Black Resistance, 1950–1960

Alan Paton offered a searing indictment of white supremacy in his famous 1948 novel entitled *Cry, the Beloved Country*. He tells the story of how the system robbed a black family of its way of life and values, its children, and its future. Paton's character John Kumalo explains to his brother Stephen, an Anglican priest, why he joined the opposition against white supremacy and rejected the Church: "The Bishop says it is wrong—but he lives in a big house, and his priests get four, five, six times what you get, my Brother."[3]

A Who's Who of Resistance to Apartheid

African National Congress (ANC): formed in 1912 with the objective of extending full citizenship to Africans, opposing all laws that separated races and discriminated against nonwhites, and advocating racial unity and cooperation. Never denying the legitimacy of the white South African government, it vigorously sought constitutional reform. The ANC advocated neither black domination nor the transfer of political power to the black majority.

ANC Youth League (ANCYL): created in 1944 to bring more young people into the ANC. However, in frustration over lack of success, ANCYL formed a new mission, to free all of Africa and South Africa in particular from European domination and to create genuine democratic rule with constitutional guarantees of the rights of minorities. ANCYL called for an "inclusive" South African nationalism that embraced people of all color who supported democratic ideals and an end to white domination. "Freedom in our lifetime" was their rallying cry.

Pan Africanist Congress (PAC): created in 1959 by ANC members who left in protest against the ANC's failure to demand the end of white domination and the return of South African land to its rightful owners. The PAC advocated for a "nonracial" society, arguing that the ANC's "multiracialism" contributed to the fragmentation that made white domination possible and did not sufficiently promote African claims. Their call for "Africa for Africans" did not exclude whites but insisted that any legitimate African government must reflect the developmental needs and aspirations of its African majority.

All three organizations were declared illegal in 1960. Many leaders were arrested and spent years in South African prisons. Some went underground and were eventually captured and imprisoned. Others fled to neighboring African countries where they carried on their resistance to apartheid for thirty years with financial support from sympathetic sources around the world.

On May 1, 1950—designated "Freedom Day"—the ANC organized a nationwide strike. The government responded by invoking the Suppression of Communism Act, charging the leaders of the Communist Party with incitement to destabilize the country. In 1952 the ANC began a "Defiance Campaign" against six apartheid laws by violating the pass laws and entering "whites-only" public facilities. Police raided ANC and South African Indian Congress offices around the country, arresting their leadership on charges of being communists. In 1954 and 1955, ten thousand African women staged protests against the pass laws that were now being extended to women as well as men.

In 1955 the ANC formed alliances with other national resistance organizations. On June 26, the third anniversary of Defiance Day, a Congress of the People convened, comprised of representatives of the ANC, South African Colored Peoples Congress, South African Indian Congress, South African Congress of Democrats (whites opposed to apartheid), and the South African Communist Party. This congress drafted a new constitution for South Africa that affirmed the right of all population groups to full political participation, cultural and language development, freedom of speech, religion, press, and political association, and equal treatment under the law. The constitution also affirmed the right of all people to own property and to receive reparation for property unjustly taken, the right of workers to protection from exploitation, and the right to adequate housing, health care, and food. Its preamble, the "Freedom Charter," is one of the most eloquent twentieth-century statements of democratic ideals.

Freedom Charter

We the people of South Africa declare for all in our country and the world to know,

That South Africa belongs to all who live in it, black and white;

That our people have been robbed of their birthright, land, liberty, and peace by a form of government founded on injustice and inequality;

That our country will never be prosperous and free until all our people live in brotherhood, enjoying equal rights and opportunities;

That only a democratic state, based on the will of the people, can secure to all their birthright without distinction of colour, race, sex, or belief.

On the second day of the congress, South African police stormed the meeting, and all 155 delegates were arrested and charged with high treason. Their trial would last for six years, focusing primarily on whether or not their views were communist.

Outside the courtroom, new dramas were unfolding. In 1958 a faction of the ANC broke with the organization over ANC cooperation with the Communist Party and with the Indian Congress. Declaring that whites and Indians were foreign minorities, this group embraced an "Africanist" position, and took as their name the Pan Africanist Congress (PAC). The PAC's rallying cry was "government of the Africans, by the Africans, and for the Africans." The PAC was most disturbed that the Freedom Charter had failed to assert African ownership of the land. Yet the PAC declared itself nonracial rather than multiracial, and defined *African* as anyone loyal to Africa and accepting of democratic rule by the majority. It was committed to the overthrow of white domination by noncooperation and nonrecognition of the white government.

The PAC organized a national anti-pass campaign for late March 1960, during which hundreds of Africans went to police stations in many townships and turned themselves in for violating pass laws. In Sharpville, a small township outside Johannesburg, hundreds burned their passes. The police panicked in the face of the large but unarmed crowd and opened fire on the demonstrators, killing sixty-nine people and wounding four hundred. In response to the massacre, nationwide demonstrations, pass burnings, and work stoppages broke out across the country. The government responded by declaring a state of emergency, and by May, eighteen thousand opposition leaders were in government detention. Nelson Mandela, one of the 120 ANC leaders on trial for issuing the Freedom Charter, wrote to Prime Minister Verwoerd, urging him to call a national constitutional convention in 1961 or risk the largest three-day strike ever staged in the country. The government refused; instead, it invoked the Unlawful Organizations Act against the ANC and the PAC. Eventually, ANC leaders fled the country or went into hiding, since their continued membership was now a crime.

4. *Cry, Freedom*: New Tactics and New Voices of Resistance

The 1960s began a new chapter in the struggle against apartheid, a chapter that included armed resistance, an intensification of opposition from Christian churches both inside and outside South Africa, and a forceful African student movement nourished by rising black consciousness that radiated into the wider African communities.

In 1961, the trial of the Freedom Chartists finally ended, with the court ruling that the government had failed to prove that the Freedom Charter was promoting communism. The verdict was no victory, however: the ANC was banned anyway. Mandela went underground the day of his acquittal, becoming both fugitive and hero of the movement. Mandela argued convincingly with the remaining (underground or exiled) ANC leadership that because they could no longer organize peaceful forms of public protest, the only way forward was resistance to apartheid by selective acts of violence against the government that would induce the government to end its apartheid policy. The ANC, with approval of the other alliance member organizations, authorized the recruitment and training of a military unit, called *Umkhonto we Sizwe* (Spear of the Nation), to engage in sporadic attacks on the government. (The PAC also developed an armed wing.) Mandela took charge of establishing Umkhonto, raising funds from other African nations, and establishing training bases in neighboring Mozambique and Angola. The intent was to engage in acts of sabotage against government property but to avoid attacks on persons. If this failed to move the government to negotiation, Umkhonto would resort to guerrilla warfare and terrorism. In December 1961, several government offices and power plants were bombed.

When the government captured Mandela in September 1962, they did not know his connection to Umkhonto. He was convicted of "inciting" the three-day strike of the previous year and given a five-year sentence. The following year, South African intelligence agents uncovered Umkhonto headquarters and implicated Mandela, who was retried and convicted of sabotage and sentenced to life in prison. But the efforts of Umkhonto continued for the next two decades, with sporadic attacks on government offices.

With the political voices of the ANC and the PAC silenced, the leadership of the resistance within the country began to shift. Activists started to emerge within the churches and among black students, "fired with the spirit of protest and rebellion."[4] We will briefly describe the growing opposition of churches and students.

The massacre at Sharpville in 1960 and the banning of all organized political opposition challenged the churches as never before. The 1960s and 1970s were marked by increasing concerted efforts of the churches and increasing levels of confrontation between South African churches and the government. The World Council of Churches (an ecumenical body of three hundred Protestant churches in one hundred countries founded in 1948), for example, concerned from its beginning with the racial attitudes and practices of Christians, became increasingly concerned with racially motivated social injustice in South Africa throughout the 1950s.

Resisting Apartheid: Clergy and Students

World Council of Churches (WCC) and South African Council of Churches (SACC)
Christian Institute (CI)
Southern African Catholic Bishops Conference (SACBC)
Black Consciousness Movement: led by theologians and university students, affirmed African culture and mobilized opposition to apartheid
South African Student Organization (SASO): established in 1969 in colleges and universities designated for Africans, inspired by the growing black consciousness movement in Africa and in the United States. SASO began as a student advocacy movement but turned its attention to health, literacy, and development within the black community. SASO initiated improvement projects in the townships.
The Black Peoples Congress (BPC): established in 1972 when SASO extended its opposition to apartheid beyond black universities.

:ranged a "consultation" in Johannesburg with
;anization of twenty-one South African Protes-
hich became the South African Council of
: joint statement these bodies issued criticized
es within church denominations, denied that
;rounds for the government's declaration that
; immoral, insisted on the right of blacks to par-
, and decried the poverty-level wages paid to
overnment pressure, most of the representatives
gned the statement recanted and the DRC with-
nd the SACC. Thus began an era of escalating
rch and state, between the DRC and other
churches, and within the DRC itself. Some within the DRC began to
criticize its consequences—namely, the economically unlivable and
impoverished homelands, the migratory black labor system, and the
resulting damage to the African family. What "separate development"
really meant at this stage of South Africa's history, they admitted, was
maintenance of white control of South Africa. The most outspoken crit-
ics within the church would soon find themselves expelled.

Beyers Naude, a well-known white DRC churchman who had
refused to disavow the WCC condemnation of apartheid in 1960,
founded the Christian Institute (CI) in 1963. Originally intended to
move the white churches to resist apartheid, the CI looked increasingly
to black Christian churches to lead the Church against apartheid and to
challenge white churches to join them. In 1965 the DRC prohibited its
members from participating in the CI and expelled Naude from the
church.

In 1968 the CI and SACC issued "A Message to the People of South
Africa" that called apartheid a "false faith," an attempt to secure salva-
tion outside of Christ. The growing church resistance to apartheid
within South Africa found support from the worldwide association of
Protestants, the WCC, which in 1970 initiated its "Program to Combat
Racism" and funded organized resistance by South African blacks in
exile in neighboring countries. The South African government
expressed outrage and banned WCC representatives from entering
South Africa. The SACC, though not endorsing armed resistance,
acknowledged that "the social order in South Africa is already to a considerable extent based on the use of violence" and blamed the inaction
of the churches for the decision of the oppressed "to use violence
against entrenched violence." The hostility of the government toward
the SACC reached new levels in 1974, when the SACC passed a

resolution calling into question the moral legitimacy of the government's security forces, urging whites to consider refusing military service in the South African Defense Forces (SADF). Prime Minister John Vorster warned the churches of South Africa that encouraging resistance would get them nowhere, saying pointedly that "if some clergy think they can do in South Africa what King did in America, forget it!"[5]

As the Southern Africa Catholic Bishops Conference issued "A Call to Conscience" in 1972, black Catholic priests became some of the most active anti-apartheid leaders among the clergy of the English-speaking churches. In 1977 the Catholic bishops also affirmed the right of conscientious objection. These were among the boldest public stands ever taken by churches against a national government. Outraged, the government passed legislation imposing large fines and prison sentences for those convicted of counseling youth to refuse military service. By the mid 1970s the government was squashing all opposition.

The black theology and Black Consciousness Movement that arose during the U.S. civil rights struggles of the late 1960s stimulated parallel movements in South African universities, seminaries, churches, and townships. The successes of the U.S. civil rights struggle encouraged the South African freedom struggle.

The Black Consciousness Movement grew, led by Steve Biko, seeking to infuse African people with new pride in themselves, "rather than regard themselves as appendages to white society."[6] Biko asserted: "There is nothing wrong with blacks. The problem is white racism and it rests squarely on the laps of white society."

The victims of police attacks on the black community were getting younger. In 1976, a group of middle school students in the township of Soweto marched in protest to a new regulation requiring that all instruction be in Afrikaans as well as English. Government forces opened fire, killing several children.

In 1977 Steve Biko died from massive head injuries sustained while in police custody. That same year, the government banned SASO and seventeen other black organizations. Also banned were the Christian Institute and Beyers Naude personally. In 1980 the government targeted the SACC, its general secretary, Desmond Tutu, Anglican Archbishop of Johannesburg, and scores of church leaders and activists.

South African National Anthem

(English and Zulu)

God Bless Africa	Nkosi Sikelel'i—Afrika
Let her fame resound	Maluphankanyisw'
Hear our prayers	Udumo Lwayo
God bless	Yizwa imithandozo yethu
Us, Your children	Nkosi sikelela
Come Spirit	Thina Lusapho Lwayo
(Come, Spirit, Come)	Woza Moya
Come Spirit	(Woza Moya Woza)
(Come, Spirit, Come)	Woza Moya
Come Holy Spirit	(Woza Moya Woza)
God bless	Woza Moya Oyingcwele
Us, Your	Nkosi sikelela
Children	Thina Lusapho Lwayo

5. Apartheid's Last Stand: 1980–1990

As bannings, arrests, and harassment continued through the 1980s, church leaders found themselves taking a stronger stand. In 1980 Tutu exhorted the SACC: "We cannot be content only to protest verbally: the Church must do more than just talk. The survival of South Africa is at stake."[7] Tutu called on the churches to challenge the government vigorously. As a result, Archbishop Tutu's passport was revoked. In 1981 the SACBC refused to participate in government ceremonies marking the twentieth anniversary of South Africa's withdrawal from the commonwealth. To protest South Africa's escalating war in Namibia, the Catholic bishops called for a day of prayer on behalf of the Namibian people. Archbishop Denis Hurley of Durban was charged with making false statements, accusing the SADF of atrocities in Namibia. This was the first time in thirty years that a Catholic bishop had been arrested for confronting the state. (The last time was in 1953, when the communist government of Poland tried and imprisoned Cardinal Stefan Wyszyński. See chapter four.) During Archbishop Hurley's trial, the government withdrew its case, and Hurley later won a suit against the government for malicious prosecution. These bannings, arrests, and incidents of harassment, however, did not silence church leaders; rather, they had the opposite effect. Now that church leaders were also suffering, their sympathies deepened for the sufferings of several generations of black South Africans. Finally, more than ever, they were committed to ending apartheid.

For every organization and activist banned, imprisoned, or exiled, others arose to take their place. In 1983 six hundred organizations in South Africa formed the United Democratic Front (UDF) under the banner "Apartheid divides, the UDF unites." The government dubbed it "a front for the ANC." The Freedom Alliance of 1955 was indeed back—and as a much larger force. Desperately seeking popular support, the government proposed constitutional changes giving Indians and coloreds—but not blacks—their own legislatures. The UDF countered by organizing countrywide boycotts, and the SACC and SACBC declared the constitutional change inadequate.

The government determination to root out opposition within South Africa and in neighboring countries was very costly. In addition to administering and policing the Bantustans and townships, and maintaining large security and intelligence networks, the cost of the SADF, the largest military in Africa, was estimated to be at least $35 billion in the first half of the 1980s. The government employed an estimated forty percent of Afrikaners directly or indirectly.

With Bantustans experiencing fifty percent unemployment, however, their populations simply could not be pacified. By 1984, the black townships were in revolt and the government declared a state of emergency, sending defense forces to occupy them. Over the next two years the army and police personnel killed more than a thousand children. On the ninth anniversary of the Soweto massacre, the SACC called for a national day of prayer "that God will replace the present structures of oppression with ones that are just, and remove from power those who persist in defying his laws, installing in their place leaders who will govern with justice and mercy." Then, in 1985, one hundred and fifty representatives of South African churches issued the Kairos Document, urging all Christians to join in active civil disobedience against the police state South Africa had now become. This was the *kairos* moment, God's appointed time to act against a situation of massive injustice.

The government no longer exercised restraint against church protesters. In a 1985 march by Protestant and Catholic church leaders, "clergy were beaten (one almost losing his eye), nuns were stripped and searched on arrival at prison, and clergy who arrived at court singing in the back of a police van were tear-gassed while still locked inside."[8] The General Secretaries of both the SACC and the SACBC were both arrested and tortured. In 1986 the Catholic bishops declared, "Let there be no mistake—we are not neutral in the current conflict in South Africa. We fully support the demands of the majority of the people for justice."[9] That support was evident in the fifty priests, nuns, and church workers currently in government custody. In 1986, with the South African Council of Churches and the black trade unions (COSATU) joining the UDF in calling for an end to the state of emergency and the release of detainees, cracks in the wall of apartheid were beginning to appear. In the wake of mass protests and burnings of the odious passes, the government had no alternative but to suspend the pass laws.

The growing instability of the country worried foreign investors. The UN Security Council passed a resolution asking UN member nations to impose economic sanctions in the form of bans on new investments and loans. Anti-apartheid lobbies around the world succeeded in getting many investors, including those in charge of government pensions and university portfolios, to divest their stock holdings of companies that did business in South Africa. In 1985 forty U.S. corporations closed their South African operations, and in 1986 the U.S. Congress passed an anti-apartheid bill over President Ronald Reagan's veto, denying tax credits to U.S. companies paying taxes in South Africa. By 1989 two hundred U.S. companies had left the country. When the loss of investment, shortages of skilled labor, and no new technologies brought the economy to a halt in the late 1980s, white South Africans registered insecurity and pessimism about their future. Finally, watching their nation plunging into deeper and deeper darkness, they were beginning to realize that apartheid could not be enforced indefinitely. As the 1980s witnessed escalating government violence against the opponents of apartheid, too many whites were being corrupted in defense of apartheid while the blood of apartheid's "enemies" was flowing freely. What would the dawn of a different South Africa look like? Would it be red with the blood of Afrikaners too? What would be the consequences of a civil war for a post-apartheid South Africa?

When the government accused the churches of encouraging and promoting violence by blacks, the churches denied the charge but countered that the government's extensive use of violence was most to blame for the desperation that drove the oppressed to take up arms. Now the DRC issued an appeal jointly with SACC for the government to release political prisoners, permit the return of anti-apartheid leaders in exile, and begin talks with the authentic leadership of the various population groups.

Armed Resistance to Apartheid? The Question of Violence

The ANC's resort to violent forms of struggle in 1961 was made, wrote Mandela, "after long and anxious assessment of the South African situation" and "when all channels of peaceful protest had been barred to us . . . [and] the government had left us no other choice."[10] Among the churches, however, the use of violence against apartheid was an issue sharply debated. An Umkhonto leader, Chris Hani, who was assassinated in 1994 by a right-wing Afrikaner group, expressed surprise and dismay that church leaders opposed armed resistance, especially since church teaching supported defensive military action against tyrannous rulers. For over twenty years, although Umkhonto denounced violence against persons, claiming that the system and not individuals was the adversary, it also trained several thousand guerrillas for possible engagement with the SADF and carried out sporadic acts of sabotage against the government. Although the deadliest act associated with Umkhonto was a car bombing in Johannesburg in 1983, those responsible insisted that they were not authorized to act by Umkhonto.

In response to the issue of armed resistance, Archbishop Hurley, in 1986, said that the churches should avoid pronouncements of the just or unjust nature of the ANC armed resistance, because the behavior of the ANC was occurring in a "bear-pit of injustice."[11] Likewise, Frank Chicane, General Secretary of SACC, called on the churches to stop debating whether violent resistance to apartheid is permissible, and to start acting boldly to remove the injustice that makes the resort to violence so compelling for those suffering the agony of its effects. Chicane implored the churches "to move from noninvolvement" to "developing and implementing nonviolent struggle [for justice]."[12]

In 1987 a book urging churches to engage in nonviolent resistance against apartheid by U.S. theologian Walter Wink was circulated to a thousand churches in South Africa. *Violence and Nonviolence in South Africa* blamed the churches for not translating their denunciation of apartheid into "risky, committed actions" in support of the ANC's Defiance Campaign twenty-five years earlier, "when nonviolent resistance might have checked apartheid before it could have become entrenched."[13] Wink argued that whites pleading for blacks to struggle nonviolently obscured the crucial moral fact of white passivity that allowed injustice to grow until its victims reached the combustion point. When the people who are urging nonviolence are the very ones who have benefited from apartheid, one wonders if their motives are self-serving: i.e., don't damage the system that works for us. They are naive if they think apartheid can be dismantled without exacting a price from them.

But Wink also argued that "the dream of violent revolution in South Africa is an opium vision with no basis in reality," given the military strength of the apartheid regime. Apartheid cannot be killed, it can only be repudiated by coming to recognize the humanity of the neighbor and actively taking up the cause of justice for those long denied it. Wink was unwilling to declare a black armed struggle a "just war"—given the inevitable level of casualties and atrocities, when a concerted nonviolent struggle through "grassroots training, discipline, organizing, and hard work" had yet to be undertaken by the churches.

By the late 1980s Mandela recognized that Umkhonto foot soldiers could engage government forces in mortal combat for years without a victory. But in his secret negotiations with the government from his prison cell, Mandela refused to commit the ANC to ending the armed resistance of Umkhonto until apartheid was dismantled. Mandela's focus was on persuading the Afrikaner government to travel a new road with nonwhite South Africans. Mandela offered reassurances of reconciliation to allay fears of retaliation, and knew that compromises would be necessary in order to ease the transfer of power. Afrikaner politicians needed to offer reassurances to their constituencies.

In February 1988 the government launched another offensive by banning the UDF and seventeen other opposition organizations. The SACC and SACBC called the action "a blow directed at the heart of the church's mission in South Africa," since the banned organizations involved church members whose activities were "central to the proclamation of the Gospel." The state, they declared, was acting "against the Church of God in this country for proclaiming the Gospel."[14] The day after the bannings, church leaders assembled in the Anglican Cathedral in Cape Town to pray, and were arrested as they marched to the Parliament with a petition of protest for President P. W. Botha. When Botha accused the churches of working for the ANC and the Communist Party, Tutu responded, "I work for God's Kingdom. For whose Kingdom with your apartheid policies do you work?"[15]

The struggle reached a turning point in 1988. With all the other organizations working for justice now banned or restricted, the churches offered the only option left with which to continue the struggle. The SACC and SACBC confronted the government more directly than ever in May of that year, announcing a "Stand for the Truth Campaign." The truths to be exposed were the government's crimes against humanity shrouded in secrecy of a "state of emergency."[16] The campaign declared that, "the role of the church is to create peace. But on the road to negotiation, reconciliation, and peace, it will be necessary to confront, pressurize, and defy."[17] The Stand for the Truth Campaign urged South African Christians to boycott local elections in 1988, on the grounds that the government no longer held the moral, theological, or legal claim to legitimacy. The campaign also encouraged the development of grassroots activism: boycotts, acts of civil disobedience, refusal to pay taxes, and the interposing of church members in situations of likely violence between police and township residents.

In 1989, COSATU and UDF with support of the SACC and SACBC organized a nationwide defiance campaign of civil disobedience against all apartheid institutions. In retaliation, authorities locked church doors and attempted to ban religious services—until the South African Supreme Court ruled that they could not prohibit exercise of religion. The headquarters of SACC in Johannesburg were bombed in August, and the Cape Town offices of SACBC were burned in October.

Under mounting pressures, President Botha met with Mandela—and a month later, Botha announced his resignation. His successor, F. W. de Klerk offered Mandela freedom—if Mandela would call off all armed resistance. Mandela declined the offer, refusing such a pledge as long as apartheid remained in place.

6. Forging a Democratic South Africa: 1990–1995

The collapse of apartheid came three months after the Berlin Wall was pulled down: two very different ideologies collapsing under the weight of their oppressiveness. In February 1990 President de Klerk announced to the South African Parliament that his government was prepared to negotiate a new constitution guaranteeing democratic rule, universal franchise, and the protection of the rights of all South Africans. He also promised that his government would immediately undertake programs for the improvement of education, health, housing, and social conditions for all of the peoples of South Africa. De Klerk "unbanned" all political groups and individuals, and announced the release of all political prisoners, beginning with Nelson Mandela. All South African political organizations would henceforth be free to join the political process. De Klerk urged an end to violence, declaring that the reasons for resorting to violence given by the opponents of the government now no longer existed.

A week later, Mandela was free. In his first address to the nation he repeated his words to the court that had sentenced him, in 1964, to spend the rest of his life in prison:

> "I have fought against white domination, and I have fought against black domination. I have cherished the ideal of a democratic and free society in which all persons live together in harmony and with equal opportunity. I place my life at the service of that ideal."

Leaders and members of the ANC, PAC, SASO, and BPC walked out of prisons or returned to South Africa to begin the work of rebuilding their political bases. As de Klerk had urged, Parliament repealed the Bantu Land Act, the Group Areas Act, the Separate Amenities Act, and the Population Registration Act. In turn, the ANC announced suspension of armed struggle. In 1991 the ANC, the Inkatha Freedom Party (IFP), led by Zulu Chief Buthelezi, and the National Party signed a National Peace Accord crafted by church and business leaders. The accord called for an end of all secret military operations, the removal of all weapons at political rallies, and the establishment of eighty local peace committees to mediate conflict and investigate public violence.

Although the churches now facilitated and mediated during the negotiation for the transfer of power, the Catholic bishops insisted that their clergy not be members of political parties, so they could be effective mediators during the transition. In the summer of 1991, the Convention for a Democratic South Africa, representing all willing political parties, met to create a new federal constitution. De Klerk's National Party proposed a transitional government of shared rule between the major political parties for five to ten years, hoping to avoid national elections while ANC's popularity was so high and the National Party's so low. The ANC insisted on general elections within two years. De Klerk scrambled for allies against the ANC, finding them among the chiefs of the Bantustans (most prominently, in Chief Buthelezi, head of the KwaZulu homeland and founder of the Zulu Inkatha Freedom Party) whose rule originated with and was beholden to the apartheid government. Because of the impasse on elections, the ANC withdrew from the convention and called for national mass protests against the government's stalling.

Although the ANC had wide popular support and the government commanded the powerful police and defense forces, neither had control over the youth, the second and third generation of apartheid's victims, whom Mandela described as South Africa's angriest and most rebellious generation. Recognizing the urgency of the situation, parties resumed negotiations in March 1993, and eventually agreed to nonracial elections to be held in April 1994 to elect a transition government to rule for five years. The parties would be represented in the government in proportion to the number of votes cast for its candidates. A Constituent Assembly of four hundred was created, its principle task being to write a nonracial and democratic constitution.

Neither Zulu Chief Buthelezi nor right-wing Afrikaner organizations would settle for less than separate autonomous states, and threatened to prevent the elections. In the end, they did not succeed. The election of 1994 was the first time Africans were permitted to vote in a national election. It was also the first time the ANC had ever participated in a political campaign. In colored and Indian population areas from which African workers were barred under apartheid, the National Party played on voter fear of a flood of Africans taking their jobs. The ANC's alliance with the Communist Party during the struggle against apartheid fed fear that a victory of the ANC would see the nationalizing of banks, industries, and mines—a fear never realized.

A month before the election, de Klerk declared a state of emergency in KwaZulu in the midst of growing violence between IFP and ANC partisans. (It would later come to light that the violence de Klerk was quelling had been supported by the South African Defense Forces which armed and trained the IFP to create instability and cast doubt on the ANC's ability to govern.) Three weeks before the election, Mandela and de Klerk worked out an agreement with Buthelezi to preserve the ceremonial status of the Zulu monarchy and allow international mediators to examine IFP's claims to greater autonomy for KwaZulu. In the three days before the election, right-wing Afrikaners detonated bombs across the country, killing 12 and maiming 145. Thirty-one terrorists were brought to justice.

The ANC won sixty-two percent of the popular votes and 252 of the 400 seats in Parliament, with the National Party finishing second and Inkatha third. Mandela became South Africa's first democratically elected president, with de Klerk as his vice president. South Africa was now blessed with a leader committed to the rehabilitation of the victims of apartheid and to reconciliation of all parties, including the chief victimizers. A contemporary South African theologian wrote that "it was [Mandela's] choice of the path of reconciliation that qualitatively heightened his moral and political stature so that even former enemies recognized that he was the key to the future, the undisputed candidate for the presidency of the new South Africa."[18]

The Government of National Unity faced the immense tasks of overcoming the past and rekindling in the dispossessed hope for the future.

> I see only one hope for our country, and that is when [whites] and [blacks], desiring neither power nor money, but desiring only the good of their country, come together to work for it. . . . I have one great fear in my heart, that one day when they are turned to loving, they will find that we are turned to hating (Fr. Msimangu, a black Anglican priest in *Cry, the Beloved Country*).

7. The Road to Reconciliation

The interim constitution of 1993 stated: "There is a need for understanding but not for vengeance, a need for reparation but not for retaliation, a need for *ubuntu* [compassion] but not for victimization." In 1995 the National Unity and Reconciliation Act created the "Truth and Reconciliation Commission" (TRC). The TRC was charged with investigating crimes committed in support of or in opposition to apartheid from 1960 (the Sharpville massacre) until the establishment of the Government of National Unity in 1994. Empowered to subpoena and question government leaders, intelligence and police officials, military officials, and anti-apartheid leaders, the TRC's mandate was:

- to uncover the nature and extent of crimes and recommend reparations and rehabilitation for victims and their families
- to determine whether those who committed such crimes should be granted amnesty
- to promote the dignity of the victims
- to create a culture of human rights in South Africa

From 1995 to1998, the TRC heard appalling testimonies of victims, their families, and some perpetrators. The depth and extent of the cruelty revealed in testimonies shocked Afrikaners outside of the police, national security, and armed forces systems. Family members of the victims relived the pain of the past. By describing to an official public forum horrific personal experiences, victims and families of victims found some release from the power of evil still holding them through memory. The testimonies of perpetrators answered questions haunting victims and families. Why, how, and by whom had these crimes been committed? On whose orders? Answers to these questions helped bring closure to years of pain. While the pain of hearing the testimonies of assassins, murderers, and torturers was intense, when it was over most of the victims wanted to rejoin the living in building a new nation, and leave the punishment to God. Remarkably, retaliation was not on their agenda.

Identifying the guilty parties and the degree of government complicity was difficult because the police, intelligence, and armed forces destroyed thousands of documents. Few members of the South African Defense Forces came forward. Inkatha Freeodm Party militants who had committed crimes against ANC supporters leading up to the 1994 election refused to participate. Many who might have carried their complicity to their graves with them, however, did come forward, but with mixed motivations: for some it was to blame others (those whose orders they had followed), for others it was to avoid prosecution. But for some, the burden of their evil past was unbearable, and they needed to talk about it, express remorse, and vent feelings of being betrayed by superiors. The granting of amnesty to perpetrators who testified fully and truthfully was controversial, meeting objections from international rights organizations, including Amnesty International.

Former President Botha defied the TRC's subpoena, paid a small fine, and refused to admit any complicity with the murderous deeds of the army, police, and security forces during the eleven years of his presidency. Under examination by the TRC's chairman, Archbishop Desmond Tutu, former president de Klerk acknowledged that the apartheid system had done enormous harm to blacks. But he incurred the archbishop's wrath by denying personal awareness of any wrongdoing by those who served in his government. Nor did the commission accept the claim of Umkhonto that its violence was legitimate in the "just war" against apartheid. Six leaders of the DRC admitted their failure: "At the very times when we should have continued to speak out clearly for the truth and against the injustice we grew tired and gave up protesting."

The testimonies forced even those whites in greatest denial to admit that the police and security forces had acted "unnecessarily" or had "gone too far." The overwhelming evidence flew in the face of attempts to minimize the harm done by apartheid. For another two years, the TRC published its recommendations for reparations and amnesty. Below is an example of one of the statements.

TRC Amnesty Decision, 6 March 2000

"Amnesty Committee of Truth and Reconciliation Commission today has granted amnesty to four senior security police involved in the killing of a Congress of South African Students leader Siphiwo Mthimkulu and Topsy Madaka in April 1992. . . . The Committee found that the four have met the requirements of the [1995] Act. They have disclosed in full how they abducted the deceased, killed them, where they killed them, and what happened to their remains."

Amnesty Committee member Ntsiki Sandi issued the dissenting view that all four applicants should be denied amnesty since Mr. Madaka's murder was not politically motivated, but "occurred because he happened to be in company of Mtimkulu that fateful evening."[19]

Although national healing remains an enormous task, the fact that apartheid's fall was not followed by violent retaliation is testimony to the commitment of the oppressed to achieve reconciliation. For white South Africans, the challenge continues: to overcome their fears and to engage in the reconciliation process. Beyers Naude urged whites to "face reality, deal rationally with your fears, commit yourself to building a united nonracial South Africa and you will be surprised to discover how ready blacks are to understand your fears and to accept you—together with your culture, language, and religion."[20]

8. The Challenge of the Twenty-First Century: Reconstructing South Africa

Although Mandela called dismantling the structures of apartheid without massive violence and civil war "a miracle," the Government of National Unity that Mandela led would need more than miracles over the five years it had to begin the reconstructing the society. Most urgently needed was the cooperation of National Party leaders, the bureaucracy which remained primarily Afrikaner, the IFP, and all who had been part of the struggle against apartheid.

A century of legally sanctioned racial separation and domination has resulted in a society of enormous extremes. Conspicuous amidst the expansive poverty and abandonment of the country are the small enclaves of the wealthy and privileged. The ANC-led government has made the poor its first priority, recognizing that the greatest betrayal in the aftermath of apartheid would be to allow the desperately poor to be "forgotten people." The government introduced its Reconstruction and Development Program (RDP) in 1995, declaring: "No political democracy can survive and flourish if the mass of our people remain in poverty, without land, without tangible prospects for a better life." Jobs, housing, food, and health care were desperately needed. Where would they come from and how soon?

The housing problem, for example, was enormous. Apartheid population relocation that began under the Group Areas Act of 1951 removed four million people from their homes. In homelands, women, children, and the elderly made do with whatever shelters they could erect. In townships, black workers built shacks to return to at night from work in white areas. When apartheid laws were repealed, many tried to return home—but to homes that no longer existed. As a result, squatter camps sprang up overnight and mushroomed on any available patch of land, beach, or wooded area, sometimes adjacent to gated white neighborhoods.

The RDP announced its intention to construct a million houses, and $3,500 would be given to those without adequate housing to purchase a small piece of ground, construct a tiny two-room house—and perhaps pay the local electric and water utilities to install services. What commonly happened was that the small allocation required families to choose between a more adequate house, and the possibility of having a safe and dependable water source and light for their children to do homework by at night. Most chose the water and electricity.

The sheer scale of needs has far outstripped the government's resources, however. For example, townships that had never had sanitation systems, paved roads, or garbage collection waited for the government to get to them. They waited a year, or even two, to be added to the list of townships to be upgraded. Although the government promised clean water, electricity, and basic health services to all rural areas, many villages received their first communal water pump, but nothing more—even after three years of waiting. Nothing comparable to the Marshall Plan that came to devastated Europe's assistance at the end of World War II followed the defeat of apartheid. Economic and social development will take much of the twenty-first century, requiring immense patience from poor Africans.

For white South Africans who survived the fall of apartheid with their wealth and earning power intact, the question is how to voluntarily redistribute wealth by supporting the higher tax levels needed to meet the basic needs of the poor. South Africa incurred a large national debt in the 1980s, much of it in military spending and pay raises for government employees (by 1994 the percentage of whites on the government payroll was about sixty percent). Those now in power must resist the temptations of power and self-gain.

The churches have an important role to play in constructing a democratic South Africa. They do so first by standing with those who remain the long-term victims of economic apartheid: the poor. Second, the churches must stand up for the human rights of minorities. The violence that marked the past four decades in South Africa has not prepared the society for civil and tolerant political discourse. Third, the Church, by its own example, must embrace diversity, and its ecumenical cooperation in the transition to democracy must be a living example for others in the society.

Clearly, formidable challenges face South Africa: redistribution of wealth, the temptation of black leadership to put personal gain above concern for the poorest South Africans, education, reforming a culture of violence and crime, and the forming of a genuinely multiracial society. The churches will continue to play an important role in the creation of a just society, especially in advocating on behalf of the poor and educating members for participation in the rebuilding of their communities. The Catholic bishops established fifteen "Justice and Peace Commissions" throughout the country to assist in education, supporting human rights, and overcoming poverty.[21]

A New South African Lexicon

South Africans: all people who claim South Africa as their home, who support a democratic society, and are committed to safeguarding the rights of all.

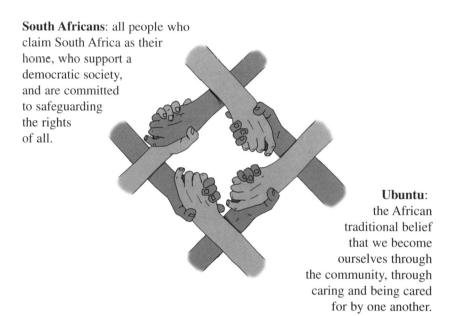

Ubuntu: the African traditional belief that we become ourselves through the community, through caring and being cared for by one another.

When questioned about his origins during a government inquiry, Archbishop Desmond Tutu answered that his parents were from different tribes and that he spoke both of their tribal languages, as well as Afrikaans and English. The government, however, had classified his race as "indeterminable at present." The archbishop then offered his opinion that "it would not be a bad thing if a few more of us were less sure of our precise identity—it might help us to find a new common identity in South Africa." Tutu expresses eloquently the hope of millions: "I long for a South Africa more open and more just; where people count and where they will have equal access to the goods of life, with equal opportunity to live, work, and learn . . . and to participate fully in political decision making, and in other decisions which affect their lives. This South Africa will have integrity of territory with a common citizenship . . . belonging to all its inhabitants"[22]

4

1980s Nonviolent Triumphs of Democracy: Poland, East Germany, and the Philippines

The suddenness of the collapse of the Soviet Union took Western governments by surprise. Equally surprising was the fact that iron-fisted authoritarian regimes of Eastern Europe were brought down by nonviolent citizen movements. Confrontations that might have led to massive bloodletting instead brought about peaceful transfers of power. Unarmed citizenry of Poland and East Germany, with critical support from the churches, defeated regimes that routinely used secret police and military forces to quell all political opposition. But these events occurred because of the groundwork patiently put in place by thousands of people over several years. The toppling of the Berlin Wall in 1989, for example, was the dramatic culmination of largely peaceful protests throughout the 1980s. All these astonishing upheavals were the fruit of a spiritual process nurtured by the churches. Through prayer, social critique, and self-disciplined protest, religious communities helped to bring about social change.

These stories from the 1970s and 1980s offer several lessons about the power of nonviolence. So, too, does the dramatic victory of the Filipino people over the corrupt Marcos regime in 1986, accomplished without the firing of a shot.

Section one narrates three decades of patient and persistent struggle in Poland against the Soviet-backed Marxist regime; section two describes the nonviolent momentum that defeated the Marxist regime of East Germany; and section three explores the equally remarkable church-supported protest against the powerful Marcos regime in the Philippines.

1. Poland's Solidarity

Poland was devastated by Hitler's war; six million Poles died, three million of them Jews exterminated in German death camps. Although the Russian Army drove the Germans out of western Poland in January 1945, Stalin's purpose was not to liberate but to plunder. "The Russians plundered machinery from factories, cut down the dockyard cranes and sent them to the Soviet Union for scrap metal; they confiscated food from the peasants and removed railway works, locomotives, and trains."[1] In gratitude for the Soviet Union's role in the defeat of Germany, the Allies agreed to the Soviet annexation of part of Poland, and accepted a Soviet-backed and communist controlled "provisional" party as the rightful government of Poland.

Within three years, however, the Communist Party had eliminated all political opposition and then trained its sights on its sole remaining opponent: the Roman Catholic Church. Despite having signed an Agreement of Noninterference with the leaders of the Catholic Church, the government attempted to silence it. By 1952, eight bishops and over nine hundred priests were serving prison terms as "enemies of the socialist revolution." Cardinal Stefan Wyszyński, Archbishop of Warsaw and primate of the Polish Church, publicly protested the assault on the religious values of Poland, repudiating the state ideology of hatred for the enemies of socialism and calling upon Christians to practice love and reconciliation. As a result of his protest, the cardinal went to prison for three years as an enemy of the revolution.

Wyszyński gathered new strength from his prison cell, however, and when he was released in 1956, he proclaimed a nine-year period of spiritual renewal that would culminate in a year-long celebration in 1966 of a thousand years of Polish Christianity. In opposition to Soviet indoctrination programs for the young, the Catholic Church sponsored a youth evangelization movement called "Light and Life." Embodying the strength of the Christian churches, Wyszyński rallied his fellow Poles by responding defiantly to the government's attempt to suppress all religious education in 1961. He declared, "If a citizen does not demand his [religious] rights, he is no longer a citizen but a slave."[2] Citizenship now required "heroic sacrifices and massive shocks to bring about the awakening of the man who no longer fights for his freedom . . . and of the nation which no longer fulfills its obligations in the name of its most important and sacred right—its freedom."[3] The Church would not easily be silenced.

Cardinal Wyszyński was a hero from the moment of his arrest. After all, what he said in public, most Poles only whispered behind closed doors for fear of the regime. A woman from Warsaw described the dilemma of teaching her children the truth while impressing upon them the ever-present danger of speaking it out loud:

> It was a question of trying to keep hold of one's interior identity and, even more importantly, that of one's children. You had to choose between bringing them up in a lie, in order to make life easier for them, or in the truth. We had to tell them things like, "Well, that's the truth, but you must not say so at school." We had to teach them to lead a double life.[4]

Against the state dogma of the necessity of class conflict and of hatred toward all who impeded the rise of the socialist state, the Church continued to preach the necessity of love and forgiveness. The Polish bishops practiced what they preached, infuriating the government when they sent a letter to the German Bishops Conference in 1965, calling for the churches of both nations to work for reconciliation and friendship between Germany and Poland. For the Polish government, the Catholic Church of Poland was undercutting the very basis for national unity that the Polish government was exploiting: suspicion and fear of everything German. The government punished the bishops by revoking their passports in order to prevent them from attending the final sessions of the Second Vatican Council in Rome.

The "heroic sacrifices and massive shocks" which Wyszyński prescribed for Polish society were not to take the form of retaliatory violence against the already pervasive violence of the regime. According to Wyszyński, reconstruction of the society would mean first of all overcoming fear of the regime. The Church would proclaim the power of nonviolent Christian love in a repressive environment by educating the people in alternative forms of political participation that avoided confrontation with security forces, riot police, and the Soviet troops that the regime might summon. Polish historian Bohdan Cywinski describes how the Church gave people courage during those years:

> People began to understand that they could gather in large numbers for religious purposes and no harm would come to

> them. They learned to keep calm, and to carry on praying or
> doing whatever they had to do. . . . It was an apprentice-
> ship—a lesson that even under a hostile regime you can
> achieve something without violence.[5]

The Church's message was soon to have a leavening effect among Poland's industrial workers. Throughout the 1960s, as the Polish economy was stagnating, everyone but the Communist Party elite suffered from chronic shortages of food and consumer goods. Workers eventually began to protest the lack of essentials and to demand reform of the Polish economy. In December 1970 thousands of workers at the government-owned shipyards in Gdansk on the Baltic Coast went on strike, demanding the right to establish a union independent of the government. A large group of workers marched from the shipyard through the streets of Gdansk to the central Gdansk government building and police headquarters. When the crowd ransacked the building, the government responded by declaring a state of emergency, severing communications into and out of the coastal region, and locking workers out of the shipyard. Unaware of the declared state of emergency, the afternoon shift of workers arriving at the rail station adjacent to the shipyard were met by government troops. For reasons never made clear, the troops opened fire on them. Although the government put the death toll at twenty-six, the number of workers who disappeared that day was much higher. The government hastily buried the bodies in unmarked graves.

One of the organizers of the strike, a worker at the shipyard at the time, was a young electrician named Lech Walesa. Walesa mourned the loss of his fellow workers and resolved to work for a movement that could produce radical change without violence. Although the possibility of violent explosions across the country was very real after years of deprivation, frustration, and repression, young Walesa saw the futility of spilling blood and splitting skulls. "The point is not to smash your head open in one day, but win, step by step, without offending anyone," he declared. A movement that becomes a mob squanders its energies and abdicates its authority. Because he saw conquering one's own fear and renouncing retaliation as keys to overthrowing violent structures, Walesa counseled patience and self-discipline among workers. While he was unwavering in his demands on behalf of workers, he also professed, "I am a believer, which is why I forgive blindly. I can be having a real go at someone, and then all at once I see standing opposite me another human being."[6]

But Walesa's recognition of the humanity of his opponents did not soften his accusations against the regime or temper his demands for radical reform. As one observer writes, Walesa "used words honestly, and gave them a truthfulness that years of doublespeak had taken from them."[7] When he was fired from his job at the shipyard in 1976, the only surprise was that it had not happened sooner.

The same year that the U.S. celebrated the bicentennial of its great experiment in democracy, Poles labored to bring forth a rebirth of democracy. In 1976 the Committee for the Defense of Workers (KOR), founded by Jacek Kuron and Adam Michnik, brought together Poles from the professions, the sciences, and the arts to join workers in demanding democratization of Polish socialism. Kuron and Michnik, too, advocated nonviolent methods for liberating Polish society. Recalling the massacre of shipyard workers in 1970, Kuron saw the necessity of a highly disciplined and nonviolent movement:

> The anti-reform policy of the Polish state leadership always contains the danger of popular explosion. The only possibility afforded to the population to ward off this danger is that of self-organization. Only by peaceful methods, like peaceful demonstrations that do not disturb public order, only by means of stubborn negotiations with the state power, can the population strive for the successful attainment of its political will and force the state power to accept its wishes for reform.[8]

The Catholic Church supported the Committee for the Defense of Workers. Pope John Paul II, in his historic first visit "home" to Poland in 1979, spoke of the dignity of work and of workers, encouraging Poland's bishops to continue to defend "fundamental human rights, including the right to religious liberty." For church-state harmony, the pope said, there must be "authentic dialogue [that] respects the rights of citizens and . . . the activities of the church as a religious community to which the vast majority of Poles belongs."[9]

In August 1980 a committee organized several thousand workers in a strike at the Gdansk shipyard. Their spokesman, Lech Walesa, vowed:

> We will not abandon the shipyards and we will not give the militia any reason for intervening. Should they try to break up the strike before it winds up, we will not do anything

> against them. We don't struggle, we won't get into fights; we
> will merely sit down and drag the peace. They can come in
> and carry us away, all sixteen thousand of us, one by one.[10]

The workers did not take to the streets or engage in any acts of violence against the government, however. The citizens of Gdansk, in support of the strikers, brought them food, and priests entered the shipyard
to celebrate Mass with them. So committed were strike organizers to
avoiding violent exchanges with government forces that they instituted
a ban on alcohol throughout the duration of the strike. Other workers
throughout the country went on strike in solidarity with the Gdansk
workers, eventually shutting down four hundred factories.

After two weeks and no sign of the strikers weakening, the government capitulated, agreeing to all twenty-one of the workers' demands,
including free and independent trade unions.[11] Polish worker "Solidarity" was now a potent social force. Later in the fall of 1980, the Soviet
Union threatened to intervene with military force to assist the regime in
defeating Solidarity. In December, Pope John Paul II wrote to Soviet
leader Leonid Brezhnev, urging him not to intervene in Poland's internal affairs and suggesting that the Catholic Church of Poland could be
a mediator in negotiations between workers and government.

Solidarity leaders avoided antagonizing the regime, neither
denouncing the socialist system nor demanding political control. After
all, Solidarity's revolutionary intent was not to oust a regime but to
work with the government to solve the country's massive economic
and social problems. Its ultimate goal was to reunite a society wracked
by class conflict, deeply fragmented by fear and distrust. Remarkably,
in the spring of 1981, the government formed a joint commission with
the Church it had set out to destroy, charging it with strengthening
national unity "regardless of the differences in world outlook or political views."[12] The Church, meanwhile, continued to set a conciliatory
tone, with the bishops advocating forgiveness and a rebuilding of
mutual trust. Cardinal Jozef Glemp, Wyszyński's successor, wrote to
the people: "Let us look at ourselves truthfully. We shall see our own
sins . . . and this will allow us to see the good done by the other
side."[13]

The capacity of the Polish people for forgiveness and trust would
be put to the test within the year, however. In December 1981, General
Wojciech Jaruzelski, leader of the regime, suddenly declared that
Poland was in a "state of war." Who had invaded Poland now? won-
dered confused citizens who heard the radio announcement. In an ironic

twist of Marxist-Leninist war against the bourgeoisie, Jaruzelski had declared war on Solidarity, the worker movement now ten million members strong. Martial law now canceled freedoms recently won, and Solidarity was banned. Walesa, Michnick, and scores of Solidarity and KOR leaders were jailed. As Jaruzelski's "war" produced yet another siege of suffering for Poles, the Church again raised the sole voice of opposition. Cardinal Glemp responded to the imposition of marital law with a plea for nonviolence: "The most important thing is to avoid bloodshed. There is nothing of greater value than human life."[14] The Polish Bishops Conference called on the regime to restore civil rights, to release all political prisoners, and to renew its dialogue with Solidarity, and the Church itself aided the families of fired or imprisoned workers.

This dark hour was soon revealed to be the hour before the dawn. Jaruzelski's power depended on his patron, the Soviet Union. But the Russians were reeling from their own failed domestic and foreign policies, and refused the general's call for help, advising him to handle his own domestic troubles. Thus, lacking both external and internal support, Jaruzelski and the Polish Communist Party simply crumbled in the face of the Solidarity movement. Jaruzelski's war against Polish workers and peasants failed because it had encountered something more powerful than armed resistance. His military threats, even if they had been made good by the Soviets, had come up against an immovable force, a collective human spirit that was firmly planted and fearless—and the victors would eventually be the Polish people. Workers and intellectuals, both believers and unbelievers, joined in a common cause.

In 1983, Solidarity leaders were released from prison and Walesa was awarded the Nobel Peace Prize. The Nobel Committee wrote:

> Lech Walesa's activities were marked by a determination to solve the problems of his country by discussions and cooperation without force. He managed to make possible the dialogue between the organization "Solidarity" and the authorities. The Committee regarded Walesa as an exponent of the active longing for peace and freedom. . . . At a time when the easing of tensions and the peaceful resolution of conflicts are more important than at any other time . . . [his] initiative is an inspiration and an example.[15]

In his acceptance speech, Walesa repeated his credo: "We can effectively oppose violence only if we do not resort to it. . . .We will defend our rights but will not allow ourselves to be overcome by hatred. . . ."[16] Walesa reflected Poland's quest for freedom, the inner freedom the people possessed that enabled them to limit the regime's ability to intimidate. Supported first by the Catholic Church and later by the workers movement, the Polish people acquired a spiritual weapon of great magnitude: the power to overcome fear and seek reconciliation with opponents.

The story of Poland and Solidarity has its martyrs, including Fr. Jerzy Popieluszko, a popular priest murdered by the regime in 1984. Eulogizing Popieluszko, Walesa said: "They wanted to kill, and they wanted not only a man, not only a Pole, not only a priest. They wanted to kill the hope that it is possible in Poland to avoid violence in political life."[17]

This story is about courage and hope and gospel love carried into politics by numerous courageous Poles. Walesa and the millions who joined the Solidarity movement bore witness to the convictions of Gandhi and King, that nonviolent resistance is a force more potent than military force. Poland's liberation soon spilled across borders, awakening the aspirations of other peoples in the Soviet bloc for freedom, emboldening them to affirm their dignity.

2. East Germans Light a Thousand Candles

In 1989 the world witnessed the toppling of the communist government of East Germany and, with it, the Berlin Wall. Overcoming the totalitarian system was the fruit of three decades of campaigns of nonviolent resistance in which the churches of East Germany played a leading role.

For forty-five years the communist regime tried to suppress Christianity. As in Poland, it did not succeed; the voices of East German churches would not be silenced. Helmar Junghans, a Lutheran pastor and professor of church history at the University of Leipzig, described the churches of East Germany as "the shield against communist attack, the shelter of action groups, the champion of the reforms, and the voice of nonviolence."[18]

Churches began in the early 1960s to promote programs to counter the ideology of the state. In 1960, the Lutheran Church initiated "Friedensdekade" ("ten days of peace"), to be observed each November for the purpose of praying for peace and discussing ways in which peace between the Soviet bloc and the West could be fostered. This annual observance concluded with a day of repentance for the sins of the nation. The Lutheran churches also introduced their "Education for Peace" youth program, challenging the official state view of the necessity of class conflict. Increasingly, churches became meeting places for study groups, places where East Germans "learned to ask the Communist government questions to which they could scarcely give an answer,"[19] and where weeklong workshops on peace were organized.

In 1980 an annual ecumenical "Bridge Worship" began in Halle, East Germany, involving weekly processions of church members moving from one church to another as they prayed for social justice and peace. In 1981 Protestant parishes in Leipzig organized weekly services in the city's most prominent church, Nikolaikirche, to pray for peace and for a reversal of plans to install intermediate-range missiles in Western and Eastern Europe. (Although the missiles were deployed anyway in 1983, the prayer groups continued to grow, only to be met with state opposition.) Also in 1981 mass arrests were made of those who, in association with the "Friedensdekade," distributed and wore patches bearing an image of a sculpture entitled "Swords into Plowshares." With dissent in Poland now galvanized into the Solidarity movement, the apprehensive German Democratic Republic (GDR) leadership sought to suppress popular opposition. The government took aim at the Monday prayer services, arresting participants on the charges that such gatherings were intended to support dissidents seeking permission to emigrate. The state's relationship with the churches was strained—and strange. To improve its image in the West, the East German government permitted East German Lutheran churches to host international celebrations of the 500th anniversary of Martin Luther's birth. Environmental protests in the mid 1980s brought more arrests and reprisals against parishioners by the Communist Party, and increased the risk that the government might deny the churches the freedom to carry out their pastoral tasks. The religious press continued to raise issues involving the environment, alternatives to national military service, popular education, legal rights, mass media policies, expatriation, and freedom of travel. The government, in turn, sought to limit circulation by withholding paper for printing.

By 1987, churches in several East German cities sponsored meetings for citizens to discuss national problems and how the churches could address them; these meetings often concluded with candle-lit processions through city centers. During this period, the churches began to negotiate secretly with the government to obtain permission for political dissidents to leave the country. The meetings with state officials could not be public because the government refused to officially recognize the existence or authority of the Church.

Finally, in the summer of 1989, confrontation between Church and government reached new levels when the churches publicly demanded an investigation of fraud in the May elections. While the arrests of those attending Monday prayer services continued to increase, the Synod of the Union of Protestant Churches, held in October, protested that "young people who demonstrate in a nonviolent fashion are oppressed through violence; participants are punished unjustly. . . ."[20] Junghans notes that, as a consequence of the estrangement of the East German Communist Party from the Gorbachev reforms, "the tanks of the Red Army had not yet been available to the government of the GDR in the fall of 1989."[21]

The decisive confrontation in October 1989 was incredible both for the absence of tanks and the nonviolent discipline of the thousands of anti-government demonstrators. Junghans describes the role of the churches in the dramatic collapse of the government and the Berlin Wall:

> More and more people began to participate in the peace prayers at the Nikolaikirche in Leipzig. Soon the church was no longer able to hold all of the people. Many thousands of them stood in the street around the church. The message was clear: The government had to act. Would it again use guns and tanks? . . . The hospitals of Leipzig had been prepared to admit a lot of wounded people. The situation was at a breaking point. The voice of the church to abstain from violence was amplified to both sides.[22]

The Lutheran Bishop of Leipzig, Johannes Hempel, urged dialogue between the government and the demonstrators, publicly pleading for calm and for no resort to violence on anybody's part. As other church leaders echoed these same pleas, thousands demonstrated nonviolently— and the police did not resort to arms against them. In the meantime, as more and more people refused to accept its legitimacy, the government was paralyzed. Church officials intervened, facilitating meetings between reform leaders and the government and negotiating the terms of the transfer of political power.

Describing the peaceful end of the communist government that was achieved in East Germany, Jorg Swoboda wrote: "Gorbachev's perestroika [political and economic reform] and glasnost [openness—a more open society] had given the people courage. God had blessed them with unyielding patience and unconquerable nonviolence. They had overcome their fear and found their voice and self-respect again."[23] After thirty years of nonviolent persistence, East Germans experienced the promise of the Gospel: "Blessed are the meek, for they shall inherit the land." And the Berlin Wall, the symbol of oppression in that land, came tumbling down.

The story of European peace movements that helped bring an end to the Cold War is much broader than these two accounts suggest. In addition to the reform movements of Poland and East Germany, other popular movements that remained largely nonviolent ousted repressive regimes in Hungary, Bulgaria, and Czechoslovakia. In August 1991, a large crowd shielded the Russian Parliament Building, protecting Boris Yeltsin and other elected officials within from a military assault. In the shadow of the Parliament building, Fr. Aleksandr Borisov, an Orthodox priest and member of Moscow's city council, moved among the tense crowd of demonstrators and the Russian soldiers facing them, distributing two thousand Bibles to soldiers and another two thousand to people on the barricades. Patriarch Alexis of the Russian Orthodox Church threatened to excommunicate any soldiers who fired on the people.[24] In West Germany, massive demonstrations were organized against NATO's nuclear deterrence policy in which Germany was to be the first line of defense in a superpower confrontation in Europe.[25] The resistance was peaceful and effective.

All of these examples illustrate the power of popular resistance when pursued patiently and without resort to violence. Like the nonviolent civil rights campaigns of Gandhi in South Africa and India, these examples illustrate the power of nonviolence to effect social and political change on a large scale. In all of these cases, the churches preached the power of nonviolence and actively supported the reform process.

Glen Stassen refers to a "new paradigm" arising from the Eastern European experience of the 1980s, involving a process by which "people who have lived in the face of oppression, violation of their basic rights, and the nuclear threat, with political scientists, Christian ethicists, and activists, fashioned realistic steps of peacemaking that enabled them to begin living in the time after the Cold War even before the Wall came down."[26] All across Europe many people began to realize that the use of violence would be self-defeating and, in the Eastern European contexts, that the counterviolence could result in massive suffering. Indeed, Eastern European protestors were no match for the military forces the regimes commanded. But what appeared to be a disadvantage proved to be an advantage: they were required to learn how to use an alternative kind of force. Nonviolence did not prove to be a "second best" means but a more certain means of overcoming oppression. Beneath its apparent weakness was a power waiting to be unleashed that could not be defeated.

3. People Power in the Philippines

Ferdinand Marcos held the presidency of the Philippines from 1965 to 1986. Over those twenty-one years he consolidated control of the economy and the military, and—along with a handful of other families—amassed fortunes by channeling government resources into personal economic enterprises. Marcos's perennial technique for dealing with charges of corruption was to warn of the imminent danger of a communist takeover of the Philippines, portray himself as staunchly anti-Communist, and deal ruthlessly with his opponents. He was the strongest U.S. ally in the Pacific—and enriched himself through that relationship. For example, President Marcos offered assurances to the U.S. that its military bases in the Philippines were secure, exchanging this assurance for financial assistance ostensibly to the Philippines, but in actuality to his family.

But the corruption of the Marcos government—nowhere more evident than in the political machinations and sumptuous lifestyle of First Lady Imelda Marcos—met ever-stronger popular opposition. When Marcos imposed martial law in 1972, claiming the threat of a communist takeover, police and military arrested thousands of Filipinos critical of the Marcos government. Among them was the leader of the largest opposition party: Benigno Aquino. Although Aquino was sentenced to twenty years in prison, he was permitted to leave the country in 1980 to undergo heart surgery in the U.S., and to return in 1983. His return lasted less than one minute, however, when he was gunned down on the tarmac of Manila International Airport while descending from the plane. The Marcos government denied responsibility, but this new act of ruthlessness galvanized the opposition against Marcos, now led by Corazon Aquino, Benigno Aquino's widow.

Traditionally the Catholic clergy and episcopacy of the Philippines were politically conservative, remaining generally supportive of the Marcos government and its anti-Communist stance. But the Church's view of the Marcos family and its cronies began to change in the early 1980s. Eventually Marcos was opposed by Cardinal Jaime Sin, Archbishop of Manila since 1974 and primate of the Catholic Church in the Philippines. The cardinal preached the eulogy at Benigno Aquino's funeral, criticizing the government "for creating an atmosphere of oppression and corruption." Sin pleaded for nonviolence amidst the growing tension between the regime and the opposition groups: "Can man liberate man without recourse to violence? Our answer to that is an unequivocal YES."[27]

In late 1985, Marcos announced that the 1987 presidential elections would be moved to February 1986—a move calculated to demonstrate to his U.S. ally that he enjoyed popular support. Jaime Sin was to play a pivotal role in this election, which would become the nonviolent revolution of 1986. Sin had been instrumental in the creation of the National Citizens' Movement for Free Elections (NAMFREL), "a watchdog group that had marshaled half a million people in a vain attempt to ensure honest polls."[28] (Many NAMFREL workers described their commitment to insuring honest elections as a Christian lay apostolate.) In December 1985 Sin took the first step in unseating Marcos by persuading Salvador Laurel, the country's second most popular opposition leader, to accept the vice-presidential spot on Corazon Aquino's presidential ticket. Without a united opposition, the resulting split-vote would have made Marcos's claim of a "mandate" easier. The Philippine Conference of Catholic Bishops met twice during the campaign and twice issued pastoral letters protesting the corruption within the Marcos camp. The week before the election, the bishops warned, "these elections can become one great offense to God and a national scandal."[29] Their letter, which was read from most church pulpits and appeared as a full-page newspaper ad, detailed Marcos-era election fraud:

> Vote-buying, bribery, unwarranted pressures, serious lies, black propaganda, the fraudulent casting, canvassing, and reporting of votes, snatching and switching of ballot boxes, physical violence and killing . . . [all] threatening to escalate to a level never before experienced.[30]

In the days leading up to the elections, Marcos workers bought votes by the thousands. So widespread was vote buying, in fact, that Cardinal Sin issued a statement that it would not be wrong for Catholics to accept bribes but that it would be seriously wrong subsequently to deliver their votes to Marcos rather than to vote their consciences. The cardinal later explained his reasoning: ". . . the people were being bribed with their own money. They were poor, they needed it badly, and certain quarters were offering it. We said, 'Take it. It's yours. There's no sin in that. But if you change your vote . . . then you have sinned.'"[31]

Despite NAMFREL's efforts, the February 7, 1986, election was, by all accounts, the most fraudulent in Filipino history. On February 9, statisticians for the national election commission in Manila, who were still tallying votes, walked off their jobs charging massive evidence of fraud in vote reporting. Fearing reprisals against them, the statisticians were given refuge in a nearby Catholic church and later hidden at an undisclosed location. On February 11, when Marcos was projected as the winner, Cardinal Sin made a trip to the NAMFREL headquarters to rally hundreds of dejected volunteers whom he exhorted to stay the course:

> I know you are doing your best to restore the freedom and dignity of the Filipino people. I know how much courage you have shown, and how much you have suffered in the recent elections. The Bible says much about the virtue of suffering . . . and you, you members of NAMFREL, have shown me how to suffer. I am inspired by you, and sometimes I am ashamed. . . . Some of you have died for your country, but now I ask you to go forth and live for your country! In you lies the Spirit, and may the Lord bless you. We will support you to the very end. . . . You cannot truly enjoy Easter Sunday unless you have suffered the pain of Good Friday. This is our Good Friday, but Sunday is coming soon. Stay here and wait for it. Don't leave us yet. You must stay and see the resurrection.[32]

Although Sin's words were interrupted with news of the assassination of a popular former provincial governor and Aquino supporter, the cardinal appeared unshaken by the news, utterly confident that the resurrection of which he spoke was at hand.

Most observers of the Church's role in the elections thought that Cardinal Sin had now mustered all his power and had still come up short against the power of the desperate and ruthless Marcos regime. Four days later, Marcos succeeded in having himself declared the winner by the members of the National Assembly who had not walked out in protest.

But the charges of fraud stuck, and what the Church did next not only helped make them stick but also denied the legitimacy of the Marcos regime: the Philippine Catholic Conference of 108 bishops prepared another pastoral letter. The letter clearly signaled a break between the Catholic Church and the Marcos regime—and was published despite the intense efforts of Imelda Marcos to stop it. After noting the widespread election fraud, the bishops drew this stunning conclusion: "These, and other irregularities, point to the criminal use of power to thwart the sovereign will of the people. . . . We are morally certain the people's real will for change has been truly manifested."[33] Having declared that " a government that assumes or retains power through fraudulent means has no moral basis," the bishops offered two options. The first was addressed to the Marcos government: recognize the people's will and relinquish power. If Marcos refused, the bishops urged the people to engage in a "systematically organized . . . nonviolent struggle by means of active nonresistance [to] correct the evil that [the government] has inflicted. . . ." [34]

The opposition that brought about the revolution of 1986 included several key players. Corazon Aquino and her running mate, Salvador Laurel, had broad popular support—a fact the U.S. conceded (after the people had taken to the streets) by acknowledging that she had won the popular vote. The day after the Marcos-dominated National Assembly declared Marcos the winner, Aquino herself declared victory and called for civil disobedience against the Marcos regime and a nationwide boycott of the economic enterprises controlled by the Marcos family and their cronies. (The next day she produced a list of those enterprises.)

The Filipino bishops and Cardinal Sin played pivotal roles as well. Marcos may have calculated that he could ride out a storm with Cardinal Sin (once referred to as "the only man in the country whom Marcos fears, the only man he'll listen to because he carried the full weight of the Roman Catholic Church"[35]), but he had not anticipated the cardinal's direct appeal to the people and the "people power" that quickly materialized.

There were other key players in the revolution, however, who were *not* committed to a nonviolent overthrow of the Marcos regime. As Aquino announced her victory, Minister of Defense Juan Enrile, General Fidel Ramos, and other military officers plotted a coup that involved capturing Marcos and his family, killing his key military leaders, and establishing a provisional committee comprised of military officers and civilians to govern the country. Although Aquino knew about the plot during the last month of her campaign, she did not know when it would occur, nor had the conspirators offered her any assurance of support beyond including her in the provisional governing committee.

The coup was planned for the night of February 23. But on February 22 Marcos's security forces discovered the plot and prepared to take action against Enrile, Ramos, and their fellow conspirators who, at that point, were at the Ministry of Defense. Enrile and Ramos panicked and called both Cardinal Sin and the U.S. ambassador for help, expecting the imminent arrival of Marcos's forces from the Presidential Palace two miles away. But Marcos did not move soon enough. It was mid-afternoon on a Saturday, and Filipinos would soon be assembling for Saturday evening Mass. Priests in churches throughout Manila were requested to urge their congregations to flood the streets and block the route that Marcos's tanks would take to the Defense Ministry. Thus, when Marcos gave orders for the tanks to move, they were stopped midway by a sea of lay people, nuns, and seminarians. Caught in the middle of a massive celebration of national liberation, the troops and tank drivers refused radio commands to proceed. During the next critical twenty-four hours, almost all of Marcos's military forces defected. On February 25, Marcos requested that the U.S. Embassy arrange safe passage out of the Philippines for him and his family.

Finally, a dictatorship dependent on a pervasive military presence was over. A military coup had failed, and its organizers had their lives spared by the courage of unarmed civilians. Loyalty to the Church (and to Corazon Aquino) and commitment to nonviolence had produced a "people power" capable of overthrowing a corrupt regime without the customary wave of retribution and vengeance against loyalists. Their lives having been saved, the rebels had no choice but to recognize Aquino's mandate.

The people had won their first victory in two decades—and at the heart of the victory was the nonviolent means by which it was accomplished. Fifteen years later, in late January 2001, the people again rallied against presidential corruption. A quarter of a million Filipinos gathered around the monument that commemorated the defeat of Marcos, demanding the resignation of President Joseph Estrada, who was charged with corruption and was facing impeachment within a few days. No shots were fired, no opponents were assassinated, and no injuries were reported during the demonstrations that climaxed three months of crisis for his scandal-ridden government. Estrada resigned—without a deal that would have permitted him to take his ill-gotten fortune with him into exile—and Gloria Macapagal-Arroyo was sworn in as president.

5

Blood Brothers
in the Balkans

In 1914 nations rose against nations, and they have continued to do so throughout the twentieth century, bloodying and burning the human family and the earth to a degree never before witnessed. The ferocity of twentieth-century wars has claimed over 127 million lives.

Some of the century's worst bloodletting began and ended in the Balkans. In 1914, the assassination of Archduke Francis Ferdinand (heir to the Habsburg throne) and his wife by a Serb nationalist ignited World War I. At the other end of the century, throughout the 1990s, ethnic nationalists made the former Yugoslavia into an inferno.

After Pope Benedict XV was elevated to the papacy in 1914, as Europe was convulsed in violence on a new scale, he spent most of his papacy aiding the victims of the Great War. He directed a massive war relief effort drawing on the Church's financial resources as well as his own family's wealth to assist war refugees.

Sections one and two describe the rise of nation-states and nationalism and the deadly dynamic of "ethnic nationalism." Section three explores how the body politic of nations ravaged by ethnic wars may be restored to health. Section four examines how Christian churches have fostered the processes of forgiveness and repentance. The fifth section considers the politics of national repentance, looking at the example of Germany after World War II.

1. Nations and Nationalism

"The twentieth century has belonged to nationalism. Nationalism has been installed nearly everywhere. . . . Of the two hundred nations which now make up the United Nations, only a score or so, nearly all European or American, possessed national consciousness before 1914."[1]

Historian William Pfaff identifies a surprisingly small list of nations that existed before the nineteenth century: France, England, Spain, Portugal, Sweden, Denmark, Poland, Russia, Japan, and the United States, pointing to France and England as the first two nations, emerging in the fifteenth century. Complex factors contributed to the rise of "English" and "French" national consciousness. In both England and France, for example, universities arose to celebrate language and culture, two sources of group identity and cohesiveness. Other factors that help build nations are shared territory, common ancestry, and shared religious beliefs. Hugh Seton-Watson observes that a nation exists when a significant number of people regard themselves as such. The result of such "national consciousness" is a political cohesiveness sufficient to support a central government and to cooperate in the maintenance of internal order and defense against external aggression.

After the Roman Empire collapsed in the fifth century, Europe was again a mosaic of fiefdoms. Nations represent the unification of these smaller units around common purposes, aided by shared language and culture. A more precise explanation of what factors have created nations would require a case-by-case examination; nations are a complicated matter. French national consciousness, for example, is founded on shared language and culture, but not on a single ethnic or racial identity. Both Belgium and India possess a national consciousness, although their citizens do not share a common language. Palestinians possess a national consciousness without having sovereignty over any territory.

The most important feature of nations, for the purposes of this chapter, is the patriotism and emotional loyalty they evoke among citizens. A nation is an idea, an object of value for its citizens beyond its organizational functions. Nations acquire mythic stature, enshrining and passing on ideals across generations, evoking pride of belonging. Nations offer their citizens an identity, impose upon them duties, and claim certain rights in relations with other nations.

It is useful to distinguish between two forms of nationalism, *civic nationalism* and *ethnic nationalism*. Both the French and the English experiences illustrate the development of *civic nationalism*. Both moved from monarchies through revolutions to representative forms of government, arriving at the point where they are today: political authority rests on the consent of the governed. These nations have evolved forms of government that guarantee a number of civic rights of the citizens. A nation in this mold, writes Pfaff, is "a practical affair, providing defense, civic order, a system of justice, economic structures as a framework for industry and commerce. . . ."[2] Nations that provide these sorts of practical benefits evoke in their citizens sentiments of "civic nationalism."

Another kind of nationalism arose in central Europe: *ethnic nationalism*. The story of ethnic nationalism begins with the Holy Roman Empire that arose in A.D. 800, while declined within a century in Western Europe, but in central and eastern Europe held together until the thirteenth century. Beginning with Holy Roman Emperor Otto (ruled 938–973), every ruler of the Empire until its final fracturing into a thousand fiefdoms was Germanic. The German Hapsburg rulers actually retained the "Holy Roman Emperor" title until 1806. From this origin, German nationalism flowered in the mid-nineteenth century. The great German nationalist was Otto Von Bismarck, whose views were fuelled by the Romantic notion that ethnic groups required national embodiment to realize their potential. Bismarck justified the annexation of Alsace and Lorraine from France on the ground that as German-speaking areas they belonged with other German peoples in a German nation. In ethnic nationalism bloodline is the basis of belonging. Pfaff writes: "The appropriation of this romantic idea that a racial origin identifies nations proved a decisive factor in Bismarck's enterprise, creating a new definition and consciousness of German nationality which has existed ever since."[3] Ethnic forms of nationalism appeared in the nineteenth century in Italy and Greece as well.

In Germany, in the Baltics, and in Eastern Europe, nationalist dogma was that the *volk* (people with a particular cultural identity) or the *ethne* (ethnic group) must be a nation in order to achieve their destiny. So German, Croats, Serbs, Montenegrins, etc. all cried out for autonomy. But ethnic nationalism was not conducive to the cause of democracy or human rights. Rather, its tendency was to exclude groups who did not share the majority's ethnic background from political participation, and to deny their rights. The recurring violence against foreigners seeking asylum in Germany and against foreign workers, for example, is rooted in the deeply held conviction of many Germans that only those of German blood belong in Germany. Thus, writes Pfaff, "children of Turkish or Yugoslav workers in Germany, born and educated in Germany, entirely German in culture, could be denied citizenship because they were not German by descent."[4] Where ethnic nationalism is strong, political leaders are able to influence public sentiments by raising fears of "aliens" within the nation

When ethnic nationalism takes hold of a society, minorities suddenly become unwelcome outsiders amidst a majority whose racial or ethnic background differs from their own. Ethnic nationalism sparked World War I. Despite President Woodrow Wilson's "Fourteen Point" program to avert future wars, ethnic nationalism actually intensified because political borders drawn after the war attempted to separate ethnic groups.

2. Ethnic Nationalism in the Balkans

By the terms of the Treaty of Versailles (1919), six republics and two "autonomous provinces" (Kosovo and Vojvodina) were created in the Balkans from the dissolution of Ottoman and Austria-Hungarian Empires after World War I. These republics and provinces were placed within a federation called "Yugoslavia." Because of the blend of many different ethnic peoples—Serbians, Montenegrins, Croats, Slovenes, Bosnians—this first Yugoslavian federation was uneasy from the start. While Serbians and Montenegrins took credit for Croat and Slovene liberation from Austro-Hungary, assuming a kind of "manifest destiny" over Yugoslavia, Croats, Slovenes, and Bosnians viewed federation as a partnership of equals. Because the creation of Yugoslavia was unification without negotiation, distrust understandably was present from the start. Later, when the Germans occupied the Balkans from 1941 to 1945, certain Croatian forces known as the *Ustase* collaborated with Hitler against the Serbs, committing atrocities similar to Nazi crimes against Jews and other Slavic peoples. Such crimes went unpunished— or unavenged—when Germany was defeated, because communist leader Josip Tito assumed absolute control over the "second Yugoslavia" and suppressed the aspirations for freedom and justice for all of Yugoslavia's ethnic groups.

We frequently hear that national identities and animosities are centuries old in the Balkans. However, consider Bosnia, in southeastern Europe on the Balkan Peninsula. When the Jews were expelled from Spain in 1492, many settled in Sarajevo, Bosnia's major city, which became a model of ethnic and religious toleration. Bosnians possess a common language, have been economically interdependent for generations, and have functioned as a multiethnic society for four centuries. Mixed marriages between Muslims and Christians were common, and Catholics and Orthodox lived side by side. In fact, Sarajevo was the site of the Winter Olympics in 1984.

Then, late in the twentieth century, ethnic nationalism visited unspeakable horrors on the Balkans. Into the void created by the collapse of Communism in the late 1980s rushed ethnic nationalism—flowing red. When authoritarian communist rule in Yugoslavia ended in the 1980s, Serbia began to realize its dream of uniting all Serbs into a "greater Serbia," gaining political control in Montenegro and in the "autonomous provinces" of Kosovo and Vojvodina. The effects of ethnic fear spread as ominously as small fissures in a dike. In 1991 Croatia and Slovenia declared independence from the federation (and, with pressure from the German government on Western nations, had their sovereignty recognized). As we shall note in the testimony of a Croatian observer, the "new Croatia" was hostile to its Serbian population, "Croatized" its public institutions, and removed Serbs from governmental posts (and most crucially, from the judiciary). Serbia sent the Yugoslavian Army and paramilitary units to assist Croatian Serbs. When Bosnia attempted to leave the federation in 1992, Serbs within Bosnia, assisted by Belgrade, carved out a Serbian enclave in northern Bosnia by "cleansing" the regions of all non-Serbs.

Thus began a decade of agony for the peoples of the Balkans. South central Europe, where Europeans and Slavs and multireligious communities of Muslims, Jews, Catholics, and Orthodox Christians had lived together for several centuries, was awash in the blood of "ethnic cleansing." Bosnia-Herzegovina, Croatia, and Kosovo were scenes of massacres, mass graves, and looted and burned villages. Numbed by shock and grief, refugees fled their homes, lands, and livelihoods across borders and into refugee camps, where they awaited news of family.

Zlata Filipovik, thirteen years old, was trapped with her family in Sarajevo when she wrote the following:
"Tuesday, May 4, 1993. I've been thinking about politics again. No matter how stupid, ugly and unreasonable I think this division of people into Serbs, Croats, and Muslims is, these stupid people are making it happen. . . . Now these maps are being drawn up, separating people, and nobody asks them a thing. Those 'kids' [politicians] really are playing around with us. Ordinary people don't want this division, because it won't make anybody happy—not the Serbs, not the Croats, not the Muslims. But who asks ordinary people?"[5]

Canadian journalist Michael Ignatieff traveled to six ethnic battle-grounds in 1994, including Bosnia in the former Yugoslavia. What he saw everywhere were societies dismembered by ethnic separatists. Efforts of every ethnic group to insure its safety in the absence of any legal protections led to violence and counterviolence, ethnic civil war, and secessions. Less than a reemergence of a feudal system, this phenomenon resembled gangland turf wars. By might and by nation-alistic rhetoric (Ignatieff calls it "a vocabulary of opportunistic self-justification"), thugs and warlords took charge of police, govern-ment, and economies. Even one's own ethnic leaders came to be feared as much as ethnic "enemies." In gangland no one was safe. Rival gang leaders waged civil war, nullifying whatever legal system once existed.

> When the Soviet empire and its satellite regimes collapsed, the nation-state structures of the regimes also collapsed, leaving hundreds of ethnic groups at the mercy of each other.[6]

Ignatieff argues that ethnically driven nationalism is a disaster—culturally, politically, and morally. An ethnic community "purified" of outsiders becomes the cultural ideal, buttressed by the political claim that each separate group naturally has a right to its own territory. When intoned as a "moral imperative," it calls upon citizens to become their neighbors' murderers in the name of preserving the nation.

Is there hope for a different future? After four decades of Josip Broz Tito's authoritarian rule, citizens had no experience of democracy. Yet, many Serbs, Croats, Albanians, Kosovars, Montenegrins, and Bosnians desperately desired peace. Political scientist Bogdan Denitch is a citi-zen of Croatia and is of Serbian ancestry. In *Ethnic Nationalism: The Tragic Death of Yugoslavia*, he examined ethnic relations and conflicts in the Balkans since 1918, concentrating on the bloody dismemberment of Yugoslavia since 1991. What follows is his assessment of how to stop the hemorrhaging and begin the slow process of bringing peace and healing to the Balkans.

1. Denitch calls for the preservation of the Balkan republics with their pre-Yugoslavian federation borders intact. He sees the first step as mutual recognition by the republics of one another. The republics must enter into a nonaggression treaty. He argues against redrawing borders for two reasons. First, new borders will fuel new

bloodletting among the majority-minorities that are created. Second, attempts to redraw the frontiers along ethnic lines "reinforce two absolutely deadly myths: first, that it is possible to draw borders in such a way; and second, that it is desirable."

2. The army of the former Yugoslavia for the most part became the Serbian Army when the federation collapsed in the 1980s. The few leaders who hold power use the military to preserve themselves and further their ethnic cleansing agendas. The Republics must agree to an equitable distribution of the military hardware of the former Yugoslav Army, permit all soldiers to return home, provide pensions for all army personnel. Military forces must be brought under control of civilian governments, local militias disbanded, and their members returned to what is often a "dull civilian existence."[7] Poor economic prospects for the young have swelled the ranks of local ethnic militias, the Balkan form of urban gangs.

3. Denitch advocates the development of mixed economies that combine public planning, self-management, regionally owned public enterprises, cooperatives, and a small-scale private sector.[8] To revive social solidarity, he argues, will require a minimally just order and commitment to the common good that a "so-called pure market economy" geared only to production and profit will not provide.

4. Denitch has long been active in the Croatian Democratic Socialist Party's efforts to establish strong trade unions. It was a training ground for the democratic participation that must draw in all of the ethnic and religious peoples in all of the Balkan republics. His prescription for peace within and among the republics depends on the emergence of democratic institutions, including multiple political parties, a free media, and strengthened labor unions, women's groups, and professional associations to help foster civil social participation and power sharing. The more broadly power is distributed within each republic, Denitch argues, the greater the likelihood of protecting people's rights. Denitch hopes for something similar to the accomplishment of the Polish workers' "Solidarity" movement in the early 1980s that overcame authoritarian state control of most Polish institutions. Solidarity furthered the cause of democracy against authoritarian regimes through nonviolent economic and political strikes, mass agitation, and peace demonstrations.

Denitch challenges political parties, media, workers, and churches in all of the republics to foster citizen participation.

5. Denitch charges that his fellow Serbian "pseudohistorians" and "yellow journalists" have distorted and politicized Croat WWII crimes against Serbs "beyond all resemblance of reality," keeping rife the atmosphere of revenge. The citizenry, he laments, proved to be "numerous passive accomplices, who thought it would be harmless to indulge in a little national assertiveness and triumphalism . . . [but] certainly did not expect the consequences."[9]

6. Denitch calls for establishment of a human rights code with monitoring and enforcement by the United Nations and the European community.

The Dayton Peace Accord signed in December 1995, suspended the Balkan conflict for a time. But elections in Bosnia the following fall demonstrated precious little movement away from the separatist frenzies of the previous five years. In 1998 Serbia carried out ethnic expulsion and "cleansing" of Albanian Kosovars in the Yugoslavian province of Kosovo; genocide was occurring once again. More than ever, the protection of human rights and the promotion of pluralism in Croatia, Bosnia, and Serbia require the involvement of other nations and the solidarity of democratic groups around the world. According to Denitch:

> For decent and fair collective decisions to be made in a state there has to be general agreement as to its boundaries, as to who exactly constitutes the demos that is entitled to make controversial allocative decisions in that polity. If the demos is defined only in terms of the ethnos, then when one ethnic group is outvoted in an election it is viewed as more than a political defeat—it is seen as exploitation and robbery of one's nation (ethnos) by other exploiting nations.[10]

3. Can Nationalism Be Reformed?

Ignatieff's tour of nationalist war zones revealed the perverse logic orchestrated by ethnic nationalist leaders: don't trust your neighbors. Drive them out or they will turn on you. While called *wars of liberation* by people who feel singularly victimized, these struggles are intended to hurt, humiliate, and punish enemies and their descendants. Ethnically driven wars, observes Ignatieff, quickly become nihilistic. As a Serbian sniper killing innocent Sarajevan civilians admitted in self-defeat: "I have no feeling for what I do. I have no life anymore."[11] This sniper and thousands like him do the work of small-time warlords and demagogues. There are no heroic national liberators or selfless statesmen here.

Ignatieff observed that ethnic homogeneity did not guarantee social cohesion; in fact, the authoritarian nature of ethnic nationalist regimes seldom produced respect for law, civility, or security. What Ignatieff saw were regimes devoted to promoting the "narcissism of minor difference," avenging old wrongs, transforming neighbors into enemies, breeding paranoia and fear, and making "unwilling nationalists out of ordinary people."[12] Like Pfaff, Ignatieff is critical of the European community's response to Serbian and Croatian talk of self-determination as both sides captured villages and drove out or exterminated hundreds of thousands of people whose chief sin was to be born a Croat, Serb, or Muslim. He asks why Western powers weren't adjudicating rival claims to self-determination, arbitrating border and property claims, and demanding that minorities' rights be guaranteed as a condition for recognition of sovereignty. Why, Ignatieff asks, was "every post-Communist demagogue permitted to exploit the rhetoric of self-determination to his own end?"

Ignatieff and Pfaff offer a litany of failed opportunities to curb the ethnic rivalries. For example, Western European leaders did little to punish acts of aggression across recognized borders or to punish systematic attacks on civilian populations: the employment of rape as an instrument of terror and ethnic purge; the razing of towns; the destruction of churches, mosques, libraries, and historical monuments—places of peoples' civilization and collective memory; genocide in internment camps. All of these atrocities were attested to in the reports of human rights abuses in the Balkans compiled by former Polish Prime Minister Tadeusz Mazowiecki at the request of the European community.[13] With impunity, Serb rebels in the surrounding hills subjected the citizens of Sarajevo to months of deadly mortar attacks and sniper fire as they stood in bread lines. Is it any wonder that the thousands of minorities who had fled their multiethnic villages were afraid to return since Sarajevo and other cities, so-called UN "protected zones," were being destroyed as the world watched?

Ignatieff examines the principle of self-determination, the modern political principle that peoples ought to be able to create or at least choose for themselves the state to which they will belong. But modern nation building requires that consideration of minorities' rights be included in the formation of the state. The acknowledgment and protection of their rights is what "civic nationalism" is about. Ignatieff criticized the hypocrisy of ethnic nationalists championing "the people" and advancing the idea of popular sovereignty while excluding everybody but those of their own kind.

To what critical standards ought claims of national "sovereignty" and "self-determination" be held? Speaking in his homeland in 1983, Pope John Paul II suggested that a state is entitled to a claim of sovereignty "when it governs society and also serves the common good of society."[14] The fundamental purpose of sovereignty is the creation of just and stable internal political order that contributes to the international common good.[15] The Catholic notion of sovereignty, asserts political theorist Jean Bethke Elshtain, arises within a society from "the multiple associations of civil society in dialogue with one another as 'subject.'"[16] Civic nationalism is nurtured by supporting minority rights, pluralist institutions, and a free press. Elshtain urges the international community to delegitimate nationalisms that exclude minorities and to denounce leadership that secures political power by inflaming ethnic fear and resentment.[17] Opposing ethno-cultural versions of national identity, Elshtain says that while "we are not all the 'same,' . . . we do share a capacity for identity with the idea of a plural body politic; we all require self-dignity; we all yearn for a decent life for our children."[18]

While Pope Pius XII acknowledged national sovereignty and protested the aggression of fascist, totalitarian, or communist regimes, he was also a thoroughgoing internationalist, committed to international cooperation and organization to realize the common good. Pius encouraged respect for international law, courts and tribunals, the UN, and the Universal Declaration of Human Rights (1948).

4. Repentance and Forgiveness of the Sins of Nationalism

The new Croatia, like some jealous goddess, wanted all my love and loyalty, and wanted to possess every part of my being. . . . The Balkans are aflame with Serbia's identity with itself. Identity without otherness—that is our curse.[19]

Theologian Miroslav Volf returned to his Croatian homeland from the U.S. in 1992. As he entered the airspace of newly independent Croatia, he reflected joyfully that Croatians now had a place of their own. But the attitudes he heard during his visit home alarmed him. For example, to be part of the new Croatia, one must wholeheartedly be loyal to all that was Croatian, renounce other loyalties, and distance oneself from other ethnic and religious groups and individuals. As a Christian, Volf recognized the idolatry of the ethnic nationalism now aflame in Croatia and Serbia.

Ethnic idolatry has become a curse upon the Balkans, and the ethnic enclaves brutalize those who are removed and those who remain. In pain and passion, Volf asks, "Does not one discover in Croatia's face some despised Serbian features?"[20] Isn't the face of the stranger our own face?

Volf reminds us that Christian identity and belonging must challenge us to develop a center of identity deeper than ethnic, racial, or religious centers of identity. "To be loyal to our Creator and Redeemer," he writes, "we must separate ourselves from the centers of our births." Volf recalls the proclamation of St. Paul: "If anyone is in Christ, there is a new creation: everything old has passed away; see, everything has become new!" (2 Corinthians 5:17) We are called to form a "catholic personality" that is not limited in its loyalty to fatherland, but rather identifies with the new creation that has come through Christ, dedicating ourselves to the "ministry of reconciliation" of the One God who "was reconciling the world to himself through Christ" (2 Corinthians 5:19).

Denitch lays partial blame for the ethnic hysteria and violence on both the Orthodox and Catholic churches, whom, he says, "labored mightily to get close to a 100 percent fit between religion and ethnic identity among Serbo-Croatian speakers . . . reinforc[ing] nationalism rather than any sort of 'catholic' universalism."[21] Denitch challenges the churches, pointing them to the promotion of the common good and of social justice that is deeply embedded in social Christianity and "even more precisely in social Catholicism."[22]

Muslim, Catholic, and Orthodox Christian religious leaders in Bosnia have tried to end the atrocities and hostilities. In Belgrade, for example, Baptists and Pentecostals assisted Muslim and Croatian refugees. Belgrade citizens also staged protests against the war in Bosnia and sent aid to the citizens of Sarajevo. In 1993 Franjo Kuharic, Catholic Cardinal of Zagreb, Croatia, implored:

> I can only beg and implore all participants in this cruel
> war . . . to make peace among themselves. . . . The coexis-
> tence of Muslims, Serbs and Croats in Bosnia-Herzegovina
> is the common destiny of this state. Intermingling and being
> together are part of that destiny. Humanly, it is possible to
> live with others—no matter how different they are—only in
> reconciliation, in the wholehearted acceptance of God's
> commandment: "Do to others whatever you would have
> them do to you" (Matthew 7:12).[23]

Other efforts to promote healing must also be noted. In Croatia, Franciscan priests sponsored seminars on nonviolence. International members of the Fellowship of Reconciliation, an interfaith peace organization begun at the end of World War I to heal French-German animosities, sponsored "listening sessions" between Muslims and Serbs. European and American Quakers and Mennonites joined secular international peace activists in relief efforts and nonviolent conflict resolution initiatives. The international Catholic organization Pax Christi brought relief aid and peace witnesses to Sarajevo.

The Dayton Peace Accord did not resolve the Balkan conflict. In fact, the damage done to human relations continued to spread further. Thus, in the wake of the horrors perpetrated in the Balkans, we must ask: Is it possible for the various peoples there to dwell together in peace? How can the damage be repaired? How can reconciliation occur?

Robert Schreiter's *Reconciliation* examines the possibility and process of forgiveness by the victims of violence and repentance by its perpetrators. He describes reconciliation as "a fundamental repair to human lives, especially the lives of those who have suffered."[24] Reconciliation involves two movements at once: liberation from injustice and healing of pain-filled memories. Those who speak as victims and those who stand with them must insist that liberation from injustice is a prerequisite for reconciliation.

Schreiter cautions those who have not experienced violence against attempting to impose a hasty peace by turning their backs on the past rather than examining it in all its painful detail. Outsiders who urge reconciliation often give in to the temptation to ignore the necessities of justice and liberation. To forget the crimes is to forget the victims as well. Attention must be paid to what was done, who bore responsibility, and what must be done to make restitution. The victims themselves possess the moral authority to guide the process. Schreiter emphasizes that "reconciliation can only come about if the nature of the violence perpetrated is acknowledged, and its conditions for continuing or reappearing are removed."[25] The healing of memory begins with the "reconstruction of memory" by repeating the narrative of the violence "over and over again to ease the burden of trauma that it carries . . . [in order to] put a boundary around the violence, as it were, to separate it from memory."[26]

Schreiter argues that "those who have suffered war and violence cannot return to a prior tranquil state. The violence of those times is burned into memory—repressed perhaps, but surely able to come to the surface and haunt and horrify the present."[27] Those who have suffered grievous harm and loss need to get to a new place, beyond the violence that stripped them of safety, self-hood, and all meaning. Only "when some sense of spiritual survival has been established" can they think of reconciliation.[28] Victims need immense courage and extraordinary faith to enter into the process of reconciliation. While the guilty party ought to approach the victims with repentance and reparation, often it is the victims who find courage and grace to begin the process.

Can Christian churches become credible agents of reconciliation? Schreiter argues that it is presumptuous for church leaders to assume that they are able to reconcile ethnic, racial, and social conflicts just because they hear and speak the gospel words of reconciliation. He suggests, rather, that the churches join in the reconciliation process only when invited to do so by the victims. When they enter into the process, the churches must fully examine themselves, acknowledging how they have abetted conflict and injustice. Have they encouraged divisions? Has the *status quo* served their self-interest and muffled their voice? Do they have the mechanisms in place to work to overcome oppressive situations and to mediate conflicts, or is their response sporadic and ad hoc?

A recent study of the role of the churches in social conflicts concludes, sadly, "the research has shown that the inter-communal antipathies present in the society at large are reflected in the attitudes of churches and their adherents. The leaders of these institutions acknowledged this problem and decried its prevalence, but they have only sporadically used their strategic position as keeper of conscience to influence and alter the ethical choices of their members."[29] The author notes the limited efforts made by clergy to address communal conflict: occasional sermons, periodic inter-ethnic and inter-communal programs, and attempts at cross-cultural activities following outbreaks of intergroup violence.

These reflections are not meant to suggest that the churches are unable to perform the ministries of reconciliation or have always failed to do so, but to acknowledge realistically the challenge reconciliation presents. It may be helpful to point out the recent efforts of Christian communities to bring about reconciliation among enemies.

- The churches of Eastern Europe have had to contend with total-itarian regimes often linked to the Soviet Union as well as with inter-ethnic hostilities. During the 1970s and 1980s the Catholic Church of Poland supported the nonviolent Solidarity move-ment for reform and freedom. Even as it took the side of thou-sands of striking workers against the regime, the Church urged the people to avoid casting all blame for Poland's economic failures on the communist government, but instead to acknowl-edge the widespread responsibility for Poland's stagnation. The Church also cautioned against any forms of retaliation against Communist Party officials. In 1965 the Catholic bishops rejected the regime's propaganda campaign against Germany that was calculated to win the loyalty of Poles to the regime. The bishops sent a public letter to the German bishops seeking reconciliation between Germans and Poles—a move that so angered the regime that it denied visas to the Polish bishops to attend the closing of the Second Vatican Council in Rome.

- In Chile, the Church established a Vicariate of Solidarity as a documentation and advocacy center for the "disappeared" and their families. Schreiter reports that "as the bishops developed the theme of reconciliation in the mid-1980s, it was written into their national pastoral plan as 'reconciliation in truth,' that is, a reconciliation that did not forget the past, did not elide over injustice, but one that would call for the truth to be revealed as a condition for reconciliation. As the Pinochet regime came to an end, they established 'houses of reconciliation' throughout the country where victims of the regime could come to tell their story, to struggle, as it were to overcome the narrative of the lie that had lain like a heavy pall over Chile for seventeen years."[30]

- Desmond Tutu and other church leaders in South Africa have assisted the work of the national Truth and Reconciliation Com-mission to confront the crimes committed during apartheid.

The Christian Gospels proclaim that Jesus Christ has overcome our alienation from God and overcome the sin that causes enmity with one another. Jesus has come to announce the healing of the rift described in Genesis 3 between humankind and God, man and woman, brothers and races. Or, as St Paul, proclaims, in Christ there is no essential distinction between race (Gentile or Jew), class (slave or freeman), or gender (see Galatians 3:28). Especially in the theology of St. Paul, the cross is central to the reconciling ministry of Christ. Jesus' life and death are the story of one that is betrayed, humiliated, tortured, and killed. But the experience of foresakenness is not the end of the story: Jesus' resurrection marks the triumph of life over death, love over sin, good over evil—forever! By the pain of Christ's cross we are reconciled and called to be reconcilers.

5. National Forgiveness

In *An Ethic for Enemies: Forgiveness in Politics*, Donald Shriver describes four actions that make forgiveness possible. First, victims cannot forget the wrong that has been done to them and must insist on acknowledgment of what they have suffered. They must identify and condemn evil "in utmost possible detail"; indeed, without the vigilance of memory, the evil may rise again. Second, victims must renounce the desire for vengeance. Their determination not to forget must be joined to an equal determination not to retaliate for what has been done. The third and fourth tasks may be even more demanding. Those who have suffered must somehow acknowledge the human faces of their former enemies and their descendants. If those who have suffered injury and injustice are able to do these things, they reach the point of reestablishing a relationship and co-existing with those who have harmed them. The acts of remembering, resisting retaliation, recognizing the co-humanity of wrongdoers, and reestablishing relationship are the strands of a sturdy lifeline that can pull us from the mire of hatred, from "the debris of national pasts"—that, tragically, are not really past.

Shriver explores the nature of forgiveness within the politics of nations. Forgiveness, he writes, is the only means of delivering the human future from repetition of the atrocities of the past. Given the scale of the politically engineered atrocities of the twentieth century, nothing could be a more practical or urgent gift to our neighbors of the twenty-first.[31]

An Ethic for Enemies explores the efforts of three nations to come to address national guilt and reconciliation through its political actions: Germany after the Nazi era, Japan after a half century of aggression in the Far East, and the U.S. in its continuing legacy of racial injustice. Let me conclude by briefly reporting the journey of reconciliation between Germany and the victims of its Nazi era. The journey of the German people, politicians, and church leaders to acknowledge guilt, seek reconciliation, and make reparation for the magnitude of Nazi crimes has been painful and divisive. But the words and gestures expressing moral guilt and shame have been equally remarkable for their courage.

Following the Nürmburg Tribunal's prosecution of the highest ranking Nazi leadership, the West German government continued to extirpate Nazis from public life, prosecuting 12,900 and imprisoning over 5,000 by 1970. Since federal legislation was passed in 1952, the government has transferred $75 billion to Jewish victims, to the state of Israel, to Germans forced to flee from Eastern Europe at the war's end, and to citizens of other nations victimized by German aggression. In 1988, the government said of this restitution:

> No matter how large the sum, no amount of money will ever suffice to compensate for National Socialist persecution. . . . But in dealing with the legacy of the Hitler regime, the Federal Republic of Germany has established a precedent, namely, that of legislating and carrying out a comprehensive system of restitution for injustice.[32]

The Cold War could have been a time for the Bonn government to vilify the Soviet Union rather than remember the crimes and aggression of its own Nazi past. But Willy Brandt, upon assuming the chancellorship in 1969, spoke of the need for Germany and its eastern neighbors "to learn how to live alongside and then with each other"[33] A year later, in a visit to Poland, he knelt at the memorial for Jews who died in the Warsaw Ghetto to express repentance for crimes against the Jews. Citizens of the Balkans should hear Brandt's words to Germans and Poles: "We have to live with the borders as they are and do everything possible to make them transparent. At some point Europe must pull out of this devil's circle of injustice, injustice, and new injustice."

In 1985 Chancellor Helmut Kohl acknowledged that steering a path away from vilification of the East and reintegration into the West "was only possible because those nations—and not least the former concentration inmates and relatives of victims—reached out their hands to us in reconciliation." His gratitude for the reconciliation offered by the West and many of its citizens who had been victims of Nazism was accompanied with his government's commitment not to forget its past, symbolized by its establishment of a national archive to study the history of Jews in Germany. As Kohl put it, "reconciliation with the survivors and descendants of the victims is only possible if we accept our history as it really was, if we Germans acknowledge our shame and our historical responsibility, and if we perceive the need to act against any efforts at undermining human freedom and dignity."[34] Kohl was not alone. The President of the Federal Republic of Germany, Richard von Weizsacker, in an electrifying speech before the Bundestag (the German federal legislature), recalled in unflinching detail the vast suffering caused by Nazism. He offered a litany of the victims: six million Jews, millions of Russians, Poles, Germans, the Gypsies, homosexuals, those who were mentally ill, those in Resistance movements. Recalling all of this, Weizsacker said, was the debt of integrity his generation of Germans owed to future generations.

How painful and yet how necessary the journey to acknowledging moral wrongdoing will be is evident in the efforts of German Christians to acknowledge the failure of the Church to resist Nazism. In 1945 the Synod of Evangelical Churches issued a "Confession of Guilt" that acknowledged the grave sin of idolatry of German Christians and the equally grave demonization of Germany's Eastern European neighbors. It was another five years before the churches could express what still had to be said: "We declare that through negligence and silence before the God of mercy, we have shared in the guilt for the crime which was committed by men of our nation against the Jews."[35] Theologian Jürgen Moltmann, who first read the Confession of Guilt as a German prisoner of war in Scotland, was stunned by Germany's confession that "through us, infinite suffering has been inflicted on many peoples and countries." He recalls:

> In my captive soul the truth of these words was slow to dawn, until I sensed the liberation to which this confession of guilt led me. . . . A person who thus admits his guilt and complicity renders himself defenseless [sic], assailable and vulnerable. But he becomes free from alienation . . . and steps into the light of a truth which makes him free and brings him into a comradeship with the victims—readiness for reconciliation. For that reason there is never an end to the admission of guilt; the Confession remains topical. It gives

me the courage to return to the "solidarity of guilt" and to the
"community of suffering" of my nation, and no longer want
to escape.[36]

As a citizen of the U.S., I am amazed to hear such reckonings of a
nation's moral failure expressed publicly by its political leaders and its
churches. Shriver is likewise so moved that he writes: "I suggest, on
behalf of Americans, that one of the gifts of postwar Germany to the
world may be its example of wrestling with the necessity and the enduring problem of breaking with an evil political past."[37] The journey has
taken many years and much dialogue. The half-century since the Nazi
era could have been an ally of forgetfulness. Instead, it has been marked
by remembering, regretting, forgiving, and healing.

6

Justice and Peace
in the Middle East

Three events of far-reaching significance occurred in Spain in 1492. Columbus's expedition was only one of them. Earlier that year Spanish forces defeated Turkish forces at the city of Grenada, expelling the Ottoman Empire from its last foothold in Western Europe. That same year the Spanish Crown issued a "Decree of Expulsion," giving three hundred thousand Jews four months in which either to convert to Catholicism or leave Spain. In the port city of Palo, Columbus's expedition was delayed because Jews going into exile in North Africa and the Middle East had already chartered most of the available ships.

The intolerance of European Christians for the other two Abrahamic faiths, Judaism and Islam, had spilled blood for several centuries before Columbus's time, setting the stage for the tragedies of the twentieth century: the genocide of the Jews under Hitler and the deadly Arab-Israeli conflicts born with the State of Israel.

In the Middle East, peoples of diverse cultures and religions live in very close proximity. To begin to appreciate just how much diversity the region contains, pinpoint the cities of Jerusalem in Israel and Mecca in Saudi Arabia on a map of the Middle East. Now draw a circle with the distance between those cities as its radius, with Jerusalem at its center. Some of the most famous cities of the ancient and modern world are within the area: Athens, Constantinople (now Istanbul), Baghdad, Mecca, Medina, Cairo, and Jerusalem. All have rich and often turbulent histories. For example, from the fourth century, Constantinople was a

Christian center as important as Rome. After the eleventh century break between the churches of the West and the East, however, it became the preeminent city of Eastern Orthodoxy. Since 1453 the city has been called Istanbul and is a center of Islamic culture and religion.

This chapter is about the conflict between Arabs and Jews in the Middle East during the last half of the twentieth century. The origin of this religious and ethnic conflict must be traced to Christian Europe, where Christians rejected their Jewish neighbors or looked the other way when governments turned against the Jews. Western animus toward the Jews and low regard for Arabs contributed much to the fatal embrace in which Israelis Jews and Palestinian Arabs are now locked. In preparation for the third millennium, Pope John Paul II acknowledged the sins of the Catholic Church against the Jewish people and has sought the forgiveness of the Jewish community. Making a pilgrimage of peace to the Holy Land in March 2000, he called upon Christians, Muslims, and Jews, all of whom recognize Abraham as their father in faith, "[to] witness to the value of solidarity and the promotion of justice." (This exhortation was a constant theme of the pope during his week in Israel and Jordan. See his speeches at www.vatican.va/ holyfather.JohnPaul2/travels.)

Section one considers the circumstances that forced European Jews to flee to the Middle East. Section two traces the unsuccessful efforts of the British administrators to balance the interests of Jews and Arabs during the British control of Palestine from 1917 to 1947. Section three describes the conflict between Israelis and Arabs since the creation of the State of Israel in 1948 and Israel's military occupation since 1967 of neighboring territories inhabited by Palestinians who had fled in 1948. Section four examines the reasons behind the Palestinian *intifada* (uprising) that began in 1987. Section five considers the frustrated quest for justice and peace that will one day allow Jerusalem to be true to the meaning of its name: "city of peace."

1. Nineteenth-Century European Jews among Nations and Empires

Chapter five discussed the rise of nationalism and differentiated between its two types: civic nationalism and ethnic nationalism. For most of the nineteenth century French and British Jews felt accepted within their respective civic national states. As the embers of prejudice seemed to be dying, Jews played integral roles in the political, economic, and cultural life of their countries. But the suspicion of Jews as different, as a foreign race, still smoldered and would soon flare up. Rising French anti-Semitism was signalled by the false accusation of espionage against Alfred Dreyfus, a high-ranking military officer and a Jew. In 1894 Dreyfus was convicted on scant evidence, dishonorably discharged, and exiled from France. Dreyfus was eventually exonerated, but the rush to judgment against him revealed the undercurrent of suspicion toward the Jews in France. A half century later, French authorities handed over their Jewish citizens to Hitler's furnaces.

Attacks against Jewish populations flamed up in Czarist Russia in the early 1880s. In western Russia, home of five million Jews, looting and burning of Jewish property began. As pogroms intensified in Russia, 50,000 Jews left in 1900, 100,000 in 1905, and 150,000 in 1907. An equally ominous note was sounded by a German professor's description of Jewish refugees in Germany: "Year after year there pours over our Eastern frontiers . . . from the inexhaustible Polish cradle, a host of ambitious trouser-selling youths, whose children and children's children will one day dominate Germany's stock exchanges and newspapers" (ca. 1890, German professor Heinrich von Treitrschke).

Early in the twentieth century the British government, which had long prided itself on its tolerance, closed its doors to increasing waves of Russian Jewish refugees, officially classifying them as "undesirable aliens." As more Russian Jews fled, Baron Edmond de Rothschild, scion of the prominent Parisian banking family, was among the donors assisting their resettlement in Palestine. Jewish immigrants established farms and commercial enterprises with the wealth they brought with them, trading with Arab businesses and hiring Arab workers. But the increasing cruelty of the Russian pogroms brought increasingly traumatized refugees. With time, the measure of their own suffering would became the measure of their aggressiveness in Palestine. By 1914 eighty-five thousand Jewish settlers lived amidst five hundred thousand Arabs. As Palestinian Arabs resisted the increasing Jewish immigration, Jews, in turn, conducted less and less business with Arabs and formed their own security force. Many Jewish immigrants nurtured a "Zionist" dream—that is, the realization of the biblical promise of a homeland for the Jews with Jerusalem (Zion) as its center.

At the turn of the twentieth century, Palestine was part of the Ottoman Empire, ruled from Istanbul by Sultan Muhammad V. By treaties between the Sultan and the European governments, European citizens—Jews among them—were accorded protection in Ottoman lands. By the outbreak of World War I, the German Kaiser was on very friendly terms with the Sultan, and Britain desired a buffer to protect the Suez Canal from German imperial aims. Thus, British national interests and Jewish aspirations for a homeland in Palestine began to converge.

2. Palestine under British Rule: 1917–1947

In 1917 Britain's Parliament passed the Balfour Declaration calling for a "Jewish National Home" in Palestine. In December 1917, when the British troops took Jerusalem from the Turks, the Ottoman Empire was no more. A British military administration took control of Palestine when the Armistice was signed in 1918. The League of Nations placed Palestine and Iraq under British Mandate (i.e., control) and Syria under French Mandate. Britain's hope was to resettle more Eastern European Jews in the Middle East, counting on the Palestinian Arabs, whom they had freed from Ottoman rule, not to object to more Jewish settlements.

Although Britain wanted a homeland for the Jews, British officials resisted the aspirations of Zionists for a sovereign Jewish state in Palestine, knowing that half a million Arabs (and sixty thousand Christians) would never consent to be ruled by a Jewish minority.

As the Zionist movement grew, however, with Jews arriving from Europe, coming at a rate of ten thousand per year, the British military government attempted to discourage Zionism. It forbade the performance of the Zionist anthem, refused to recognize Hebrew as an official language, banned land transfers to Jews, and curbed immigration.

"Give me your tired, your poor, / Your huddled masses yearning to breathe free, / The wretched refuse of your teeming shore. / Send these, the homeless, tempest-tossed, to me, / I lift my lamp beside the golden door."

The American Jewish poet Emma Lazarus wrote these words in 1883 with the plight of Russian Jews in mind. Her words were affixed to Lady Liberty's pedestal in the 1930s. Ironically, the U.S. had already closed its doors to mass immigration in 1924, causing many more Jews to seek refuge in Palestine.

In the late 1920s conflicts broke out between Jewish and Muslim worshipers in Jerusalem. The worst occurred in August 1929, leaving 133 Jews and 110 Arabs dead. Meanwhile, German Jews were facing increasing attacks in Germany, and were eventually barred from employment in government, media, and teaching in the early 1930s. Their businesses were boycotted, and the Nürmburg Laws of 1935 deprived German Jews of citizenship. By 1936 an estimated half of the Jews in Germany were unemployed—and they streamed to Palestine. Between 1922 and 1937 the Jewish population of Palestine rose from 84,000 to 400,000.

Arab discontent with the British Mandate was growing: it was colonial rule; it was rule of Muslims by Christians; and it was marked by increasing encroachment by the Jews. As the British came under increasing pressure to extend greater self-rule to the Arabs, in 1936 the Arab Higher Committee demanded a halt to Jewish immigration. The British agreed to cut Jewish immigration quotas for that year by half, leaving Britain caught between Jewish intent for a nation and Arab demands for autonomy—with Nazi rearmament complicating the matter further. Hearing the thunder of threatening war, Britain knew it needed to be on good terms with Arab countries; in the event of war, its access to Middle East oil would be essential.

In 1937 Britain convened a commission in Palestine to examine the possibility of partitioning Palestine. But the testimony of both Arabs and Jews revealed deep opposition and fear, no support for partitioning, and little hope of creating a pluralist Palestinian state. When Jewish militants bombed the Arab market in Haifa, Palestinian leaders appealed to other Arab nations for help—and anti-Jewish sentiment began to spread into Syria, Iraq, and Lebanon.

In 1939, on the eve of the outbreak of World War II, Britain declared that there would be neither partition nor a Jewish state. Instead, Jewish immigration to Palestine would end in five years and an independent Palestinian state would be created within a decade. Despite the lack of British support for a Jewish state, the Jews supported the British against the Nazis, and Jewish volunteers underwent British military training in the event of a Nazi attack on Palestine. In 1941 Muslim leaders in Iraq fomented revolt against the British, and violence against the Jewish community of Baghdad broke out. By 1943 Menachem Begin, a Polish freedom fighter, was commanding Jewish freedom fighters in Palestine.

The Faces of Palestine

Israeli Jews: constitute seventy-nine perscent of Israel's population of almost six million. There is much ethnic diversity among them. Sephardic Jews came to Palestine from Spain, North Africa, and elsewhere in the Middle East. Some trace their presence in Palestine to biblical times and have lived side by side with Muslims for centuries in what is known as Jerusalem's "Old City." Ashkenazic Jews are culturally European, immigrating to Palestine because of the European anti-Semitism of the late nineteenth century. By the time the State of Israel was founded, Ashkenazic Jews outnumbered Sephardic Jews three to one. Israel's "Law of Return" grants anyone with a Jewish grandparent full immigration rights. Many Sephardic Jews have immigrated from the Middle East. After the break up of the Soviet Union 400,000 Ashkenazi Jews immigrated to Israel.

Israeli Arabs: constitute eighteen percent of Israel's population. The 150,000 Arabs who did not flee in 1948 automatically became Israeli citizens. However, they too lost much of their family wealth when the Israeli government did not honor land titles of the Ottoman period. The Arab system of community-held wealth (called *waqf*) administered by Muslim clerics for the benefit of the Muslim community was taken over by the government.

When areas of large Arab populations were placed under Israeli military rule in 1967, the second generation of Arabs to live under Israeli rule were less willing than their parents to accept second-class status. In certain respects, Israeli Arabs did find themselves better off than Arabs in the Mandate or Ottoman periods in terms of health, earnings, and education— and better off than Arabs in other countries today. Nonetheless, the standard of living and schools for Israeli Jews were better. The Jewish distrust of Arabs in general increased the hostility of young Israeli Arabs. Since Israel banned all Arab nationalist political parties, the only legitimate non-Zionist party open to them was the Israeli Communist Party. By the late 1970s fifty percent of the Communist Party was Palestinian.

Palestinian Arabs in Gaza and the West Bank: those who sought refuge there in 1948 and who were never offered Egyptian citizenship—and thus have remained "stateless" since Israel's occupation in 1967. Gaza, twenty-five miles long and eight miles wide, located in southern Israel on the Mediterranean Coast, is one of the most densely populated areas on earth (current population, 400,000). Israeli Defense Forces targeted Arab resistance movement in Gaza, conducting house-to-house searches and interrogations, demolishing parts of refugee camps, effectively destroying the Palestine Liberation Organization's (PLO) Gaza base.

Palestinians who fled to the West Bank became Jordanian citizens. Since the Israeli occupation of the West Bank, most Palestinians have retained Jordanian citizenship, rejecting the offer of Israeli citizenship. Half a million Palestinians live in the West Bank.

Palestinians Arabs outside Palestine: Palestinians living in Lebanon, Syria, and Jordan (approximately 1,300,000), where they are often treated as outsiders. Palestinian liberation movements originated in and are supported by neighboring Arab states. Islamic fundamentalist movements champion the Palestinian cause and the more fanatical elements are committed to the destruction of Israel. In 1974 the Arab Summit at Rabat recognized the PLO as the sole representative of the Palestinian people.

Bedouin: a semi-nomadic tribe that has lived for 2,500 years in the Negev Desert of southern Israel. Since 1950 Israel has limited their agricultural and animal grazing activity and attempted to settle them in seven towns designated for Bedouin, although these towns lack the infrastructure found in other Israeli municipalities. Some forty Bedouin villages are not officially recognized by Israeli authorities and are often without water or electricity. Christian Arabs constitute the remaining two percent of Israel's population.

Christian Arabs: constitute two percent of Israel's population. One percent is Roman Catholic and one percent is Eastern Orthodox.

As the war ended and the full horrors of the Holocaust were revealed, Britain lifted all restrictions on Jewish immigration to Palestine, again supported the establishment of a Jewish state, and requested the UN to mediate the claims of Jews and Arabs to Palestine. The UN Special Commission on Palestine recommended in 1947 that the mandate end as soon as possible and that Palestine be partitioned into a Jewish state and an Arab state with an international zone created around the holy sites of Jerusalem. In November of that year the United Nations General Assembly voted to accept the recommendation: 33 in favor, 13 against (all 11 Arab states), with 10 abstentions (including Britain). When Britain announced that its mandate would end May 15, 1948, tensions in Palestine could not have been higher, and Jewish forces prepared for war with the Arab states. Could a Jewish state survive the inevitable hostility from both the Palestinian Arabs and the surrounding Arab states? In April 1948, when Menachem Begin's Jewish forces crushed an Arab revolt and killed 250 Arab civilians in the Arab town of Deir Yassin (three miles west of Jerusalem), thousands of Palestinian Arabs fled in panic from Jewish-held areas. British troops in the meantime prepared to withdraw, refusing to enforce partitioning. Several hours before the expiration of the British Mandate on May 14, 1948, David Ben-Gurion proclaimed the State of Israel.

3. Israel: The First Forty Years: 1948–1987

The next day Egyptian fighter planes bombed Tel Aviv; Jordan, Syria, and Lebanon also attacked. Israeli forces battled the Egyptian Army, pushing west and occupying the Sinai Desert, a peninsula in northeaster Egypt. They also secured a corridor to the small Jewish community in the Old City of Jordan-controlled Jerusalem. Under pressure from the UN, Israel signed a cease-fire with Egypt and eventually withdrew from the Sinai. Israel negotiated treaties with Syria, Lebanon, and Jordan, its treaty with Jordan specifically giving Jews access to the Western Wall in exchange for Jordanian control of Arab neighborhoods of West Jerusalem.

As many as half a million Palestinian Arabs fled their homes in Israel in fear of Israeli military forces, taking refuge in camps hastily erected by the UN in Gaza and in Jordan's West Bank. Arabs refer to 1948 as "the disaster."

The military defeats of Egypt, Jordan, and Syria brought to power hard-line regimes that vowed to destroy Israel. In 1954 the Israeli Air Force bombed Arab guerrilla bases in Gaza in response to Arab raids on

Tel Aviv, Israel's capital. In 1956 Israeli forces invaded Gaza and pressed on into Egypt's Sinai, driving back Egyptian troops to within thirty miles of the Suez Canal. In protest against Israel's aggression against Egypt, the UN General Assembly voted 65-1 for Israel's immediate withdrawal from the Sinai. Israel withdrew its forces and an international force under UN command patrolled the Suez Canal. For ten years an uneasy peace prevailed between Israel and its neighbors.

Then, in 1967, the Middle East peace was shattered when Israel launched devastating air strikes on the Egyptian, Jordanian, and Syrian air forces. Israeli ground forces occupied Egypt's Gaza strip, Jordan's West Bank (already home to a million displaced Palestinians), and Syria's Golan Heights, and then took control of East Jerusalem. Israeli military leader Moshe Dayan exalted, "We have returned to our most holy places . . . and we shall never leave them."[1] Israel effectively cut off access to the holy sites of Islam (the Dome of the Rock and the El Aqsa Mosque) and confiscated Arab property in the Old City in order to restore the Jewish Quarter that had become a Palestinian refugee camp in 1948. Jewish housing projects would soon surround Jerusalem, displacing Arabs.

In response to the "Six Day War" in1967, UN Security Council Resolution 242 called for the immediate:

> . . . withdrawal of Israeli armed forces from territories occupied in the present conflict . . . and acknowledgement of the sovereignty, territorial integrity and political independence of every State in the area, and their right to live in peace within secure and recognized boundaries.

Israel returned the Sinai to Egypt and the Golan Heights to Syria on the condition that those territories would be designated demilitarized zones, but declared that the West Bank was part of "greater Israel."

When Egyptian President Anwar Sadat made peace overtures in 1971, Israel refused to draw back its fortifications on the western side of Egypt's Suez Canal. Egypt, in turn, launched an attack during the Jewish observance of Yom Kippur (the Day of Atonement) in October 1973. Simultaneously, Syria attacked across Israel's northern border. Israeli air and land forces counterattacked on both fronts, crossing the border into Syria and engaging the Egyptians in the largest tank battle in history. Israeli forces led by Ariel Sharon crossed the Suez Canal, and later that month, a cease-fire was negotiated between Israel and Egypt. Although Israel had again prevailed, this latest attack left the

Israelis with a permanent defensive posture in relation to the Arab world.

By the late 1970s, Sadat was again pushing for peace with Israel and found an ally in U.S. President Jimmy Carter. In a courageous gesture of his serious intentions, Sadat made a historic trip to Tel Aviv where he was welcomed by President Menachem Begin and addressed the Israeli parliament, the Knesset. Then, at Camp David, Maryland, in 1979, President Carter successfully brokered an Egyptian-Israeli peace treaty between Sadat and Begin.[2] Finally, a first step toward peaceful coexistence between Israel and its neighboring states had been achieved.

The most volatile threat to this peace, however, were half a million Palestinian Arabs displaced since 1948 and living under Israeli military rule in the occupied territories of the West Bank and the Gaza Strip since 1967. The cycle of violence between Israelis and Palestinians was now in its second generation. The sons of the Jews who had taken up arms in 1948 and had expelled the Palestinians were now called upon to police another generation of Palestinians living with memories of their homes, farms, and villages and waiting for the day they could return.

Since 1973 the Israeli government had encouraged Israelis to establish settlements in the West Bank. Jewish settlements were to be a first line of defense for Israel proper and the beachheads for the eventual incorporation of the territories into Israel. The land for the settlements and the roads to reach them were expropriated from Arabs. The settlers would require permanent military protection from the antagonized Palestinians who surrounded them.

In 1982, when Palestinians staged strikes and rioted throughout the occupied territories, the ensuing cycle of riots and repression took the lives of thirteen civilians. Frustrated that the "comprehensive peace process" being advocated in the UN did not address the issue of sovereignty for Palestinians, the Palestine Liberation Organization (PLO), led by Yasser Arafat, sought allies in neighboring countries. In June of 1982 Israeli forces crossed into southern Lebanon and took control of two Palestinian refugee camps. Two months later several hundred Palestinian refugees were massacred by Lebanese Maronite (Christian) forces that the Israeli Defense Force (IDF) had sent into the camps to apprehend suspected Palestinian terrorists. Israel was widely condemned for the massacre, and within Israel, both Arabs and Jews protested.

In 1987, yet a third generation of Israelis donned combat gear against the next generation of Palestinians in the West Bank and Gaza, facing off against youths throwing stones, burning tires, and setting explosives.

4. *Intifada:* Palestinian Uprising of 1987

Voices of Palestinians in the Occupied Territories[3]

"The Jordanians took our national identity but you [the Jews] took everything and left us the living dead."

"The 1200 new laws to deprive us of our land and traditions, and honor [make the occupied territories] a great big prison that [Israelis] hope we'll escape from and never be able to return."

"I have no life outside of work. Only dirty work. No one cares about my life, no one thinks that this also is a human being who wants to do something with himself" (a Palestinian who commutes to Israel to work).

"Before I went to jail, I didn't even know I was a Palestinian. There they taught me who I am. Now I have opinions. The average Palestinian is not a fascist and hating type, but you [Israelis] and the life under your occupation pushed him into hatred" (a thirty-year-old Arab, jailed for the previous ten years).

Like South African natives forced from their homes and land to live in townships, Palestinians lost their homes and land in 1948, were forced into exile or became refugees in the West Bank and Gaza, and have been subject to military rule since 1967. Economically, they have been forced to live on less than one-third of the income of Israelis. Although many Palestinians have professional degrees from one of the five universities in the West Bank or from foreign universities, the only work most of them find in Israel are low-status jobs as restaurant workers, as laborers in warehouses and sweatshops, or as gardeners or domestics. Although one hundred thousand of them commute to Israel for work, they cannot stay overnight in Israel without an official permit.

From its beginning in 1948, Israel's efforts to "pacify" the occupied territories failed. Israeli authorities arrested and imprisoned suspected terrorists and militants—and bulldozed their families' homes as additional punishment, imposed curfews, and shut down Palestinian schools and universities. Because Israeli citizens' civil rights do not extend to Palestinians in the occupied territories, an Israeli suspected of a crime may be held only for two days without being charged—whereas Palestinians in the occupied territories may be held for eighteen days and do not have the right to meet with an attorney. Only since the creation of the Palestinian Authority in 1994 have Palestinians in the occupied territories had any police protection: Israeli defense and police protect only Jewish settlers.

The explosion came in December 1987, when rioting broke out in a Gaza refugee camp over the killing of four Palestinians following the murder of an Israeli visiting Gaza. Protests spread to the West Bank and Jerusalem, with more Arabs dying at the hands of Israeli forces. These incidents soon developed into a well-organized uprising in which thousands of Palestinians took part. Known as the *intifada* (shuddering, shaking), the uprising unified Arabs of the occupied territories as never before and, for the next three years, Palestinians staged strikes, stayed home from their jobs in Israel, set up roadblocks with burning tires, and pelted Israeli soldiers with stones. Israeli Defense Forces tried to stop the *intifada* with increasingly violent means; beatings of those suspected of participating in the *intifada* became routine. Over the next eighteen months, military prisons were filled, military courts were jammed with Palestinians, and Israeli soldiers killed over five hundred Palestinians, wounded eleven thousand and beat as many more. The Arab world was inflamed and the Israel's public image was blackened. Israeli society was divided, reflecting "an enormous crisis of confidence and conscience within the soldiers themselves, who were neither equipped nor trained to carry out such extraordinary orders . . . some reacting with horror and refusing to participate . . . others who seemed to relish the chance to settle scores with Palestinians."[4]

Israeli Jewish journalist Yoram Binur posed as a Palestinian from a West Bank refugee camp to experience what it was like for Palestinians in Israel and the occupied territories. Because of his fluency in Arabic and his familiarity with Palestinian customs, his true identity was not discovered until he published the account of his experience (*My Enemy, My Self*, 1989).

Pretending not to understand Hebrew, Binur heard many Israelis' comments about Arabs—including himself! Working as a "Palestinian" worker for Israelis, he also experienced how they are treated. His book offers powerful testimony regarding the sufferings of the Palestinians and suggests the inevitability of the *intifada* that broke out just as he was ending his pose.

"For twenty years the Palestinians have lived among us. During the day, we were the employers who profited by their labor and exploited them for all they were worth; in the afternoon we were the police; in the evening we were the soldiers at the roadblock on their way home; and finally at night we were the security forces who entered their homes and arrested them. While many Israelis regarded the Palestinian Arabs primarily as cheap labor and as a potential security risk, the Palestinians studied (sometimes unconsciously) Israeli society with all its characteristic weaknesses and vulnerabilities. They know exactly how the average Israeli thinks and feels; they know what is important to him and how he can be hurt. They know how to identify the military units that are sent to repress their demonstrations, and can tell you which are tougher, which are more lax . . . "[5]

Palestinian resistance to occupation and demand for independence had never been stronger. Many of the faces of the participants in the *intifada* were those of children; seventy-five percent of the West Bank population was under twenty-eight years of age, and forty percent were students (300,000 students were no longer in school because Israeli military authorities shut down the schools). An Israeli entering a camp in Gaza reported that the stone throwers "ranged in age from three to twelve . . . and could be found on all points of the perimeter of the camp, armed with improvised slingshots and creating an atmosphere of apocalypse and anarchy."[6]

The *intifada* had grassroots support from women's groups, trade unions, student and professional groups, farmers, and business organizations. As a Palestinian national leadership emerged in the Unified National Leadership of the Uprising (UNLU), the PLO and other political groups united. In addition to new levels of Palestinian solidarity, the *intifida* proved to be an exercise of Palestinian self-government. The

UNLU mobilized emergency medical services, aid for families of the imprisoned, and financial assistance for those whose property was destroyed or confiscated.[7] In 1988 Jordan renounced its claim on the West Bank and Arafat endorsed UN Resolution 242, renouncing terrorism and recognizing Israel's right to exist and to secure borders.

Israel has responded to the *intifida* as a nation under siege. Three years of military service is now required of all Israeli men and women, followed by reserve duty each year until age forty-five. As a percentage of its annual budget, the state of Israel defense spending is twice that of the U.S. It maintains a massive intelligence operation both at home and abroad to counter terrorism. Many Jewish Israelis are deeply paranoid regarding Arabs. Arabs, in turn, have old and new grievances toward Israel and its two main allies, the U.S. and Britain. Diplomatic efforts have often derailed, leading to resumption of very violent and deadly confrontations between the IDF and a variety of Palestinian and other Arab revolutionary forces. For example, Palestinians cheered in 1990 when Iraq president Saddam Hussein fired missiles at Tel Aviv and briefly took up their cause, an episode that plunged Israeli-Palestinian relationships into the abyss, with renewed rioting in Gaza and more killings of Palestinians by Israeli soldiers in 1992.

This conflict has painfully divided Israelis. Many called to military service have no stomach for policing the occupied territories; some have, in fact, refused military duty in the territories. An Israeli public opinion poll in 1992 reported that eighty-one percent were willing to give up Gaza and fifty-eight percent were willing to relinquish part of the West Bank for peace. In 1993 a hopeful development began in Oslo, Norway, where negotiations for Palestinian autonomy were held. Israeli prime minister Yitzhak Rabin and PLO Chairman Yasser Arafat signed a "Declaration of Principles" that would create a Palestinian Authority to govern the Gaza Strip and the West Bank city of Jericho, while allowing Israel to retain control of its Settlements, army bases, and access roads in the West Bank. Israeli troop withdrawals from the occupied territories were to begin in seventeen months. Speaking to the Palestinians the following year at the ceremonial signing of this historic agreement at the White House, Rabin said:

> We are destined to live together on the same soil, in the same
> land . . . we the soldiers who have returned from battle

stained with blood . . . we who have fought against you . . .
we say to you today in a loud and clear voice: "Enough of
blood and tears. Enough."[8]

While the dream of a Palestinians state seemed to be approaching
reality, how much of the West Bank would belong to the Palestinians,
the extent of a Palestinian government's authority, and the status of the
holy sites of Jerusalem remained unresolved issues.

In 1995, when Rabin was assassinated by a militant Jew, Israelis
remained highly divided over exchanging "land for peace" with the
Palestinians. Seven years after the Oslo Agreement, a Palestinian state
was still not a reality. Instead, Israel was expanding Jewish settlements
in the occupied territories at a rapid pace. In the face of mounting Palestinian frustration, the levels of militant Islamic guerrilla warfare rose

5. Peace?

Michael Lerner, an American Jew, calls for

> . . . a new form of discourse [recognizing that] we are pre-
> sented with two peoples who are equally entitled and equally
> in error. With that foundation in place, we will be able to
> move to the next stage, requiring the Jewish people to rec-
> ognize that it is our responsibility to take the most decisive
> stop to rectify the current situation, not because we are more
> wrong, but because we are more powerful.[9]

Where are the Israelis leaders who can muster the political will necessary to make peace with the Palestinians by dealing with the issues of
refugees and compensation and resolving how Jerusalem can again be
shared among Jews and Arabs? Are there Palestinians able to tap the
nonviolent strength of the people, to stand against their oppressors with
dignity and truth that will set them free?

There are many such people on both sides of the conflict. The following graphic identifies some of the groups that are committed to nonviolent achievement of justice and peace. Too often, however, their
efforts are obscured by those committed to victory through violence.
They, too, are identified.

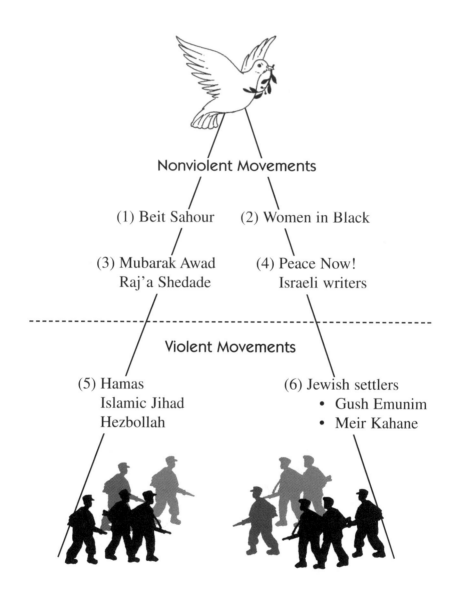

Nonviolent Movements

(1) Beit Sahour   (2) Women in Black

(3) Mubarak Awad   (4) Peace Now!
    Raj'a Shedade   Israeli writers

Violent Movements

(5) Hamas   (6) Jewish settlers
    Islamic Jihad   • Gush Emunim
    Hezbollah   • Meir Kahane

(1.) **Beit Sahour** is a predominately Christian (Greek Orthodox) Palestinian town in the West Bank, approximately two miles from Bethlehem. The leaders of this town of ten thousand did not passively accept Israeli occupation but developed their own unarmed police force to protect their homes and property, initiated an alternative education system, community gardens, and a low-cost medical treatment program. After the *intifada* began, Beit Sahouris opened a community center that Israeli authorities immediately declared illegal and closed, detaining several town leaders. Mobilizing in the town churches, women and children marched in protest. When Israeli soldiers and Jewish settlers killed several of the town's youth, the women held a church vigil in which they wrote appeals to women of the world, the UN, and the Vatican to help end the occupation. In 1989 the townspeople began a tax protest and the Israeli Army blocked roads into the town. Israeli authorities confiscated cars and personal possessions, and fined and jailed those who refused to pay taxes. While the Beit Sahouris suffered for their resistance, they demonstrated a freedom from the occupation that occupying forces could not shackle.

(2.) **The Women in Black** is a group of Jewish and Arab women that conducted weekly protests beginning in 1987 against the occupation and violations of Palestinians' civil rights. Their protests began in Jerusalem at a crowded intersection where the women endured constant verbal abuse by Israeli motorists. The protests of the Women in Black spread to many other sites and continued for several years.

(3.) Palestinian nonviolent resistance in the occupied territories, promoted by **Mubarak Awad** in the 1980s, especially advocated active resistance by a wide variety of means, from noncooperation to sabotage of Israeli efforts to administer the territories. Awad promoted many of the "civilian-based defense methods" studied and reported by Harvard theorist Gene Sharp. **Raj'a Shehadeh**, an internationally known Palestinian human rights advocate, promotes a "third way" that both resists the temptation to violence and refuses to surrender to Israel occupiers. His way is a patient unwillingness to be defeated or to leave and a continual calling attention to the injustices Israel is committing.

(4.) **Peace Now** is the largest grassroots peace organization in Israel and has affiliates in the U.S. and other countries. Founded in 1978 by over three hundred Israeli reserve officers and combat soldiers, Peace Now believes that Israel's security is best insured by peace. It advocates a Palestinian state "subject to strict military limitations," a negotiated peace with Syria, a withdrawal of Israeli forces from the Golan Heights, and "an undivided Jerusalem that accommodates the national aspirations and religious needs of both Israeli and Palestinian residents."[10]

Israeli writers such as David Grossman, Yoram Binur, and Amos Oz have stirred the consciences of Israelis regarding the plight of Palestinians. Grossman's interviews of Palestinians and descriptions of the moral, personal, and social tragedy of the occupation are widely read in Israel. Grossman asks Jewish readers to reflect on what the long-term effect of the occupation will be on Israel. He recalls asking a group of Jewish settlers "to imagine themselves in their Arab neighbors' places" and discovering that "they did not allow themselves even a split second of empathy [for] those whose fates are intertwined and interwoven so much with theirs." Grossman observes that "we are social creatures . . . and when we accustom ourselves to relations like those between slave and master, that division is stamped within us as well." He asks his readers: "Can it be—and this each one of us must answer himself, alone—that in the very making of this dramatic separation you do not turn yourself, in the course of time into just such an impenetrable mechanism, a mechanism that you sometimes control and that sometimes controls you and is capable of deeds that were once only imagined . . . ?[11] Binur not only invites readers to imagine the world of Palestinians but his undercover experience allowed Israelis to see themselves through the eyes of Palestinians.

(5.) Several Islamic militant groups actively work for the liberation of Palestine through the destruction of Israel. **Hamas** has conducted terrorist attacks against Israelis since 1994. **Islamic Jihad** also engages in terrorism against Israel. Under the Oslo Agreement, the Palestinian Authority is charged with controlling Islamic militants, many of whom have been imprisoned by the Palestinian Authority. **Hezbollah**, a Shiite Muslim paramilitary organization, operates from Lebanon and receives support from Iraq.

(6.) Especially strong among **Jewish settlers** in the West Bank and Gaza is the movement called **Gush Emunim** ("block of the faithful"), numbering 350,000. They believe that God intends the land of Israel for the Jews and that they must defend this inheritance to the death. They also believe that their religious claim to the land trumps all Palestinians claims, opposing the return of land to Palestinians. The settlers are viewed by many Israelis as dangerous fanatics, although the Israeli government since 1977 has assisted in building and defending the settlements. **Meir Kahane** is an Israeli terrorist organization whose slogan is "Only by force." Rabbi Meir Kahane spearheaded a movement to rebuild the Temple. In 1983 his followers tunneled under the Muslim holy sites to establish an underground Jewish community. He was later assassinated.

In July and August of 2000, Yasser Arafat and Israeli prime minister Ehud Barak met at Camp David to try to work out the issues still remaining after Oslo. Arafat complained bitterly that Israel had not implemented four of the key Oslo agreements, demanding nothing less than Palestinian sovereignty over East Jerusalem. Barak, on the other hand, offered some Palestinian control but not sovereignty. Although President Clinton praised Barak's offer and showed no patience for Arafat's refusal, we must understand why Arafat was unwilling to compromise: Arafat viewed the Dome of the Rock and the El Aqsa Mosque as sites holy to Arabs and Muslims everywhere. Arab determination to defend the holy sites in Jerusalem has increased with each new episode of fanatic violence against Muslim worshipers.

Jerusalem's Destiny

When the Israelite King David took Jerusalem from the Jebusites he ordered that the Ark of the Covenant be brought there (see 2 Samuel 6:12–23). The Bible says he danced for joy before this symbol of divine presence that the Israelites had carried from Mt. Sinai through their dangerous passage into the promised land. David's son Solomon then built a magnificent Temple to Yahweh on Jerusalem's Mt. Zion and placed the Ark of the Covenant in the "holy of holies," its innermost sanctuary. The spot chosen for the Temple was a place held sacred by the city's former rulers, the Jebusites, and its splendor recalled Yahweh's greatness and reminded Israel to revere God by observing his commandments.

Three centuries later, the prophet Isaiah brought to his fellow Jerusalemites the painful message of Yahweh:

> I will hide my eyes from you;
> even though you make many prayers,
>   I will not listen;
>   your hands are full of blood . . .
> Cease to do evil,
>   learn to do god;
> seek justice,

>> rescue the oppressed,
> defend the orphan,
>> plead for the widow (Isaiah 15–17).

If the Israelites do not honor Yahweh by upholding his justice, their city will be made desolate, like an abandoned and barren vineyard. But Isaiah offers a profoundly different hope for Jerusalem in the plan of Yahweh:

> Afterward you shall be called the city of righteousness,
>> the faithful city.
> Zion shall be redeemed by justice,
>> and those in her who repent, by righteousness
>> (1:26–27)..

*

> In the cays to come
>> the mountain of the LORD's house
> shall be established as the highest of the mountains
>> and shall be raised above the hills;
> all the nations shall stream to it (2:2).

*

> On this mountain the LORD of hosts
>> will make for all peoples
>> a feast of rich food, a feast of well-aged wines . . .
> And he will destroy on this mountain
>> the shroud that is cast over all peoples,
>> the sheet that is spread over all nations;
>> he will swallow up death forever.
> Then the LORD GOD will wipe away
>> the tears from all faces (25:6–7)

*

> For the hand of the LORD will rest on this mountain . . .
> The high fortifications of his walls will be brought down
> (25:10, 12).

In 587 B.C.E. Isaiah's warning came to pass when the armies of the Babylonians conquered Jerusalem and destroyed the Temple. In bitter exile in Babylon, the Jews longed for Jerusalem, until half a century later, when they were permitted to return and rebuild the Temple. But their sojourn in Babylon had also given birth to a spiritual insight: wherever and whenever they are faithful to Yahweh and act justly, they are in the presence of Yahweh.

A thousand years after David, Jerusalem now under Roman rule, an obscure Galilean named Jesus came preaching the reestablishment of Yahweh's rule. He came to Jerusalem to remind Jewish religious leaders that God's presence is found in human acts of love and justice. After Jesus and his message were rejected and he was executed, followers of Jesus proclaimed that he was himself the presence of God. In the wake of the destruction of the Jewish Temple by the Romans in A.D. 66, those faithful men and women would look to the risen Jesus as Yahweh's indestructible temple and await his return, which would signal the wedding of God and his people. In the Book of Revelation, John envisions the "new Jerusalem coming down out of heaven from God, prepared as a bride adorned for her husband" (21:2).

In the fourth century Christians under the patronage of Emperor Constantine built shrines in Jerusalem commemorating Jesus' life, death, and resurrection. But Christians also "indulged in some rather unholy gloating when they contemplated the fate of the Jews who had dwelt in this city before them."[12]

Then, in 610, in the city of Mecca, a man named Mohammed preached a message of total surrender (*islam* is Arabic for "surrender") to God. He instructed his disciples in Mecca and later in Medina to face toward Jerusalem when they prayed, for it was the place where David, Solomon, the Israelite prophets, and Jesus had all worshiped the one true God. Thirty years later, Arabs in the region of Jerusalem who had converted to Mohammed's teaching gained control of the city, not for religious reasons but as a strategic location in their struggle with the Persian Empire. They built a house of prayer (the El-Aqsa Mosque) where Herod's palace had once stood on the Temple Mount.

Arab officials permitted Jews to build a synagogue near the "Western Wall," all that remained of the foundation of the Temple Mount. Admiring Jerusalem's Christian shrines, Muslims undertook the construction of a shrine they called the Dome of the Rock, completed in 691 and built on the Temple Mount on what was traditionally believed to be the site of the "Holy of Holies." This place was regarded as the spiritual center point of the earth, the bridge between earth and heaven that Mohammed himself had crossed when the angel Gabriel carried him to the highest realm of heaven.

When Pope Urban II called upon Christian kings to take back Jerusalem from the Muslims in 1096, several thousand crusaders, accompanied by crowds of pilgrims, set out for Jerusalem, attacking Jewish neighborhoods in European cities along the way. Their assault of Jerusalem took the lives of thirty thousand Muslims. Four more crusades followed until Holy Roman Emperor Frederick II signed a treaty with the Sultan of Egypt that protected access to Christian shrines, provided for Muslim worship at the Dome of the Rock and the El Aqsa Mosque, and ordered the expulsion of the Jewish community from Jerusalem.

When the Ottomans added Palestine to their empire in 1516, Sultan Suleiman repaired the city and invited Sephardic Jews expelled from Spain to settle in Palestine and to resume their custom of prayer at the Western Wall. The Ottomans remained until World War I, Muslims and Jews living and worshiping in close proximity, although not always harmoniously; Muslims often resented Jews praying so close to Islamic holy sites. The schism between Roman Catholicism and Greek Orthodoxy was reflected in Jerusalem as well. The clerics who maintained separate shrines commemorating the life of Jesus for their respective churches periodically assaulted one another.

The Jerusalem envisioned by Isaiah and the Gospel writer John requires that the peoples who stream to Jerusalem must make peace if they are to encounter God. Although the pilgrims often recognized the city's holiness, they intensely despised others, as if the divine holiness was diminished by the presence of "others." Jerusalem bespeaks the human yearning for God. Jews praying at the Western (Wailing) Wall are a reminder of generation upon generation of Jews reaffirming Yahweh's covenant with them. For Christians, Jerusalem is at the heart of the mystery of God's divine compassion assuming humble human form. Christian pilgrims come to the Church of the Holy Sepulcher, the place associated with Jesus' glorious resurrection. Muslims ascend to the Noble Sanctuary to pray at the Dome of the Rock and the El Aqsa Mosque, bridges to the divine.

Finding Peace in the Eyes of One Another

In September 2000, a month after the Camp David meeting, Ariel Sharon and other members of his Likud Party entered the Noble Sanctuary accompanied by Israeli security forces, ending Israel's thirty-three-year-old policy of not entering the area in deference to Islamic sensibilities. Why had the Israeli government allowed this potential for conflict to occur during the stalled Israeli-Palestinian negotiations regarding the sovereignty of Jerusalem? Did Barak feel that politically he had to allow Sharon to make his point, that Jews must have access to their holy places close by? Sharon's visit precipitated clashes, which very quickly escalated into the worst violence between Israelis and Palestinians since the Six Day War in 1967. Did the Palestinian Tanzim (a paramilitary organization) and a dozen other Palestinian militant groups encourage the making of "martyrs" to galvanize Palestinians and garner more sympathy and support outside of Israel? A month after Sharon's provocative gesture, the death toll was 128, mostly Palestinians killed by Israeli soldiers. Shootings of rock-throwing Palestinian youths, retaliatory murders of Jewish settlers and soldiers, assassinations of Palestinian leaders in the occupied territories, and terrorism in Jerusalem and Israel continued to escalate. Over the next twelve months, almost nine hundred people had died and Barak's government had collapsed, to be replaced by a hard-line government led by Ariel Sharon.

For two millennia the Jews have suffered grievously, mostly at the hands of Christians. Although, with the rebirth of Israel in 1948, they had vowed "never again" to be victims, their children and grandchildren certainly have been. The Palestinians, too, have been victims. Should their "never again" not apply to other victims as well? The *Gush Emunim* movement reduces the expression of Jewish faith to defense of the promised land and the expulsion of the Arabs from their homes. The Palestinians have also suffered greatly. They have been a people disowned like Ishmael, Abraham's son by his concubine Hagar, while Israel assumes the role of Isaac, Abraham's legitimate heir. Islamic fundamentalists rally Muslims to defend holy places by the unholiest of means. How long will the pain of the past decide the future? David Shipler writes:

> Whatever happens in war or diplomacy, whatever territory is won or lost, whatever accommodations or compromises are finally made, the future guarantees that Jews and Arabs will remain close neighbors in this weary land, entangled in each other's fears. They will not escape from one another. They will not find peace in treaties, or in victories. They will find it, if at all, by looking into each other's eyes.[13]

Jews and Arabs of today and tomorrow must "choose life" by negotiating borders, water rights, refugee rights and compensation, and peace in Jerusalem.

What can Christians do? Catholic social teaching reminds us that our faith must bear fruit in acts of justice and charity, in the seeking and the offering of forgiveness. As Christian churches prepared to enter the third millennium they acknowledged Christian crimes against Jews and Muslims. Pope John Paul II expressed contrition for the Catholic Church's contribution to the anti-Semitism that produced the Holocaust. Other churches have also made similar overtures. Christians must also want peace in Palestine, Israel, and Jerusalem. Without peace there, we have delayed the gift of God's peace readied for all who seek God's righteousness.

Jerusalem, City of Peace

Feisal Husseini, the PLO representative in Jerusalem, said in a 1995 speech: "I dream of the day when a Palestinian will say 'Our Jerusalem' and mean Palestinians and Israelis, and an Israeli will say 'Our Jerusalem' and mean Israelis and Palestinians."

In response, seven hundred Israelis signed this statement: "Jerusalem is ours... Muslims, Christians, and Jews . . . a mosaic of all the cultures and religions . . . that enriched the city. Our Jerusalem must be united, open to all. . . . Our Jerusalem must be the capital of the two states that will live side by side in this country. . . . Our Jerusalem must be the Capital of Peace."[14]

7

Race in the United States: Where Do We Go from Here?

This chapter is about the challenge of justice that faces the citizens of the United States of America: race and the relationship between black and white Americans. Earlier chapters dealt with Latin Americans, South Africans, people of the Balkans, English and Irish, Poles and Germans, Filipinos, Jews, and Arabs. These people were ancestors to those who live in the U.S., immigrating to the "land of opportunity" and entering into what once was called the great "melting pot." This chapter concerns the African people who came to America's shores as men, women, and children in bondage, and who have known a long history of suffering and survival—people who, for all of their victories through the years, still do not know full inclusion in the collective population of "Americans."

The struggle, however, is not only for black Americans to have their dignity affirmed and to enjoy the belonging and the prosperity that they, more than any other people, created in the course of the history of the United States. Rather, the struggle belongs to white Americans as well. The courageous struggles for justice, reconciliation, and reparations seen in earlier chapters prepare the American people, somewhat at least, to respond to the moral issue confronting the nation today: What kinds of wounds have whites inflicted on blacks? What must Americans do to overcome racial injustice? How is America to heal its own deeply wounded society?

For many people, the subject of race relations in the United States is both emotional and frustrating. I recently visited my university library in search of a particular book on the subject and was overwhelmed to find that the library offered approximately eight hundred titles dealing with present-day issues of race in the U.S. In this sampling of works I found, the very titles clearly echo the depth and durability of America's racial divide:

The State of Black America, National Urban League (published annually since 1980)

Racial Healing: Confronting the Fear between Blacks and Whites, Harlon L. Dalton (1995)

The Trouble with Friendship: Why Americans Can't Think Straight about Race, Benjamin DeMott, (1995)

Two Nations: Black and White, Separate, Hostile, Unequal, Andrew Hacker (1995)

Another America: The Politics of Race and Blame, Kofi Buenor Hadjor (1995)

Integration or Separation? A Strategy for Racial Equality, Roy L. Brooks (1996)

Black and White Together: The Search for Common Ground, Danny D. Collum (1996)

The Coming Race War? Richard Delgado (1996)

Race Rules: Navigating the Color Line, Michael Dyson (1996)

"Color Blind" Racism, Leslie Carr (1997)

Long Way to Go, Jonathan Coleman (1997)

Color Blind: Seeing Beyond Race in a Race Obsessed World, Ellis Cose (1997)

Civil Rights and Social Wrongs, John Higham, ed. (1997)

The Color of Faith: Building Community in a Multiracial Society, Fumitaka Matsuoka (1998)

By the Color of Our Skin: The Illusion of Integration and the Reality of Race, Leonard Steinhorn and Barbara Diggs-Brown (1999)

Race matters in the U.S.—it matters a great deal. It divides citizen against citizen, leaving millions of people suspicious, uncomfortable, angry, confused, and totally unequipped to start a conversation that could close the gap, bring people together, and allow the nation's diverse population, in Rodney King's plaintive words, to "just get along." The subject of race is one that many would prefer to avoid. Minorities speak of "race fatigue"—the frustration of trying to pull down racial barriers while the majority deny that there is a race problem.

If there is to be racial reconciliation in the American society, there must be a willingness to confront personal and societal assumptions. Section one considers one such assumption, that the civil rights legislation of the 1960s has essentially "solved the race problem." Section two describes how racial perceptions in the U.S. often dictate how people live and interact. Section three suggests how the words that are used to talk about the issue of race sometimes impede that conversation. Section four asks citizens of the U.S. to look at the nation's history as it really was in order to confront its present race challenges. Section five examines U.S. Christianity, the reality of its racial divisions and the potential it holds for assisting in the racial healing process. The final section lists some of the creative, concrete proposals being offered in the U.S. to close its racial divide.

1. Martin Luther King, Jr.

Martin Luther King, Jr., and a courageous army of Southern blacks are hailed for overcoming segregation, for unlocking the door to opportunity so that a fully integrated society could eventually emerge.

Throughout the United States, Martin Luther King, Jr., has become a national icon of supposed racial harmony. His life, in fact, is honored with a national holiday, soothing racial anxieties with an uncritical reassurance that through his efforts and the accomplishments of the Civil Rights Movement, freedom has been won for black Americans. If we are to know King for who he really was and what his legacy ought to be, however, we must consider more than his "I Have a Dream" speech. We should listen closely to the man during the last two years of his life, by which time far-reaching federal civil rights legislation had been signed into law.

Throughout 1966 and 1967, King addressed America's three social sins as interrelated: racism, poverty, and militarism. Committed to freeing his people from the ghettos of large cities, King marched for opening housing in Chicago in 1966, and was pelted by angry whites. In his wisdom, he recognized that many white Americans were also poor, but they could easily be pitted against blacks.

In 1967 Martin Luther King, Jr., became the first national leader to publicly denounce the war in Vietnam and urge an immediate cease-fire. On April 4, 1967, a year to the day before his assassination, King delivered an electrifying speech at the famous Riverside Church in New York City in which he argued a host of reasons that the war was morally wrong: its violence had killed a million Vietnamese civilians, liberating no one but turning an entire people against the U.S. as a nation; it was a diversion of resources away from dealing with societal ills in the U.S.; it sent black Americans to kill another people of color and to die in disproportionate numbers. Instead, King called the U.S. to take the lead in a nonviolent social revolution.

A true revolution of values will soon look uneasily on the glaring contrast of poverty and wealth. . . . A true revolution of values will lay hands on the world order and say of war: "This way of settling differences is not just." . . . A nation that continues year after year to spend more money on military defense than on programs of social uplift is approaching spiritual death. America, the richest and most powerful nation in the world, can well lead the way in this revolution of values (from "A Time to Break Silence").

King's work was far from over the day he died. In April of 1968 he was in Memphis, Tennessee, to march with garbage workers in their bid to form a union. A month before, in his last major speech, aptly entitled "Where Do We Go from Here?" King laid out the unfinished agenda: the legacy of slavery was that "psychological freedom, a firm sense of self-esteem" still needed to be won.[1] The other basic challenge facing black Americans, King noted, was how to obtain economic and political power. "The problem of transforming the ghetto is a problem of power. . . . Power properly understood is nothing but the ability to achieve purpose. It is the strength required to bring about social, political, and economic change."[2]

King urged the nation to intervene in the "blind operation of our economic system" with its dislocations and discrimination to insure that everyone can work and thereby find security and eliminate want. "The poor transformed into purchasers," King argued, can do a great deal on their own. A nation spending $35 billion annually to wage an unjust war in Vietnam and investing $20 billion to put a man on the moon "can spend billions of dollars to put God's children on their own two feet right here on earth." King called on the U.S. "to ask questions about the whole society": Why are there forty million poor people in the U.S.? Why is the nation's great wealth not more broadly distributed? Why does the economy that produces so much wealth also produce beggars? Such questioning, King insisted, "means coming to see that the problem of racism, the problem of economic exploitation, and the problem of war are all tied together."[3]

Martin Luther King, Jr., America's great twentieth-century prophet, was telling Americans three decades ago where they needed to go from there. It is now up to a nation, a generation older, to consider again where the country needs to go from here. Recalling Jesus' message of personal and social transformation, King called for the structure of our society to be changed:

> A nation that will keep people in slavery for 244 years will "thingify" them—make them into things. Therefore, they will exploit them, and poor people generally, economically. A nation that will exploit economically will have to have foreign investments and everything else, and will have to use its military might to protect them. All of these problems are tied together. What I am saying today is that we must go from this [Southern Christian Leadership Conference] convention and say, "America, you must be born again!"[4]

Today, the transformation that King called for has yet to occur. As the "black power" movement gave vent to the frustration and anger over the lack of progress, King tried, until the end, to keep the black struggle nonviolent. When his birthday is observed each January, the nation would do well to acknowledge that his dream is not the reality of these times. As Leonard Steinhorn and Barbara Diggs-Brown note in their work entitled *By the Color of Our Skin*, "There is nothing wrong with looking back to the 1960s as an era of possibility. But sadly, it just doesn't apply to racial integration."[5] Rhetoric about integration "is another form of racial denial, sustaining the illusion, while keeping real integration a distant and unreachable dream."[6]

2. Race Matters

In June 2000, the *New York Times* published a six-article series entitled "How Race Is Lived in America." The second article follows the fortunes of two Cubans who have lived in Miami since 1995: Joel Ruiz is black and Achmed Valdez is white. When they lived in Cuba they were best friends, playing soccer together and visiting in each other's homes. The social world they encountered in Miami, however, changed all of that. The writer who interviewed them notes:

> The two men live only four miles apart . . . yet they are separated by a far greater distance, one they say they never envisioned back in Cuba. . . . For the first time, they inhabit a place where the color of their skin defines the outlines of their lives—where they live, the friends they make, how they speak, what they wear, even what they eat.[7]

Joel Ruiz, a black Hispanic who was assisted by relatives upon his arrival in Miami in 1995, stepped into his first experience of living with an absence of whites rather than the mixing of races he was accustomed to in Cuba. Within three months, he had a formative experience, when he and four black Cubans were stopped by the police in Little Havana, a white Cuban area in Miami. An officer said to him in Spanish: "I saw you leave [a restaurant] and I saw so many blacks in the car, I figured I would check you out." Ruiz recalls that "up until that day, I thought all Cubans were the same," and since then he has learned the rules for blacks in public: don't make any sudden motion or reach for anything if stopped by the police; don't stare at another driver; walk fast in stores to avoid security guards but slower in the streets to avoid the attention of the police; avoid confrontation in general.

Ruiz's friend Achmed Valdez, a white Hispanic, moved into a white section of Miami with his wife. They are learning English, have held a succession of jobs that pay increasingly more, and are experiencing upward mobility. Achmed has made a smooth transition and hardly feels like an immigrant. His friend Joel, however, cannot cross into that world:

> For the most part, blacks are outsiders in this racially charged city, the scene of some of America's worst race riots. Blacks, especially black Cubans, lack economic and political power and resent the white Cubans who have both. Steadily, relentlessly, the problems of Miami's poor have become Mr. Ruiz's, too.[8]

Miami's race problems are dramatically examined in "Eyes on the Prize," a documentary history of the U.S. Civil Rights Movement from the mid 1950s to the 1980s. ("Eyes on the Prize" is a series of a dozen sixty-minute videos produced between 1986 and 1990 by Blackside, Inc.) But Boston, Los Angeles, Milwaukee, rural Texas, and most of the rest of the country are not much different. Yet, white privilege and racism are realities many whites refuse to admit—a refusal that serves as one more frustration for blacks. Peggy McIntosh, a white woman, reflects that she "was taught to see racism only in individual acts of meanness, not in invisible systems conferring dominance on my group."[9] In "White Privilege: Unpacking the Invisible Knapsack," McIntosh offers a long list of positive conditions that exist for her but often do not exist for her black co-workers and friends. Among those conditions, McIntosh notes that she can:

- "arrange to be in the company of people of my race most of the time"
- rent or purchase housing she can afford, where she wants to live
- "be pretty sure that my neighbors . . . will be neutral or pleasant to me"
- go shopping and not be followed or harassed
- "turn on the television or open the front page and see people of my race"
- be sure than when her national heritage is discussed she will be "shown that people of my color made it what it is."
- "count on my skin color not to work against the appearance of financial responsibility" when writing a check or using a credit card
- expect to see a person of her race if she asks for "the person in charge"
- "arrange to protect my children most of the time from people who might not like them"
- do well "without being called a credit to my race"
- be sure she will not be asked to speak for all the people of her race
- ignore people of other races and languages without negative consequence

- be sure she was not singled out because of race if stopped by the police
- take a job without fear that fellow workers will think she got it through affirmative action
- use public accommodations without fear of being mistreated
- criticize government without appearing to be an outsider
- participate in organizations without feeling isolated, outnumbered, unheard

Blacks remain separate from and unequal to the rest of the population; they are the most spatially isolated population in U.S. history. As a result, "millions of white Americans have no regular contact in their neighborhood with blacks."[10] It is the same in education; urban public schools are predominantly black, with small percentages of Hispanics and Asians. A student at a major American university responded to the issue of race relations on campus, saying, "I don't remember any overt racial hostility. You need a certain amount of contact to have hostilities."

> What makes the failure of integration even more tragic is that blacks may be the most American of all ethnic groups, people who have worked hard, played by all the rules, and deferred gratification literally for centuries (from *By the Color of Our Skin*).

By the time landmark civil rights legislation was passed in 1965, racial patterns in housing, education, behavior, and culture had made real integration a very difficult proposition. The 1990 census offers some striking statistics:

- The average net worth of white households is ten times that of blacks.
- Black family incomes are fifty-four percent that of whites.
- Most black families require two incomes to reach the income level of a white family.
- The infant mortality rate for blacks is twice that of whites.

- The chance of a black person under age twenty being murdered is ten times higher than for a white.
- A black male born in 1991 has a twenty-nine-percent chance of going to prison—compared to a sixteen-percent-chance for Hispanics and four-percent-chance for whites.

The various facets of African American human and socioeconomic situations—joblessness, drugs, crime, family collapse, homelessness, suicide rates—are bound into structural interdependence by the power of this racial stratification; they cannot be coped with as discrete "problem areas." Trends in corporate restructuring and globalization of the economy further separate the races.

3. Speaking of Race

Current Classifications Used by the U.S. Census Bureau

American Indian/Alaska Native*
White, non-Hispanic**
Asian/Pacific Islander*
Black, non-Hispanic**
Hispanic*
Other***

* Based on region or culture of origin
**Based on race
***Biracial or multiracial

Words do more than describe; they convey assumptions and values. Words used to classify people and to talk about relationships among groups need to be used with critical care.

Race, for example, refers to skin color, and categorizes persons as red, yellow, black, and white. Since human beings are not really any of these colors, the words are only conventions—or better, *inventions.* Although categorizing people as "red" or "yellow" has become less socially acceptable, "black" and "white" remain the most powerful word pair in America. "Black" and "white" function as correlative terms, reducing persons to one or the other; in the widely held "one drop of blood" view, anyone with any black ancestry whatsoever is black. The U.S. abandoned the classification "mulatto" (comparable to the category "colored" in South Africa) in the 1920s, not because society became less color conscious but because whites did not want an intermediate category through which people could, over time, pass into the white category. Both color labels designate who and what someone else thinks we are. I, for example, do not identify myself as "white" but as Irish-German American, except when asked to check a box on an official form. But when I identify another person as being "black" or "white," I put that person into a box that collapses race, ethnicity, and culture into one. "Black" or "white" becomes a single group of people perceived as essentially alike in all the ways that evidently are important. Designating a person by color tells us very little about the whole person. Labels of color are as much evaluators as they are descriptors. For example, "whiteness" usually suggests privilege and "blackness" often suggests stigma that survives the efforts to affirm that black is beautiful.

Racism has become an emotionally charged word in U.S. politics. It has an accusatory connotation that brings responses of denial. I offer the following definition of the word *racism*, and distinguish it from a second word: *prejudice.*

"Racism" is action—of individuals, social systems, or structures— that gives advantage and power to one race over another. For example, the "Jim Crow" legislation passed in Southern states during Reconstruction was thoroughly racist because its intent was to advantage whites and subordinate blacks. "Prejudice" is negative regard for another group of persons believed to possess certain characteristics. Persons can and do exhibit prejudice toward members of other groups. But racism, unlike prejudice, permits one group to use its control over structures to inflict substantial harm on other groups.

To further the conversation about racism in American society, the following question must be addressed: How do social structures and systems work for or against groups of citizens based on their skin color or physical characteristics?

"Color blindness" is another important term to consider carefully in the U.S. conversation about race. The claim of color blindness is that black and white polarization can and should be overcome by ignoring race in the formulation of policy and the enforcement of law. Many recognize that such blindness is neither possible nor useful as a means of overcoming the nation's racial gulf. Social realities cannot be so easily dismissed.

Leonard Pitts, a black columnist for the *Miami Herald*, wrote of giving his son a special kind of driving lesson: What to do and what not to do when stopped by a police officer while driving in a white section of the city. Pitts notes that a few incidents involving blacks behaving badly are quickly generalized to apply to the entire black population. "If we were truly free," he writes, "we would be judged upon our individual merits." Addressing whites who want to believe that only a few "vestiges of racism" remain, Pitts describes the "vestiges of slavery" that blacks know all too well:

> Vestiges mean the black couple leaving the mortgage office, dreams broken for reasons having nothing to do with creditworthiness. It means the heart patient dying because he didn't get a life-saving test he certainly, by God, would have received had he been white. It means me trying to school that son of mine about how it is with black men and cops. Trying to teach him before it's too late. . . . See, what some call vestiges, others call mom, dad, sister, brother—real people denied basic rights.[11]

Pitts knows that the mention of slavery will be met with "forget slavery—that was four lifetimes ago." Yet, he wants whites to know how the effects of slavery are still felt. The point is that the stories need to be told, stories of slavery, of the reconstruction period and the Jim Crow south, of the Civil Rights Movement, of burning northern ghettos, and of what black people still experience. Language needs to be rightly connected with past and present realities.

4. Telling the Story

Harlon Dalton offers wise counsel about how both whites and blacks can contribute to the healing of the racial wounds of the U.S., encouraging blacks to continue telling the stories of their people even though the reactions of others are discouraging. For example, telling the story often brings accusations of dwelling in the past ("Nobody in the previous several generations was a slave or a slave owner"), not acknowledging progress made and opportunities that exist ("Look at the many successful blacks"), and making excuses for human failings (crime, drugs, family breakdown within the black community). When blacks tell the story of their experience in America, he notes, "and leave to our audience the task of drawing the moral, we fairly invite a dismissive response."[12] But stories need to be heard.

An Early American Story (ca. 1790)

Josiah Henson, born a slave in Maryland in 1789, describes the day he and his mother and five siblings were sold at auction in 1795, following the death of their master, a Dr. McPherson.

"Our term of happy union as one family was now, alas! at an end. Mournful as was the Doctor's death to his friends, it was a far greater calamity to us. The estate and the slaves must be sold and the proceeds divided among the heirs.

"Common as are slave-auctions in the Southern states, and naturally as a slave may look forward to the time when he will be put upon the block, still the full misery of the event—of the scenes which precede and succeed it—is never understood till the actual experience comes. The first sad announcement that the sale is to be; the knowledge that all ties of the past are to be sundered; the frantic terror at the idea of being 'sent south'; the almost certainty that one member of a family will be torn from another; the anxious scanning of purchasers' faces; the agony of parting, often forever, with husband, wife, child—these must be seen and felt to be fully understood. Young as I was then, the iron entered into my soul. The remembrance of the breaking up of McPherson's estate is photographed in its minutest features in my mind. The crowd collected around the stand, the huddling group of Negroes, the examination of muscle, teeth, the exhibition of agility, the look of the auctioneer, the agony of my mother—I can shut my eyes and see them all.

"My brothers and sisters were bid off first, and one by one, while my mother, paralyzed by grief, held me by the hand. Her turn came, and she was bought by Isaac Riley of Montgomery County [Maryland]. Then I was offered to the assembled purchasers. My mother, half distracted by the thought of parting forever from all her children, pushed through the crowd, while the bidding for me was going on, to the spot where Riley was standing. She fell at his feet and clung to his knees, entreating him in tones that a mother only could command, to buy her baby as well as herself, and spare to her one, at least, of her little ones. Will it, can it be believed that this man, thus appealed to, was capable not merely of turning a deaf ear to her supplication, but of disengaging himself from her with such violent blows and kicks as to reduce her to the necessity of creeping out of his reach, and mingling the groans of bodily suffering with the sob of a broken heart?

"I seem to see and hear my poor weeping mother now. This is one of my earliest observations of men; an experience which I only shared with thousands of my race, the bitterness of which to any individual who suffers it cannot be diminished by the frequency of its recurrence, while it is dark enough to overshadow the whole after-life with something blacker than a funeral pall."[13]

Benjamin DeMott criticizes *Roots*, the history of slavery made for television, for portraying slavery as a "succession of generations passing through purely physical torments that left them intellectually and psychologically untouched."[14] The docu-drama portrays the intrepid courage and strength of blacks to survive but leaves out a host of realities: the "iron stratification; deprivation of skills, opportunity, hope, and education; destruction of self-esteem; and forced adoption and transmission of defensive, outside-the-mainstream codes and strategies of survival."[15] DeMott also makes a critical observation about the popular documentary, *The Civil War*, produced by Ken Burns:

> . . . instead of drawing the audience close to the struggle against slavery long waged by blacks themselves, instead of helping viewers to grasp the influences of that struggle on Lincoln's own ultimate conception of the war . . . [Burns] repeatedly deprecated contentions that the war was about "human dignity," contending that the war was meaningless and pointless.[16]

The documentary failed to make the point that the Civil War marked the beginning of the journey of an enslaved people toward freedom and equality. Neither *Roots* nor *The Civil War* conveyed the reality of "two centuries of labor bondage" and "a century of post-Emancipation repression," thus stripping the public image of slavery in the U.S. of any "vital sense of a grinding devastation of mind occurring generation after generation."[17]

An Inner-City U.S.A. Story (ca. 1990)

DeMott tells the story of a single mother in her twenties put on trial for homicidal negligence in the tragic deaths of five of her six children in a house fire during her absence. DeMott examines her life through the court records: she never completed high school or received any vocational training. She migrated from Mississippi to the Midwest, having her children by three different men, raising them alone on an impossibly little amount of public assistance. DeMott describes the "primary forces visible in her life" as "need, ignorance, abuse, frustration, confusion, and dislocation." She has been "acted upon, done unto" since adolescence and is one of America's "bottom caste" (DeMott, 102). At her trial, these social facts were not acknowledged. According to court testimony, she and her boyfriend were out trying to find money to buy food when the fire occurred. Although she had arranged for a sitter who never came, the prosecution argued that she willfully chose to leave her children home alone, putting her own gratification ahead of her parental obligations. Her court-appointed attorney contended that she was doing the best she knew how, as an impoverished and uneducated woman of color. The prosecutor countered that such a characterization was "racist," denying her dignity as a free person capable of making choices. The jury found her guilty and she was sentenced to seven years in prison and denied contact with her remaining child.

This woman was tried as someone equal under the law and judged by a "jury of her peers." But she was never equal, nor is it likely that the jury of ten whites and two blacks were her peers in terms of life experiences severely limiting her ability to control the events of her life.

Three facts regarding the past and the present must be understood. First, although blacks have been victims, they have been incredibly resilient, struggling, rising up, and keeping faith. Second, slavery has left an indelible mark upon blacks: "At a deep level, slavery stamped black people as inferior, as lacking in virtue, as lacking the capacity to order their own lives."[18] Black leader Malcolm X said that the worst crime whites have committed against blacks was to make blacks hate themselves. Third, changes in American cultural and economic life have been most destructive of black Americans. Author Cornel West speaks of a "black nihilism," "the combination of the market way of life, poverty-ridden conditions, black existential angst, and the lessening of [black youths'] fear of white authorities" that has directed "most of the anger, rage, and despair toward fellow black citizens, especially toward black women."[19] A black man laments his no-win situation: "If I stand, I'm loitering. If I walk, I'm prowling. If I run, I'm escaping."[20] The experience of being watched, controlled, suspected, and presumed inadequate deepens the despair that West believes can only be overcome within the black community by love and care for one another.

Too Many Stories to Tell

In 1972 the U.S. prison population was less than 200,000. Thirty years later, in 1993, the size had multiplied almost tenfold. In 1986 Congress passed new and harsh legislation mandating automatic prison sentences for first-time drug offenders. Possession of five grams of crack cocaine or five hundred grams of powder cocaine meant a mandatory sentence of fifteen to twenty years. Crack cocaine is the poor people's drug. Since 1986, the U.S. prison population has doubled twice, with 650,000 inmates being first-time drug offenders. These are people like Dorothy Gaines, who has served six years of a twenty-year prison sentence for her involvement in a small-time crack ring. These are African American and Latino men who will be locked up for most of their prime years, devastating losses to families and communities. United States District Court Judge Clyde Cahill charges that the legislation "has been directly responsible for incarcerating nearly an entire generation of young black American men for very long periods . . . a situation that reeks with inhumanity and injustice."[21]

5. Black Christians, White Churches;
Black Churches, White Christians

It is a miracle that African slaves received and accepted the gospel message from the very people who enslaved them and made their existence "blacker than a funeral pall," as Josiah Henson described the experience of witnessing his family being sold at auction. While those profiting from the slave trade may have uttered pious thoughts about bringing Africans to Christianity, many plantation masters opposed allowing slaves to learn about and become Christians. But as Africans heard about the God whose power had freed the Israelites enslaved in Egypt, learned about the judgment coming upon those who mistreated others, and experienced the consolation of Jesus' suffering love for them, they "joined up," holding clandestine meetings at night so that the master would not discover them. Especially during the religious revivals that occurred in the 1740s in the colonies, large numbers of slaves became Christian, predominantly Methodists and Baptists. But the ambivalence of white Christians toward the black members of their congregations contradicted the unity professed by Christians. During the U.S. struggle for independence, for example, the Methodist Church condemned slavery, but later backed away from its position because of political unpopularity. In 1792, the white elders of St. George Methodist Church in Philadelphia decided that blacks and whites would no longer sit together. When black members of the congregation were informed of this decision on a Sunday morning they walked out and eventually founded the African Methodist Church.

Although legislatures of the Northern states had abolished slavery, beginning with Pennsylvania in 1780, black Christians struggled against slavery without much northern white support. In 1831 a "People of Color" convention passed a resolution urging blacks to set aside the 4th of July "as a day of humiliation, fasting and prayer . . . to beseech Almighty God to interpose on our behalf, that the shackles of slavery may be broken."[22] That same year Maria Stewart, a black activist from Boston, wrote:

> America, America, foul and indelible is thy stain! Dark and dismal is the cloud that hangs over thee, for thy cruel wrongs and injuries to the fallen sons of Africa. The blood of her murdered ones cries to heaven for vengeance against Thee. . . . You may kill, tyrannize, and oppress as much as you choose, until our cry shall come up before the throne of God; for I

> am firmly persuaded that he will not suffer you to quell the
> proud, fearless and undaunted spirits of the Africans forever;
> for in his own time, he is able to plead our cause against you,
> and to pour out upon you the ten plagues of Egypt.[23]

Following emancipation and the failure of Reconstruction, between 1865 and 1900, prophetic black Christians protested the denial of political and economic participation. Black churches decried the horrific lynching of blacks by white mobs occurring more than ten times a month throughout the 1890s and continuing for over sixty years, into the 1950s.

Although Blacks have resisted enslavement and racism since the 1700s, the black resistance we know most about began in the 1930s. The Civil Rights Movement that achieved full force in the 1950s and 1960s was incubated in Southern black churches, whose many members and clergy were in the vanguard of marches, boycotts, and sit-ins in defiance of segregation statutes. Eventually, the long struggle against "separate and unequal" status for African Americans burst into national consciousness through the leadership of black clergy (the Southern Christian Leadership Conference), the bravery of hundreds of black students (the Student Nonviolent Coordinating Committee), and the courage and sacrifices of thousands of blacks in every walk of life. Martin Luther King, Jr., who grew up in the black church tradition of opposition to segregation, joined the struggle after earning a doctorate in religion from Boston University and accepting the pastorate of a large black Baptist church in Montgomery, Alabama. King's words were like a trumpet sounding, bringing unmatched exhilaration to the movement. During the Montgomery bus boycott, for example, he told a packed church of protesters:

> If we will protest courageously, and yet with dignity and
> Christian love, when the history books are written in future
> generations, the historians will have to pause and say, There
> lived a great people—a black people—who injected new
> meaning and dignity into the veins of civilization.[24]

King's nonviolent approach drew criticism from and was challenged by other blacks for achieving too little too late. The Black Power Movement was born in 1966 in response to frustration and hopelessness, and that summer, northern urban ghettos went up in flames. The leadership of black churches called upon their members to embrace the

Black Power Movement "as an expression of the need for Black Authenticity in a white-dominated society." In the midst of the heat and tension, the National Conference of Negro Churchmen (later called the National Conference of Black Clergymen) spoke an important truth: the power held by whites is corrupted because "it meets little meaningful resistance from Negroes." Likewise, the consciences of blacks are corrupted because they have no power to act on "the demands of conscience, the concern for justice."[25] In 1967, after a second summer of rioting in northern cities, the black clergy caucus of the National Council of Churches declared:

> Historically the Black Church in America represented an authentic expression of Black Power. It grew out of the needs of Black People to glorify God, affirm their own humanity, find a sense of identity, to have something controlled by Black People . . . to celebrate, preserve and enhance the integrity of Blackness under the Lordship of Christ, to be responsive to the needs of Black people, and to be responsible to them.[26]

At that same meeting, the white clergy caucus declared that "the problem of race in America is centered in white America. The white church is a racist church."[27] When the National Conference of Black Clergymen meeting in Chicago in April 1968 received news of Dr. King's assassination, it immediately adjourned and its participating members returned to their congregations around the country. The conference did, however, issue the statement they had been preparing at the time, calling upon white churches to surrender resources to assist the work of the black churches in the depressed economic situation of most black communities.

The most dramatic challenge to the churches of the white establishment was "The Black Manifesto" written by James Forman, adopted by the Black Economic Conference, and presented by Forman to the congregation of Riverside Church, New York City, in May 1969. The manifesto demanded transfer of $500 million from white churches to black churches as reparations for past suffering and ill-gotten wealth. With only a few exceptions, white churches did not respond. With time, black power began to frightened whites, who found it hard to accept "blackness" and "power" in the same breath.

Forman, an activist with the Student Nonviolence Coordinating Committee who had traveled to Zambia and Tanzania to witness African freedom struggles, expressed in the manifesto concern for black people everywhere and sympathy for Africans and for Vietnamese who were suffering "under the domination of racist America."[28] As the struggle of blacks against U.S. racism was witnessed around the world and the call for black power was heard, the most immediate effect was the establishment of the Ecumenical Programme to Combat Racism by the World Council of Churches to end neocolonialism and racism in Africa through direct financial assistance to liberationists.

Black Catholics were a small minority within the U.S. Catholic Church, and although the Church mirrored the racism of the wider society, the Catholic Church did not split into white and black branches. Rather, blacks remained Catholics despite their official neglect, ministered to by white clergy, often in poor parishes. In fact, no blacks were trained for the priesthood until the 1850s, and then only a handful. Not until the 1950s did Catholic seminaries in the U.S. accept black candidates. The first seminary to actually train blacks for the priesthood opened in 1920. As a whole, the Catholic Church was minimally involved in the Civil Rights Movement.

It is little wonder that some blacks rejected Christianity. Malcolm X denounced Christianity as "the perfect slave religion, keeping blacks passive and in their place at the bottom of the social order,"[29] With many other African Americans, he eventually embraced the Nation of Islam, a religious movement founded in the U.S. in 1934. The majority of African American Christians, however, remained with the faith and worked against the racism that was crippling Christian churches. What emerged was a "black theology," applying the liberating message of the gospel to the experiences of black people and critiquing the racism of white churches and theology. Cone's work and that of other theologians of color, men and women, linked the Civil Rights Movement to Christian faith in a way that spoke to not only African Americans but also to peoples seeking liberation everywhere. Cone's black theology played an important role in the South African freedom struggle. The University Christian Movement organized seminars on black theology, and the South African Student Organization, led by Steve Biko, embraced Cone's challenge to white churches (see chapter three).

James H. Cone earned a Ph.D. in religious studies at Northwestern University, began his teaching career at Adrian College in Michigan, and is Distinguished Professor of Systematic Theology at Union Theological Seminary in New York City. In his many books and articles, Cone has developed themes of the liberating mission of Christianity, insisting that black power and black spirituality, that is, politics and religion, are inseparable. The following excerpts offer a sampling of Cone's thought:

Black power: "an inner sense of freedom from the structures of white society which builds its economy on the labor of poor blacks and whites."[30]

The Church: "that people called into being by the power and love of God to share in his revolutionary activity for the liberation of man." Knowing God requires "being on the side of the oppressed, becoming one with them, and participating in the goal of liberation."[31] "Christ is to be found, as always, where men are enslaved and trampled under foot; Christ is found suffering with the suffering; Christ is in the ghetto—there also is his Church" (from *Black Theology and Black Power*).

White churches: "If the real Church is the people of God, whose primary task is that of being Christ to the world by proclaiming the message of the gospel (*kerygma*), by rendering the services of liberation (*diakonia*), and by being itself the manifestation of the nature of the new society (*koinonia*), then the empirical institutionalized white church has failed on all counts."[32]

Cone charged that "as long as the south was the target, northern churchmen could assure themselves that it was a southern problem, totally unrelated to their own northern parishes. But when King brought his work north, many retreated and complained that he was confusing politics and religion. King only regained his popularity among northern churchmen after the emergence of the concept of black power. They came to view King's nonviolence as the lesser of two evils."[33] The white church, Cone wrote, is enmeshed in "exploitative, profit-oriented capitalism . . . a way of life fundamentally alien to human value in general and black humanity in particular."[34] He called upon the white church "in this situation of revolution and reaction [to] decide where its identity lies. Will it continue its chaplaincy to the forces of oppression, or will it embrace the cause of liberation, proclaiming in word and deed the gospel of Christ?"

Black theology began with the experience of African Americans, who historically accepted the gospel from their masters but were excluded from white churches. Protesting the falseness of such a racist Christianity, prophetic black leaders asked white churches how they could proclaim the gospel while their members daily devalued the lives of their black brothers and sisters. Black theology recognized that black churches historically had sustained the souls and bodies of black people. As it criticized the white churches for their hypocrisy, it also criticized the failure of black churches to address the nihilism of contemporary society and its sins against women, homosexuals, and other minorities. Black theology announces God's liberating action that demands solidarity with those struggling against oppression. Its counterpart, womanist theology, draws on the experience of black women to affirm that the struggle against oppression is three-fold: against racism, sexism, and classism. The purpose of black theology, writes Cone, is not the survival of the black church but "what is best for the liberation of the black poor in particular and the poor of the whole world in general."[35]

Sunday morning in the U.S. is still the most segregated time of the week; the color line still separates Christians. Christian faith has the power to effect a critical transformation, challenging Christians to break out of the comfortableness of their social location to learn more deeply the truth of belonging within the universal human family. Everything about "us" versus "them" must be critiqued within the framework of how together "we" will find fulfillment.

6. Solutions

As Americans raise the question, Where do we go from here to overcome the racism in our society? they must begin with the call to personal discernment, public discussion, and community commitment.

Conversations about race must occur in schools, churches, workplaces and marketplace. Beverly Daniel Tatum has facilitated such conversations and has taught a college course titled "The Psychology of Racism" for over a decade. In an article describing her teaching experiences, Tatum notes three sources of resistance to talking about race.[36] First, a powerful taboo surrounds the subject. Second, we are initially unaware of our prejudices. Third, we have been socialized and educated with the presumption that ours is a just society. Tatum quotes from a student's journal after the class had seen the first episode of "Eyes on the Prize": "I never knew it was really that bad just thirty-five years ago. Why didn't I learn this in elementary or high school?"[37] Tatum works to overcome resistance by providing a classroom in which black and white students feel safe to express themselves, by creating assignments that are opportunities for "self-generated knowledge," and by exploring in class "strategies to empower students as change agents."[38] Commonly, she notes, at about the fourth week of the semester, students feel overwhelmed by the topic and aren't sure they want to think about it anymore. Tatum's familiarity with theories of black and white stages of racial identity development helps her lead students through the pain of the discussion to grow beyond racism.[39]

There is much wisdom in the suggestions offered by some of the authors mentioned in this chapter. For example:

Leonard Steinhorn and Barbara Diggs-Brown, in *By the Color of Our Skin*, challenge the American society to:

- reconsider the concept of "minority" in reference to blacks. In historical and moral perspective, a slave caste and their descendants differ from all other immigrant groups
- continue to support affirmative action programs in order to achieve further integration than has been achieved to date
- undertake a national media campaign to educate us about the pervasiveness of subtle discrimination and the racial hurt it incurs

Harlon Dalton, in *Racial Healing* challenges both whites and blacks:

- Whites must reconsider the myth of "self-made" people.
- Whites must recognize the privileged status that being white carries.

- Whites need to admit that in the U.S. they all have a problem with race—it isn't a problem that belongs to blacks alone and which they as individuals and communities are responsible to fix.
- Blacks must tell their own stories in all of their complexity.
- Blacks must pull together as a community, resisting the assault of popular cultural on black families, and subordinating sub-group interests to the needs of the community.
- Blacks must be welcoming to other groups, recognizing the issues of "pecking order" and bias among themselves.
- Blacks and whites must engage one another without fear, without the presumption that they already know everything about each other, wanting to hear from each other as individuals rather than racial representatives, listening carefully and responding honestly.

Ellis Cose, in *Color Blind*, challenges the nation to:

- discard the belief that time will heal America's race wound and that surmounting racial hatred equals healing
- recognize that despite the end of legalized segregation, the vast social and economic separation between blacks and whites still leaves an apartheid nation
- ask, How can we all succeed at this? and What means can we develop to boost achievement for those most in need? instead of projecting blame on one another
- keep the heat on to eliminate all forms of discrimination in society
- engage in both conversation and active collaboration whenever and wherever possible

Cose is surely correct: "The reality is that the [race] problem has no single or simple solution. If there is one answer, it lies in recognizing how complex the issue has become, and in not using the complexity as an excuse for inaction. In short, if we are to achieve our country, we must attack the enemy on many fronts."[40]

Late in the Day of the Republic

In the pre-dawn of the United States, men, women, and children stacked in ships were brought to ports and sold as slaves to the owners of tobacco and cotton plantations. At noon the nation was rent by a civil war that broke these peoples chains and made them "free," but the heat of the afternoon of Jim Crow laws and white lawlessness was still stifling. In the late afternoon a mighty wind whipped up, and they marched, staged sit-ins, and boycotted, demanding justice and liberty for all. Then there was a brief storm followed by a brilliant sunset, bringing the end to a century of segregation. But a dark and starless night has descended on most black people: neighborhoods turned into no-man's land by poverty, poor education, too few and too low paying jobs, the drug traffic. What nightmares will midnight bring to this nation? Will its citizens awaken tomorrow to find themselves not one but two nations, black and white, and even more "separate, hostile, and unequal"? All citizens of the United States have the power and the responsibility to shape whatever tomorrow will be.

Although Steinhorn and Diggs-Brown are not hopeful that the U.S. can reach the racial "promised land" anytime soon, they urge the American society to seek a racial "honest land" by admitting that white America "isn't going to make integration a national cause and black America is unwilling to put up with the frustration of trying." They propose that people focus on "racial coexistence, acknowledging racial separation but keeping the lines porous," while working for "real solutions and guarantees to make . . . coexistence work."

Fortunately, there are examples of people crossing the color line that divides. There are blacks and whites working together, rebuilding neighborhoods in central cities; there are churches, synagogues, and mosques cooperating in order to put political and economic power back into the hands of the people; there are those struggling together to create sustainable rural environments. It is a hopeful sign that churches are encouraging their members to talk about race. The Archdiocese of Chicago has initiated parish workshops on racism, and a similiar project, called Recovery from Racism, has been undertaken in the Archdiocese of Detroit.[41] All over the country, blacks, whites, Hispanics, Asians, are gathered in local settings and learning to listen to one another, to build relationships, and to "reweave the fabric of their communities" for the benefit of ordinary families.[42]

Dalton provides a vision of the future by describing the "Salt and Pepper Gospel Singers," the integrated choir to which he belongs:

> No one has changed color. No one's culture has been lost or sacrificed. We have managed to blend and be respectful of differences at the same time. The only thing we have given up is the right to dominate one another. No one's history has been altered. But together we have the power to transform the future. That is my vision of the Promised Land. It is not grand, but it is real. And it is attainable. All it takes is a genuine commitment to the process of racial healing.[43]

8

Women Struggling for Justice and Peace

On behalf of the Church, Pope John Paul II asked pardon for its treatment of women, who have "suffered offenses against their dignity and whose rights have been trampled." John Paul acknowledged:

> [T]he equality of your sons and daughters has not been acknowledged, and Christians have been guilty of attitudes of rejection and exclusion. . . . Forgive us and grant us the grace to heal the wounds still present in your community on account of sin (Day of Pardon, March 12, 2000).

Not only must we recognize the suffering of women in its many forms, but we also must reform social systems that harm women and stand with them in their courageous struggles.

Today an estimated seventy percent of the world's 1.3 billion people living in poverty are women and children, constituting the majority of the world's refugees. Mary Robinson, UN High Commissioner for Human Rights (and former President of the Republic of Ireland), laments that women and children are increasingly the casualties of war and victims of domestic violence that is global. Women are denied rights in regard to property, inheritance, marriage and divorce, and employment, and girls are frequently denied education. Both young girls and women are often kidnapped and sold into slavery.

The Convention on the Elimination of All Forms of Discrimination against Women, adopted by the United Nations General Assembly in 1979, is an international bill of rights for women. To date, one hundred and sixty-five nations, but not the United States, have ratified the convention, pledging to work for gender equality and the elimination of discriminatory laws and practices, and "to take measures against all forms of traffic in women and exploitation of women."[1]

The 1993 UN World Conference on Women urged nations to renew their commitment to ending discrimination against women. Seven years later, in 2000, a UN report on the status of women since the Beijing Conference on Women (1995) noted the continuing economical and political inequalities between men and women, and again urged greater efforts by governments to protect women's rights and to promote educational, economic, and social opportunities for them.

Section one of this chapter describes aspects of the present war on women and children. Sections two and three offer examples of the instrumental role of women in the affirmation of human rights, the doing of justice, and the promotion of human welfare and dignity. Section four describes the disturbing rise of forced labor and sexual exploitation of the world's poorest and most vulnerable that has been called the "new slavery." Section five invites us to see and respond, in the light of the deepest truth of Christianity, to the situation of poor women of color the world over.

1. Wars against Women and Children

Hundreds of thousands of civilians perished in World War II, victims of the German *blitzkrieg* against British cities, the retaliatory bombing of major German population centers by the Allies, and the nuclear annihilation of the Japanese cities of Hiroshima and Nagasaki. War in the twentieth century meant weapons of increasing destructiveness and increasingly higher proportions of civilian among the dead. The high-tech war on Iraq and the ten-year embargo that followed, for example, have demonstrated how conventional weaponry can systematically destroy a nation's infrastructure (electrical power grids, water treatment plants, and production and distribution facilities), causing a public health crisis and the deaths of half a million Iraqis.

Not only high-tech warfare produces mass death and destruction, however. Terrorists also target civilian populations. Ethnic warriors in the Balkans, for example, murder women, children, and the elderly, and paramilitary units in Latin America wage "low intensity" wars against poor people. James Garbarino writes that "in today's wars, with their emphasis on 'national liberation,' 'low intensity warfare,' 'counter-insurgency,' and 'guerilla warfare,' more than eighty percent of the direct and indirect victims of military action are children and women."[2] Amnesty International reported that Serb police in Kosovo regularly and "deliberately targeted houses [of Albanian Kosovars] regardless of the fact that often women, children and unarmed men were sheltering in them." An estimated 200,000 Kosovars, primarily women and children, fled to refugee camps, without homes to return to and with little hope of joining Kosovar men fleeing across borders to safety. The report also described scenes of women and young children "wait[ing] within sight of their houses for hours, even days, before the spectacle of destruction and looting finally forces them to give up any hope of going back."[3]

More heinous still is the fact that in many contemporary conflicts, the targeting of women is part of the strategy for defeating the enemy. In conflicts from Guatemala to Bosnia, for example, women are attacked because they are wives or mothers of guerrillas or "leftists" or ethnic "enemies." The raping of Bosnian and Kosovar women was more than the brutal behavior of a few Serb soldiers. Degrading women, impregnating them to bear children with Serb blood, were means of wiping out a culture in order to make way for a "Greater Serbia." Slavenka Drakulic tells horrific stories of the crimes committed against women during the Balkan Wars of the 1990s.[4] In Chiapas, Mexico, sixty thousand Mexican federal troops have continuously occupied indigenous lands since the Zapatista rebellion (led by Emiliano Zapata and his rebel group called the Zapatista National Liberation Army) began in 1994. The Mexican army's sexual harassment, rape, and prostitution of indigenous women have weakened community and family bonds, creating fatherless children and general terror among the indigenous.

Increasingly, children's victimization in wartime includes recruiting them for combat. Amnesty International reports that since 1998 at least 300,000 youths between the ages of seven and seventeen have served in combat roles in thirty war zones.[5] Children as young as eight are recruited by paramilitaries and civilian defense forces in Colombia, Peru, Sierra Leone, Rwanda, and Cambodia. The government of Uganda recruits thirteen year olds, the Congo drafts fifteen year olds, and Pakistan and Bangladesh, sixteen year olds. Because their violent experiences do not bode well for their return to civilian life, child soldiers, if they survive, will carry physical and psychological damage into adulthood.

Other wars against women and children rage far from battle zones reported by the media. In homes and workplaces, for example, men abuse women and children with impunity. The United Nations Children's Emergency Fund (UNICEF) has estimated that between twenty and fifty percent of women worldwide experience domestic violence at one time or another. It goes so far as to call violence against women and girls "a global epidemic that kills, tortures and maims—physically, psychologically, sexually, and economically."[6]

Domestic violence, a product of male domination, is particularly rampant in societies where other forms of subjugation are practiced. In racist cultures, for example, where whites dominate people of color, the white male role of "master" is reflected in the attitudes and behaviors of white men toward white women. Men of color dominated by the white masters, in turn, vent their rage on wives and daughters.[7] In the U.S., slavery, segregation, and now poverty have taken immense tolls on black families. Black women, in fact, have suffered doubly: the abuse of both white men and black men. What harms black families harms women the most, for they are the ones who, against great odds, struggle to raise their children. In her novel *July's People*, South African author Nadine Gordimer illustrates apartheid's destruction of black families and the impoverishment of women when husbands were forced to migrate to "white areas" to find work and to live permanently apart from their families. Her story portrays a black man who serves a white family and lives in the family's servant quarter, while his own family must remain in the Homeland. His white master, totally disregarding July's wife and family, encourages July to have a town woman live with him, hoping to keep July, a valued servant, content and loyal.[8]

2. Women and Human Rights Struggles

Because their pain is universal, women around the world are organizing to defend the vulnerable, to bring justice, and to reknit societies that have been torn apart. Thousands of women in Guatemala and El Salvador, for example, have experienced tragedies similar to the death of Rigoberta Menchu's parents and brother (see chapter one). In Guatemala alone, an estimated forty-two thousand people were victims of massacres (ninety-three present by government forces or paramilitaries) between 1980–1983. The official report of the Archdiocese of Guatemala detailing massive human rights of Guatemalans drew special attention to the courageous work of women:

> The search for relatives who have been disappeared has been
> one of the most anguishing struggles arising from political
> repression, and one that has been spearheaded by women. . . .
> The search became the only means of standing up to the
> army and defying the terror behind the disappearances. It
> turned into the most unwavering stance in defense of human
> rights during the worst years of the armed conflict. Mothers,
> wives, daughters, and sisters of the disappeared were the
> ones who dared to defy the raging violence. Never before
> had they been considered protagonists in the political life of
> the country, yet they displayed courage, resolve, and hope on
> countless occasions.[9]

Women in Argentina also found the courage to stand up to a murderous regime when a right-wing military dictatorship took control of the country in 1976 and thirty thousand Argentine opponents disappeared within a matter of months. In April 1977 the mothers of fourteen "disappeared" children assembled in the central plaza of Buenos Aires to protest the government's silence regarding the fate of their children. The protest of the "Mothers of the Plaza de Mayo" drew international attention to Argentina when other groups—including the leaders of the Argentine Catholic Church paralyzed by fear of the regime—were mute. Despite government intimidation and the abduction and disappearance of the group's founder and several of its members, the Mothers of the Plaza de Mayo relentlessly continued weekly protests for twelve years. Maria Adela Antokoletz, a founding member of the Mothers, remembers:

> We endured pushing, insults, attacks by the army, our
> clothes were ripped, detentions. . . . But the men, they would
> not have been able to stand such things without reacting.
> They would have been arrested . . . and, most likely, we
> would not have seen them ever again.[10]

Although they succeeded in exposing the criminal deeds of the regime, the successive governments of Argentina have refused to cooperate with the women. Although the government's campaign to intimidate the Mothers of the Plaza de Mayo continues, the women refuse to give up their search for the truth.

> A society that does not fight for its rights becomes a sick society, a society that lives in fear and horror that it can happen again. That is what happened here in Argentina, this is what makes us, the human rights organization, survive. We can't sit peacefully at home (Maria Adela Antokoletz).

In El Salvador, novelist Claribel Alegria calls her work as activism, "a shrill cry of defiance" in support of Salvadorans ("sixty percent of whom earn less than eleven dollars per month"). The next generation, she vows, must be allowed "to learn the alphabet and thus gain access to the great literature of the world: a basic right that has been denied most of their elders."[11]

Recall the peace activism in Belfast initiated by Mairead Corrigan and Betty Williams (see chapter two). Although they were criticized as politically naïve and too compromising by both sides of the sectarian struggle, the Peace People persevered, and by the 1980s, the political process included increasing numbers of women. Sinn Fein's Gerry Adams acknowledged:

> [W]e have decided internally that because of the discrimination against women in Irish society we will have a politics of positive discrimination. . . . The fact that women have historically not enjoyed a significant role in deciding policy in the movement can be related to the status of women in society as a whole.[12]

Adams also notes that Irish women, especially, are addressing housing problems, children's issues, and better wages, and are doing much of the election work. In the mid 1980s, for example, a quarter of the places on Sinn Fein's highest council was reserved for women, and women headed seven of the party's national departments. Women, writes Adams, "humanize politics, are more radical, more open, and less macho."[13]

In South Africa a group of white women organized the "Women's Defense of the Constitution" in 1955 to protest the disenfranchisement of coloreds (that stripped nonwhites of the vote), the Bantu education laws (that denied adequate education to natives), and the forced removals of Africans to "homelands." Because they wore black sashes at their public protests to mourn the death of the South African constitution by the enactment of apartheid laws, their movement became known as the "Black Sash." Although their activities violated laws prohibiting public protest, Black Sash participated in the mass action campaign of the late 1980s. Later, after the fall of apartheid in 1990, Black Sash advocated for reparations to the millions of people who were robbed of everything as a result of apartheid policies and practices. Sheena Duncan, the president of Black Sash since 1975, knows that the dismantling of apartheid "will not make any difference to the dispossessed in the foreseeable future," since most of the nation's wealth remains in the hands of whites. Since the early 1990s Duncan and Black Sash have vigorously advocated the payment of reparations to the four million South Africans who were dispossessed under apartheid. The right of private property, she insists, must bow before "a prior right—that of people to basic protection from rain, wind, and heat . . . [and] to the use of land for the production of food for family"[14] Black Sash continues to speak out in behalf of the millions of homeless and landless Africans whose lives have yet to be substantially improved by the dismantling of apartheid.

In the late 1950s in South Africa Ruth Mompati joined thousands of other women in protest against laws requiring black women to carry passes. In 1963 she was forced into exile for her work with the African National Conference (ANC). But Mompati continued to work from outside the country. In 1990 she participated in the negotiations with the de Klerk government to establish democratic rule. Mompati says simply, "We cannot separate women's liberation from national liberation."[15]

With Mompati, Albertina Sisulu is a member of the National Assembly in South Africa. Married to ANC leader Walter Sisulu, who spent twenty-six years in prison, Sisulu herself was banned for two decades, including house arrest for ten years and three months in detention. As she struggled to raise her five children and watched them go into exile or to prison, she also saw the pain of other mothers whose children died in Soweto. "It is our obligation," she says, "to participate in the next phase of the struggle, which is the fight for the rights of our children and the rights of women, together with the rights of all human beings in the new South Africa. We cannot leave this to men. There are certain things that we can actually do better than they can." [16]

Also committed to the equality of women in South Africa is Ela Gandhi, granddaughter of Mahatma Gandhi, and also a member of the National Assembly. (Of the four hundred members of the National Assembly elected in 1994, one hundred of them are women.) As long-time South African union organizer Rachel Alexander explains, "Women realize that liberation that excludes women's rights is not liberation at all."[17] These five South African women—Sheena Duncan, Ruth Mompati, Albertina Sisulu, Ela Gandha, and Rachel Alexander—are among the thousands of women who have struggled for economic, political, and gender equality in South Africa.

The Bill of Rights of South Africa's 1996 Constitution reflects the active role of many women in the struggle against apartheid. Article 9, Section 3, for example, forbids discrimination "directly or indirectly against anyone on one or more grounds, including race, gender, pregnancy, marital status, ethnic or social origin, colour, sexual orientation, age, disability, religion, conscience, belief, culture, and birth." Article 12, Section 2 asserts that women possess "the right to bodily and psychological integrity, which includes the right (a) to make decisions concerning reproduction; and (b) to security in and control over their body."

Finally, a group of Israeli Jewish and Arab women in Jerusalem courageously keep a weekly vigil at a busy intersection, appealing to Israel to honor the rights of Palestinians. These "Women in Black" speak for Palestinian women in the occupied territories who live in constant fear that their teenage sons will die at the hands of the Israeli military for throwing stones at tanks. They speak for Israeli mothers of sons who have died in the conflict.

3. Weaving Solidarity

A century ago Pope Leo XIII affirmed the dignity of workers and protested against the injustices they were suffering. Today, the situation is different. Unlike a hundred years ago, the majority of the clothing, electronics, and home goods purchased today in the U.S. are manufactured or assembled in factories throughout the Third World. Women and children do much of the work in sweatshops that are owned by multi-national corporation that are not subject to the laws of host countries and have little stake in the well being of workers' communities.

Women and children sew clothing, assemble athletic shoes, and weave carpets in Asian factories across China, Pakistan, India, Nepal, Bangladesh, and Indonesia. In Guatemala, Honduras, Mexico, El Salvador, and Nicaragua, young women produce most U.S. designer and discount-store clothing, working long hours in miserable conditions for subsistence-level wages. Their only hope is to develop strong unions to push for labor reform within their countries and to bargain for just wages with employers. A Honduran worker explained her reasons for seeking a union: "I had to defend myself, and the union is the way a worker can defend herself." Factory owners routinely fire workers for their union organizing activities, and in the face of successful union organizing, close the factories and reopen them where unions do not yet pose a threat.

In 1992 a delegation of U.S. women traveled to Guatemala to a conference of Guatemalan unions. Recognizing their common struggle for dignity, job security, health care for themselves and their children, these women developed an organization called STITCH: Support Team International for Textileras (women textile workers). Its goals include:

- building relationships between workers, women and organizers across borders
- supporting strategic organizing campaigns
- training women as organizers

Feeling the sharp effects of the power of women, factory owners have started hiring male workers—workers who do not require time off to have or care for children, and who are less inclined to form social relationships in the factory and offer each other mutual support. What has emerged, however, is strong cooperation among male and female workers to build strong unions.

Weaving Solidarity

STITCH and **UNITE** (Union of Needletrades, Industrial, and Textile Employees) are U.S. labor groups that support workers in Third World countries who are attempting to form unions.

The **Worker Rights Consortium** and **Fair Labor Association** monitor working conditions in foreign factories licensed by colleges and universities to produce sports clothing.

United Students against Sweatshops encourages colleges and universities to insist that manufacturing of college apparel and athletic clothing is done in factories that honor worker rights.

The National Labor Committee, Committee for Labor Rights, and Labor Education in the Americas Project (LEAP) provide education on sweatshop issues, conduct fact-finding missions, and organize citizen advocacy in the U.S.

Although the right of workers to organize is a fundamental principle of Catholic social teaching, the reality for workers in poor countries is that their struggles to establish unions will be long and difficult. They deserve the support of the corporations, stockholders, and consumers in wealthy nations who are the beneficiaries of their daily labors.

4. The New Slavery

The greatest threat to human beings is poverty. Seventy percent of the world's poor are women and children, making them the casualties of chronic hunger and disease, and especially vulnerable to a form of exploitation that is hidden from the world's view.

In regions of the world where poverty is dire, poor people are entrapped in what is called the "new slavery." The "old" slavery is gone: nowhere is it legal for persons to own other persons. But by conservative estimates, twenty-seven million people today are enslaved in other ways for often long and indefinite periods of time: someone else owns their labor. Two-thirds of the people in Asia, for example, work in fields, make bricks, weave carpets, work metal, polish gems, and make jewelry—for wages that are not enough to provide for basic human needs. Haitians cut sugar cane on plantations in the Dominican Republic; Brazilians dig in mines and haul timber. Some young women brought into the so-called First World countries work as domestic laborers, lured by promises of education. Once in a household, however, they are powerless to quit or to protest. The most brutalized are young women sold into prostitution. All of these people are today's "new slaves."

Such forced labor is reminiscent of Nazism—but how can this be happening in the twenty-first century? Extreme poverty is the driving force, putting people at the mercy of those who can control their very means for survival. Impoverished families desperately needing money, for example, are often approached by labor "recruiters" offering them loans, the collateral and repayment of which is the labor of one of their children for a certain period of time. The exchange of laborers for small loans creates a situation of "debt bondage." What's more, families in rural villages are often misled by urban recruiters regarding the nature of the work, the working conditions, and the length of time their children must work to satisfy the loan. Those who own the right to someone's labor will also determine when the debt has been satisfied—and that could easily mean years of "debt bondage." Very low "wages" and charges for interest, food, and shelter insure that the loan repayment period will be long.

Kevin Bales traveled to five regions where the new slavery is flourishing. He found systems of "slave holding" more profitable than the "slave owning" of the past. The cost of "buying" them is very low—a small loan. There is no need to keep their "human investments" healthy and safe so that they can be productive. When they are no longer able to work they will be put out. They are disposable because they can be cheaply replaced. Until then all of their waking hours will be working hours. They may sleep near their workspaces. Those who hold workers in debt bondage have no certificates of ownership. What they do have are security forces to prevent workers from running away or to capture and punish them if they do. Bales writes: [The new slavery] is not just stealing someone's labor; it is the theft of an entire life. It is more closely related to the concentration camp than to questions of bad working conditions."[18]

"Slaves" today are generally very young and can be controlled with lesser amounts of violence. Girls in particular are preferred for many reasons. Manual dexterity, for example, suits them for intricate work, and they are readily available for the sexual gratification of their male overseers. If they become pregnant and have a child to support, they are less likely to attempt escape or pay down their debt. Then, in just a few years, the child will become another working body.

Perhaps the most tragic exploitation is the delivery of young women into prostitution. In Thailand, for example, girls are drawn from rural areas with promises of jobs in factories and restaurants. Once removed from the protection of their families, however, the girls are sold to brothels or exported to other countries where they will be freed only when they are able to repay their purchase price through prostitution. Brothel owners usually manage to keep young women for years (or until they test positive for HIV), deducting rent and expenses from the income derived from their sexual exploitation.

In 1989 the United Nations passed the "Convention on the Rights of the Child," acknowledging that "in too many countries children's lives are plagued by armed conflict, child labor, and sexual exploitation," that children born into rural areas have little opportunity for health care or education, and that even in wealthy countries, some children face homelessness, violence, and poverty.[19] Of the 187 member nations of the U.N., only Somalia and the U.S. have not signed the convention.

5. Jesus and Poor Women of Color

The majority of the world's poor people have been dispossessed; they have little or no productive land to work. When they migrate to urban areas to sell their labor, the conditions under which they live and work are a denial of their dignity. Without productive land or dignified work at living wages, clearly there is no hope to escape the grinding poverty.

Mexican poet Rosario Castellanos describes the heavy burdens that indigenous women of Chiapas, Mexico, must carry each day:

Indian Mother

She always walks with a load on her shoulders: her
baby and then her simple wares.

Wearily she crosses the mountains that imprison her
and descends to the hostile city below.

Once her goods are sold (or pilfered or despoiled) the
Indian mother seeks rest. . . .

In her brief moments of repose, she holds her baby on
her lap . . . She contemplates him with eyes filled
with love and guilt. The shadowy depth of her gaze
has a name: despair.

. . . Her hands (hands that motherhood should have
filled with gifts) are empty. They will never be fully
able to stifle her child's hungry cries, nor pour oil on
wounds made by the burdens he must bear. . . .

Oh, may sleep elude our brows, may friendship piece
our hearts like thorns, and may songs offend our
mouths, as long as the hands of this woman, this
Indian mother, remain unable to give her child bread,
light, and justice.[20]

Theologian Shawn Copeland examines the oppression suffered by
poor women of color, offering this observation:

From the middle of the fifteenth century forward, a totaliz-
ing dynamics of domination, already obvious in anti-Semitism and misogyny, began to make itself felt in so-called
"new worlds" through genocide and racism, cultural imperi-
alism and colonialism.[21]

To the degree that Christianity has been part of the dominating force, it
shares responsibility for the wretchedness of the lives of millions. The
poor, the malnourished, the chronically ill, and those who are enslaved
are reduced to statistics for the small minority of those who live in
affluence and who fail to see the poor as human subjects, who ignore
"the humanity and realities of poor red, brown, yellow, and black
women."[22] But as Copeland notes, Jesus is "the incarnation of divine
compassion" who was himself "among the multitudes of history's victims."[23] Thus, in solidarity, we must recognize and regard "exploited,
despised poor women as who they are—God's own creation."[24]

Perhaps the suffering of women seems distant and remote; perhaps
the mistreatment of women is not immediately visible to everyone. Hattie Gossett's poem invites us to open our eyes.

World View

there's more poor than nonpoor
there's more colored than noncolored
there's more women than men

all over the world the poor woman of color is the mainstay of
the little daddy centered family which is the bottom-line of big
daddys industrial civilization
…
she is holding up the whole world
what you gonna do?
you can't stop her
you gonna just stand there and watch her with your mouth
open? or are you gonna try to get down?
you can't stop her
she is holding up the whole world[25]

Some of the Indian women of Chiapas, "with loads on their shoulders" walked onto the world stage and spoke to us in January 1994. They were among the leadership of the Zapatista movement, demanding freedom and justice. These women pledged Zapatista support for women's rights to land, health care, education, and economic enterprise. (The movement also encourages the communities' banning of liquor, a major contributor to the squandering of family resources and domestic abuse.) Chiapan women in the autonomous communities describe their own journeys to great self-realization. Otelina, representative of a women's cooperative, says:

> When women don't participate it's because we are afraid, embarrassed, we feel ashamed. We feel timid and we don't speak up in the community assembly. We feel that we don't know anything: we don't know how to participate, we don't know how to read even one word, we don't speak Spanish, and we don't know about our rights as women. There are still very few women who participate because we don't have much experience. When we begin to participate, we learn to get over the fear. … In the [EZLN] organization women's lives began to change and we are not as oppressed. (Otelina, representative of a women's cooperative store)[26]

Another woman explained:

> Before '94 we had never seen a woman participating, or
> women that left their communities to travel to other places.
> In some communities where the soldiers attacked us in 1995,
> many women organized to defend their communities; they
> protested, they spoke out against the soldiers and drove them
> out of their communities. (Segunda, health promoter)

Women have increasingly participated in community assemblies,
the church, and women's collective enterprises. ("In the women's stores
we work well as a collective . . . learning how to sell in the store, how
to go buy merchandise." Josefa) One of the most hopeful signs in the
indigenous communities' struggles is the growing recognition and
respect of women.

Copeland argues that preferential option for poor women requires
us to take responsibility for their exploitation and to form responsible
relationships with those too long invisible to us.

> The shouldering of responsibility obliges us in the here-and-
> now to stand between poor women of color and the powers
> of oppression in society, to do all that we can to stop their
> marginalization, exploitation, abuse, and murder. In memory
> of the cross of Jesus, we accept this obligation, even if it
> means we must endure rejection or loss.[27]

If we are to join Pope John Paul II in asking forgiveness for the
"rejection and exclusion" of women and the consequent suffering to
them and their children, we must recognize their plight. We must find
ways to join these women and work side by side for the justice long
denied them.

Afterword

We have encountered spirit-filled, courageous, and persevering women and men in South Africa, Northern Ireland, Poland, the Philippines, and many other places around the globe—people struggling to heal the consequences of human sinfulness. They and thousands of others in Latin America, the Balkans, and the Middle East give us hope that justice and peace are possible. Yet justice and peace are as much aspirations as they are achievements; they will always be works in progress.

What are we called to do? If we look around us as well as within us, the answer will appear. The needs are close at hand. Gandhi reminded us that work for justice and peace is always as much an interior work as a commitment to others. For we must confront our own conflicted selves if we are to engage in patient and peaceful conflict with others. "*We* must be the change we wish to see," Gandhi said. We must pass on to the next generation a hunger for justice and a capacity for peacemaking.

God's work of creation and redemption continues to transform the world and its peoples. In our strivings for justice and peace, we witness to what God intends for all creation. We are part of that plan, summoned to be justice to the needy, health to the wounded, and peace to the divided human family. Isaiah describes how God's creative energy will overcome barriers:

> Do not remember the former things,
>   or consider the things of old.
> I am about to do a new thing;
>   now it springs forth, do you not perceive it?
> I will make a way in the wilderness
>   and rivers in the desert . . .
> to give drink to my chosen people,
>   the people whom I formed for myself
> so that they might declare my praise (Isaiah 43:18–20).

Just as Yahweh freed the Israelites from bondage in Egypt, through his sons and daughters he also freed Poles from repression, delivered Filipinos from the hands of the greedy, began to break down the walls between Catholics and Protestants in Belfast, and restored to South Africans their birthright.

God's work with us and for us is not yet finished, however. Jews and Palestinians in deadly embrace, marginalized indigenous peoples, oppressed women and children, despised people of every hue and culture call out to be recognized as God's children. God promises, "See! I am making all things new!" (Revelation 21:5) God's work of renewing the earth will one day be accomplished. If we join ourselves to God's work in the time that we have been given, we will know the divine joy that only sharing in the activity of God can bring.

> Lord of the world, Father of all, through your Son you
> asked us to love our enemies, to do good to those who hate
> us and to pray for those who persecute us. Yet Christians
> have often denied the Gospel; yielding to a mentality of
> power, they have violated the rights of ethnic groups and
> peoples, and have shown contempt for their cultures and
> religious traditions: be patient and merciful towards us, and
> grant us your forgiveness!
> —Pope John Paul II, "Confession of Sins" March 12, 2000

Appendix

For teachers using this book with courses in religion, ethics, or social studies, the chapters are intended to:

- inform students of the principles of Catholic social teaching
- inform students of several contemporary situations of injustice and the work of people to bring justice and peace
- help students make connections between Christian faith and social action and strengthen their commitment to respond to injustice both globally and in their own communities
- teach students how to update their knowledge of current events through use of Internet and other sources

Discussion questions and suggestions for projects are included with students in mind. The web sites listed in the chapter notes and Additional Resources are intended to help readers update their knowledge.

Other resources for enriching understanding of the struggles discussed in the chapters have also been included. They are listed for each chapter in four categories:

A. books by journalists, scholars, and activitists

B. works of literature

C. documentaries (doc) and commercial films

D. web sites

Introduction

Questions for Discussion

1. What economic situation in the late nineteenth and early twentieth century aroused the conscience of the Catholic Church?

2. In the 1960s what did the Church assert was authentic national development?

3. What did Pope John Paul II mean by rich nations' "moral under-development"?

4. How are our civic ideals contradicted by our actual practices?

5. Which of the ten social principles reminds us that we human beings are social in nature?

Chapter 1: The Way of the Cross: Central America Past and Present

Questions for Discussion

Sections 1–3

1. Bartolomé las Casas went "against the crowd" when he stood up for the native peoples. How do you think his family may have reacted to his stand? What gave him the courage to do what he did?

2. Why did Columbus believe he could simply claim everything discovered for Spain?

3. How could the New Testament quote in section 3 apply to the *mestizos*?

4, What are some of the reasons political and economic progress has been frustrated for so many people in Latin America?

5. How is the Church in Latin America challenging the *status quo*?

Sections 4-6

1. Do you think indigenous people should have autonomous territories in which to preserve their cultures? Explain.

2. Do Bishop Ruiz and the Mayan struggle going on in Chiapas matter to us? If not, why? If so, what can we do about it?

3. Which Catholic social principles are particularly relevant to the situation of Mexico and Central America?

4. Maquiladoras are defended for providing employment opportunities. NAFTA is claimed to promote higher standards of living for all. Are these claims accurate? Explain.

5. How has the colonial past of Latin America contributed to its economic, social, and political problems of today?

Terms to Know

accompaniment
encomienda
mestizo

Names to Know

Guadalupe event
North American Free Trade Agreement
Zapatistas/Emiliano Zapata

Additional Resources

A.

George Collier, *Basta! Land and the Zapatista Rebellion in Chiapas*
Marguerite Feitlowitz, *Lexicon of Terror* [El Salvador]
James Goldston, *Shattered Hopes: Guatemalan Workers*
Elaine Katzenberger, *First World: Ha, Ha, Ha*
Rigoberta Menchu, *I, Rigoberta Menchu*
John Ross, *Rebellion from the Roots: Indian Uprising in Chiapas*
_____, *The War against Oblivion*
Jon Sobrino, S.J., *Romero: Martyr for Liberation*
Diana Taylor, *Disappearing Acts*
John Womack, Jr., *Rebellion in Chiapas*

B.

Julia Alvarez, *The Time of the Butterflies* [Dominican Republic]
Manlio Argueta, *One Day of Life* [El Salvador]
Sandra Benitez, *Bitter Grounds* [El Salvador]
Eric Carlson, *I Remember Julia* [Guatemala]
Mario Payeras, *Days of the Jungle* [Guatemala]
Demetria Rodriguez, *Mother Tongue* [El Aalvador]

C.

Central America Close Up (Maryknoll Films)
Disappeared
El Norte
The War against the Poor
Missing
A Place Called Chiapas

Chapter Two: Northern Ireland:
War No More

Questions for Discussion

Section 1

1. Explain how the English-Irish conflict became a conflict over religion.

2. What does it mean for religion to be "established"?

3. How was religion a factor in the colonization of America?

4. Was the U.S. struggle for independence violent, nonviolent, or both? Explain.

5. In what circumstances is revolution justified?

6. Why does dividing ("partitioning") a country to end ethnic, racial, or religious conflict often fail to resolve the problem? How may it, in fact, create greater problems?

Section 2

1. Have you ever experienced discrimination? In what way?

2. What would be the political effect if U.S. citizens who rent apartments rather than own homes were not permitted to vote?

3. Should people be permitted to demonstrate or march, even if it offends others and may result in a civil disturbance? Why?

4. If you were a government leader in Northern Ireland in 1969, what could you have done to prevent violence that summer?

5. Look up the word boycott in the dictionary. What is the origin of the word?

6. What other nonviolent forms of protest could be used?

Section 3

1. The IRA claimed it was fighting for democracy. The IRA also claimed their revolutionary methods were morally justified because the present government was illegitimate. Do you agree or disagree? Explain.

2. How were British soldiers unsuited for the policing role they were given in Northern Ireland? What is internment?

3. What are "paramilitaries" and why are they formed? In what ways are they dangerous—in addition to their use of violence? Can you think of any movements in the U.S. today that are similar?

4. What protections do U.S. citizens have against internment. During WWII, whom did the U.S. government place in internment camps? Was it a violation of the Constitution?

5. Amnesty International is an organization that advocates on behalf of persons whose human rights are being violated. Go to its web page and see what cases it is currently working on. Where are people currently being detained without charges and imprisoned without fair trials? What can be done to help these people?

Section 4 and 5

1. How did the pope challenge Sinn Fein? How did Sinn Fein challenge the Church?

2. Identify each of the groups that were eventually involved in the years of negotiations between 1985 and 1995.

3. What is a mediator? What is the difference between wants and needs? What did the unionists have to give up? What did the nationalists have to give up?

4. What political principles were discussed and consented to?

Section 6

1. Seeking forgiveness or offering forgiveness is difficult and complex. What do you personally think must be the steps in the forgiveness process?

2. What caused Spence, Hutchinson, and Doherty to change their minds about violence?

3. A U.S. historian conducted a research project in Northern Ireland that explored ways to overcome prejudice. Neighboring Catholic and Protestant churches held joint meetings for several weeks at which parishioners discussed their attitudes toward one another. The study found that personal encounters between individuals do not break down stereotypes, but that encounters between groups do. Why are group encounters more successful than relationships between individuals?

Section 7

1. What kind of self-examination must parties in a social conflict undertake?

2. How can politicians help the peace process? Why is it risky for them?

3. The government is responsible for preserving law and order. What

are the most and the least effective ways it can discourage violence?

4. How can the churches be involved in the peace process? How is memory important?

Terms to Know	Names to Know
internment	Orangemen
decommissioning	Northern Ireland Civil Rights Association
shared rule	the Peace People

Additional Resources

A.
Martin Dillon, *God and the Gun: The Church and Irish Terrorism*
John Feehan, *Bobby Sands and the Tragedy of Northern Ireland*
Bobby Sands, *Diary of Bobby Sands*

B.
John Montague, *A Slow Dance.*
Brian Moore, *Lies of Silence*
Daniel Gerard Morrison, *West Belfast*
Glenn Patterson, *Burning Your Own*
Graham Reid, *The Hidden Curriculum, Remembrance, The Billy Plays, Ties of Blood* (plays)

C.
The Crying Game
In the Name of the Father
Patriot Games

D.
Amnesty International (www.amnesty.org//ailib/countries)
The "Conflict Archive on the Internet" (CAIN) gathers information about several conflict areas throughout the world, including Northern Ireland. See www.incore,ulst,ac,uk/cds/countries/nireland
For general information about peace activities in Ireland, see www.peacejam.org
Irish Newspapers provide the most up-to-date information on the

peace process. For example, see the *Irish Times* on line (www.irish-times/paper/1999)
Most political parties also have web sites. For example, see www.sinnfein.ie

Chapter Three: South Africa's Stain of Apartheid

Questions for Discussion

Sections 1 and 2

1. How did the Boers' experience with the British affect their attitudes toward native Africans?

2. Respond to the claim of Afrikaner political leaders that tribal peoples would be corrupted in urban settings and thus belonged in rural areas.

Sections 3 and 4

1. How did the political objective of the ANC differ from that of the PAC?

2. What was the Congress of the People and why were its members charged with treason?

3. After the anti-apartheid political parties were banned, what organizations continued the struggle?

4. How did racial issues in the U.S. in the 1960s affect racial issues in South Africa?

5. In what ways did churches outside of South Africa influence racial issues in the country?

6. Who was Steve Biko and what was the Black Consciousness Movement?

Sections 5 and 6

1. What made the churches' stand against apartheid more effective in the 1960s and 1970s?

2. What were the churches doing in the 1980s that brought government retaliation?

3. What was the attitude of the churches toward the use of violence in the struggle?

4. What events brought about the virtual collapse of the government in 1989?

5. What tactics did the Afrikaner National Party use to blunt the political popularity of the ANC?

Sections 7 and 8

1. We can respond to injustices and harm done by trying to blot out their memory, by attempting to bring to justice all those who were responsible, or by overcoming them with forgiveness and reconciliation. Discuss the pros and cons of each response.

2. In your view, what is the most impressive achievement of South Africa since 1990?

3. How were whites affected by the collapse of apartheid?

4. What are the most critical problems facing South Africa today?

Terms to Know	Names to Know
banning	Boers
homelands (Bantustans)	Dutch Reform Church
amnesty	Black Consciousness Movement

Additional Resources

A.

Steve Biko, *I write What I Like*
Allan Boesak, *Farewell to Innocence*
Frank Chicane, *No life of My Own*
Cosmos Desmond, *The Discarded People*
Brian Frost, *Struggling to Forgive: Nelson Mandela and South Africa's Search for   Reconciliation*
Trevor Huddleston, *Naught for Your Comfort*
Govan Mbeki, *Learning from Robben Island: The Prison Writings of Govan Mbeki*
Allister Sparks, *Tomorrow Is Another Country*
Desmond Tutu, *No Future without Forgiveness*
Michael Worsnip, *Michael Lapsley: Priest and Partisan*

B.

Mark Behr, *The Smell of Apples*
J. M. Coetzee, *Age of Iron, From the Heart of the Country*
Nadine Gordimer, *Crimes of Conscience, July's People, None to*

Accompany Me
Alex la Guma, *In the Fog of the Season's End*
Alan Paton, *Ah, But Your Land Is Beautiful, Cry, the Beloved Country*
Sindiwe Magona, *Mother to Mother*
Beverley Naidoo, *No Turning Back*

C.
Cry, Freedom
Witness to Apartheid (a documentary by Sharon Sopher)
Last Grave at Dimbaza (doc.)
The Power of One
Cry, the Beloved Country, Long Night's Journey into Day (doc.)

D.
Southern African Catholic Bishops Conference
(www.sacbc.org.za)
Government of South Africa (www.polity.org.za/govdocs

Chapter Four: Nonviolent Triumphs of Democracy: Poland, East Germany, and the Philippines

Questions for Discussion

1. Why do oppressive social situations often produce spiritual and moral renewal of societies?

2. What kind of victory was the Church in Poland and Lech Walesa seeking?

3. Nonviolent resistance has been used especially by groups with little military capability. In what sense is their weakness also their strength?

4. How can people who are not experiencing oppression and powerlessness cultivate nonviolence?

Terms to Know

Friedensdekade
"People Power"
solidarity

Chapter Five: Blood Brothers in the Balkans

Questions for Discussion

Section 1

1. Describe some of the distinguishing features of a "nation." How do nations differ from empires? Identify a historical empire.

2. What kind of political units did Otto Von Bismarck unify in the mid nineteenth century? What kind of argument did he make for their unification?

3. As typologies, what values do "civic" and "ethnic" forms of nationalism exhibit?

4. Explain the notion "national self-determination"? Do you think the notion will prevent or cause war?

Section 2

1. What kind of political unit was Yugoslavia?

2. In what ways was Bosnia and its capital city of Sarajevo a more tolerant society than other areas of Europe from the fifteenth through the nineteenth centuries?

3. What sort of democratic practices could help to restrain the forces of ethnic nationalists?

4. Group Denitch's recommendation for peace in the Balkans into political, economic, and cultural categories and discuss how they could concretely be implemented?

5. On a map of pre-World War I, locate the borders of the six Balkan republics. How do they compare to the present borders?

6. Look up the "Dayton Accords" (1995) on the Internet. How might the renewed ethnic violence against Albanian Kosovars that broke out in 1998 have been prevented?

Section 3

1. According to Ignatieff, how do wars waged to achieve ethnic unity actually destroy that unity and become nihilistic?

2. Many argue that ethnic purity is a fiction and that a pure ethnic community is an impossibility. Do you agree or disagree? Explain.

3. In Catholic political thought, sovereignty is not only a nation's right but also its leaders' responsibility. What kind of responsibility is it?

4. Are national sovereignty and internationalism opposing or complementary ideas? Explain.

5. Croatia claimed national sovereignty in 1991. According to Elshatain, how would an authentic Croatian sovereignty be manifested?

Section 4

1. What did Cardinal Kuharic insist is part of preserving one's humanity in the Balkans?

2. According to Schreiter, how does memory function in the process of reconciliation between people?

3. Although Christians have often failed to engage in reconciliation, how does Christian theology oblige them to do so?

4. Imagine you are the leader of a religious community in the Balkans. Why will it take a great deal of courage to be an agent of reconciliation?

Terms to Know	**Names to Know**
civic and ethnic nationalism	Holy Roman Empire
sovereignty	Balkans and "balkanization"

Additional Resources

A.
Zlata Filipovic, *Zlata's Diary: A Child's Life in Sarajevo*
Roger Rosenblatt, *Children of War*

B.
Slavenka Drakulic, *"S": A Novel about the Balkans*
Dan Fesperman, *Lie in the Sark*

C.
Welcome to Sarajevo
Underground

Chapter Six: Justice and Peace in the Middle East

Questions for Discussion

Section 1

1. Why did so many European Jews emigrate to Palestine in the late eighteenth century and early nineteenth century?

2. Who ruled Palestine at the time?

3. What was Britain's self-interest in helping the Jews establish a homeland in Palestine?

Section 2

1. What is Zionism?

2. What was the difference between a Jewish homeland and Jewish state in Palestine?

3. Why did the Jewish population of Palestine quintuple between 1922 and 1937?

Section 3

1. What effect did the declaration of the State of Israel in 1948 have on Palestinians?

2. What was the effect of Israel's occupation of the West Bank and Gaza in 1967?

3. Where were Jewish settlements established beginning in the 1970s and what was their purpose?

Section 4

1. What does *intifada* mean?

2. Look up *Black Like Me* by Howard Griffin and compare it to the expose of Israeli journalist Yoram Binur.

3. How did the military service laws of Israel bring the Palestinian situation "home" to many Israelis?

4. New hopes for peace and a Palestinian state were kindled in the Oslo Accords (1993). What happened to the peace plan?

Section 5

1. What kind of nonviolent resistance has been attempted by the Palestinians?

2. What makes Jerusalem so important to Israelis and to Palestinians? What kind of an arrangement could be made regarding Jerusalem that would preserve what is important to all parties?

3. What should Christian churches be doing in the cause of Middle East peace?

Additional Resources

A.
See chapter endnotes.

B
Amos Oz, *Lebanon*
_____, *The Smile of the Lamb*
Elie Weisel, *Dawn*

C.
The Oasis of Peace (documentary produced by CNN in its "Waging Peace" series)
Cup Final (in Hebrew with subtitles, First Run Features)

Terms to Know	**Names to Know**
Zionism	"Law of Return"
intifada	West Bank and Gaza Strip
	Noble Sanctuary/Temple Mount

Chapter Seven: Race in the United States: Where do we go from here?

Questions for Discussion

1. How aware are you of race and racial tension in your daily life? What are your own assumptions about race as we discuss the topic?

2. How are self-esteem, economic power, and political power connected?

3. Is "color blindness" desirable? Would there be both positive and negative social effects? Explain.

4. Compare the life experiences reported by Josiah Henson, the former slave, and the life of the mother whose children died in the house fire in 1990.

5. What concretely could Christian congregations do to overcome the fact that "Sunday mornings in the U.S. are still the most segregated time of the week"?

6. Propose ideas for making a difference about race in each of these areas: (1) personal discernment; 2) public discussion; and 3) community commitment.

<table>
<tr><td align="center">**Terms to Know**</td><td align="center">**Names to Know**</td></tr>
<tr><td align="center">racism and prejudice
race fatigue</td><td align="center">Black Power Movement
Black theology</td></tr>
</table>

Additional Resources

A., B., and C.
Prose, poetry, plays, and films dealing with race issues in the United States are too numerous to name here. In fall 2001 the City of Chicago Public Library system sponsored a program encouraging Chicagoans to read and discuss with one another *To Kill a Mockingbird,* Harper Lee's compelling story of courage in the face of racism.

Chapter Eight: Women Struggling for Justice and Peace

Questions for Discussion

1. In what ways do women in U.S. society continue to experience oppression?

2. What are some of the special strengths of the women you read about in this chapter?

3. What other women-led activism can you name?

4. Why has the U.S. government refused to sign the Convention on the Rights of the Child and the Convention on the Elimination of All Forms of Discrimination Against Women?

5. What can be done to resist modern forms of slavery? (Consult the Appendix of *Disposable People* by Kevin Bales for a list of advocacy organizations.)

Terms to Know	Names to Know
noncombatant immunity	Mothers of the Plaza de Mayo
debt bondage	Black Sash
low intensity warfare	Women in Black
	STITCH

Additional Resources

Prose, poetry, plays, and films dealing with discrimination against women and women struggling for justice are numerous. The following sources address children and war and child labor.

A.

Roberta Apfel and Bennett Simon, eds., *Minefields in Their Hearts*
Rene Cohn and Guy Goodwin-Gill, *Child Soldiers*

B.

Marjorie Agosin, *A Map of Hope*

C.

"Soon We Will Finish" (UNICEF film about children carpet-makers in Nepal)

Endnotes

Introduction

1. John Paul II, "On Social Concern" no. 8.

2. Catholic moral teaching has developed eight criteria to help political and military leaders and citizens consider the moral permissibility of warfare. Six of them address *whether* resort to arms is justifiable: (1) justifiable cause, (2) legitimate authority, (3) right intention, (4) last resort, (5) probability of success, and (6) the good to be realized through warfare may not be outweighed by the probable harm caused. The remaining two criteria address the *manner* in which war is waged: (7) the lethal force used against a nation's military personnel must not exceed what is sufficient to achieve the justifiable objective, (8) civilians may not be directly attacked. For a discussion of these criteria, their meaning, their historical development, and their application to the Gulf War (1991), see Michael Duffey, *Peacemaking Christians: The Future of Just Wars, Pacifism, and Nonviolent Resistance* (Sheed & Ward, 1995).

Chapter One

1. Cristobal Colon, *Journals and Other Documents,* trans. Samuel Morrison (New York: 1963), vol I, 90.

2. Ibid., 91.

3. Ibid., 149.

4. For a fuller account see David Traboulay, *Columbus and Las Casas: The Conquest and Christianization of America, 1492–1566* (Lanham, MD: University Press of America, 1994).

5. Miguel Leon-Portilla, *Fray Anton de Montesinos (*Mexico City: Fondo de Cultura Económica, 1982), 12.

6. Bartolomé de Las Casas, *History of the Indies,* 3 vols., ed. Augustin Millares Carlo and Lewis Kanke (Mexico City: Fondo

de Cultura Económica, 1951; English trans. New York: Harper and Row, 1971), book 3.

7. Helder Camara, "CELAM: History Is Implacable," *Cross Currents* (Spring 1978), 56.

8. Synod of Bishops, "Justice in the World," (Rome, 1971), no. 36.

9. Gary MacEoin, *The People's Church: Bishop Samuel Ruiz of Mexico and Why He Matters* (New York: Crossroad, 1996), 26.

10. Ibid., 37, 26.

11. Virgil Elizondo, *Galilean Journey* (Maryknoll, NY: Orbis, 1983).

12. Pope John Paul II, "Opening Address at the Puebla Conference" (January 28,1979), III, no. 1.

13. Ibid., I, no. 5.

14. Ibid., III, no. 7.

15. Pope John Paul II, "Address to the Indians of Oaxaca and Chiapas" (January 29, 1979).

16. Global Trade Watch, "NAFTA's Broken Promises: The Border Betrayed 1996" (January 1996), 43. Document is available at www.tradewatch.org

17. Penny Lernoux, "The Long Path to Puebla," in *Puebla and Beyond,* John Eagleson and Philip Scharper, eds. (Maryknoll, NY: Orbis, 1979), 17–18.

18. Brian Willson, "NAFTA Versus Life," Report of a U.S. Veterans Delegation to Southern Mexico (April 7–24, 1997), 2.

19. José Saramago, "Chiapas, A Name of Pain and Hope," trans. Gregory Rabassa. Foreword to *Our Word Is Our Weapon: Selected Writings of Subcomandante Insurgente Marcos.* Juana Ponce de León, ed. (New York: Seven Stories Press, 2001), xx–xxi.

Chapter Two

1. William Gladstone, *Speeches on Home Rule,* quoted in P. S. O'Hegarty, *A History of Ireland Under the Union* (London: Methuen and Co., 1952), 553.

2. Tim Pat Coogan, *The Troubles* (London: Hutchinson, 1995), 90.

3. Ibid., 74.

4. Ibid., 88.

5. Ibid., 82.

6. Carolyn Kennedy-Pipe, *The Origin of the Present Troubles in Northern Ireland* (London: Longman, 1971), 54.

7. John Hume, *Personal Views: Politics, Peace and Reconciliation in Ireland* (Dublin: Town House, 1996), 156.

8. Gerry Adams, *Before the Dawn: An Autobiography* (New York: William Morrow, 1996), 326–327.

9. Quoted by Adams, *Before the Dawn*, 287.

10. Gerry Adams, *Free Ireland: Toward a Lasting Peace* (Dingle, Ireland: Brandon, 1885), 243.

11. "Mairead Corrigan, Betty Williams Biographies" (www.gale.com/gale/cwh/corriga).

12. Quoted in David McKittrick, *The Nervous Peace* (Belfast: Blackstaff Press, 1996), 110.

13. Quotations of McGoldrick, Armstrong, Hill, Kerr, Clarke, and Porter are from transcripts of interviews associated with "For God or Ulster: Northern Ireland Takes a Leap of Faith Toward Peace," *Christianity Today,* vol. 41, no. 11 (October 6, 1997), 74–78, found at www2.Christianity.net/ct/archives.

14. Quoted by McKittrick.

15. Billy Hutchinson is quoted in Darina Molloy, "Decommissioning Dogs Peace Process," vol 14, no. 6 (December 31, 1998).

16. Joe Doherty is quoted in Brian Rohan, "The Prisoner" *Irish America,* vol. 14, no. 5 (October 31, 1998), 38.

17. *Milwaukee Journal Sentinel* (August 23, 1998), 3A.

18. "In Northern Ireland Guns Turned to Scrap," *Milwaukee Journal Sentinel* (December 19, 1998), 3A.

Chapter Three

1. Trevor Huddleston, quoted in Charles Villa-Vicencio, *The Spirit of Freedom* (Berkeley: University of California Press, 1996), 134.

2. Ibid.

3. Alan Paton, *Cry, the Beloved Country* (New York: Scribners, 1948).

4. Nelson Mandela, *Mandela: An Illustrated Autobiography* (Boston: Little, Brown and Company, 1994), 148.

5. John Vorster, quoted in Mokgethi Motlhabi, *Challenge to Apartheid: Toward a National Moral Resistance* (Grand Rapids: Eerdmans, 1988), 151.

6. Steve Biko, *I Write What I Like* (London: Heinemann, 1978), 51.

7. Desmond Tutu, quoted in Tristan Anne Borer, *Challenging the State: Churches as Political Actors in South Africa, 1980–1994* (Notre Dame, IN: University of Notre Dame Press, 1998), 52.

8. Borer, 64.

9. SACBC, "The Bishops Speak" vol. 4, 1986–1987 (Pretoria: SACBC, 1989), 8.

10. Nelson Mandela, *The Long Walk to Freedom* (Boston: Little, Brown and Company, 1996), 246.

11. Quoted in Borer, 81.

12. See Charles Villa-Vicencio, *Theology and Violence* (Grand Rapids: Eerdmans, 1988), 301.

13. Walter Wink, *Violence and Nonviolence in South Africa* (Philadelphia: New Society Publishers, 1987), 6.

14. Borer, 71.

15. Ibid., 73.

16. Ibid., 74.

17. Ibid., 77.

18. John W. DeGruchy, "The Dialectic of Reconciliation" in *The Reconciliation of Peoples: Challenge to the Churches,* ed. Gregory Baum and Harold Wells (Maryknoll, NY: Orbis Press, 1997), 18.

19. Government of South Africa, Truth and Reconciliation Commission (www.polity.org.za/govdocs/pr/2000).

20. Beyers Naude, quoted in Villa-Vicencio, 231.

21. See the SACBC Website (www.sacbc.org.za/justice)

22. Desmond Tutu, quoted in Villa-Vicencio, 283.

Chapter Four

1. Quoted in Mary Craig, *Lech Walesa and His Poland* (New York: Continuum, 1987), 56.

2. Craig, 114.

3. Craig, 125.

4. Craig, 85.

5. Craig, 125.

6. Craig, 204.

7. Craig, 182.

8. Craig, 193.

9. Pope John Paul II, "Church and State in Poland: Address to the Polish Bishops" (June 5, 1979).

10. Quoted in Rainer Hildebrand, *From Gandhi to Walesa* (Berlin: Verlag Hausam Checkpoint Charlie, 1987), 146.

11. For a full list of the demands, see Jean-Yves Potel, *The Promise of Solidarity* (New York: Praeger Publishers, 1982), 219–220.

12. Craig, 195.

13. Craig, 214.

14. Craig, 234.

15. Quoted in Hildebrand, 142.

16. Craig, 271.

17. *Time* (November 12, 1984), 58.

18. Helmar Junghans, "The Christians' Contribution to the Non-violent Revolution in the GDR in the Fall of 1989," *Philosophy and Theology* 6, 1 (Fall 1991), 79–93, at 80.

19. Junghans, 81.

20. Junghans, 91.

21. Junghans, 89.

22. Junghans, 91.

23. Jorg Swoboda, *The Revolution of the Candles* (Wuppertal und Kassel: Oncken Verlag, 1990), 5.

24. See Timothy G. Ash, *We the People: The Revolution of Eighty-Nine*.

25. The West German peace movement arose precisely out of the perception of the futility of a war in Europe, particularly a war involving the use of nuclear weapons. The protests on behalf of human rights in Eastern Europe and on behalf of nuclear disarmament in West Germany drew on a variety of sources and attracted a variety of participants. Among the extensive literature on European peace movements, see *West European Pacifism and the Strategy for Peace*, Peter van den Dungen, ed. (New York: St. Martin's Press, 1985).

26. Glen Stassen, *Just Peacemaking: Transforming Initiatives for Justice and Peace* (Louisville: Westminster/John Knox Press, 1992), 18.

27. Quoted in Lewis Simons, *Worth Dying For* (New York: William Morrow, 1987), 43.

28. Bryan Johnson, *The Four Days of Courage* (New York: The Free Press, 1987), 46.

29. Johnson, 53.

30. Johnson, 53.

31. Johnson, 53.

32. Johnson, 49.

33. Johnson, 57.

34. Johnson, 60.

35. Simons, 94.

Chapter Five

1. William Pfaff, *The Wrath of Nations* (New York: Schuster, 1993), 30.

2. Pfaff, 23.

3. Pfaff, 46.

4. Pfaff, 47.

5. *Zlata's Diary: A Child's Life in Sarajevo*, trans. by Christina Pibichevich-Zoric (New York: Viking, 1994), 145–146.

6. Michael Ignatieff, *Blood and Belonging: Journeys into the New Nationalism* (New York: Farrar, Straus, and Giroux, 1994), 9.

7. Bogdan Denitch, *Ethnic Nationalism: The Tragic Death of Yugoslavia* (Minneapolis: University of Minnesota Press, 1994), 49.

8. Denitch, 77.

9. Denitch, 36.

10. Denitch, 71.

11. "A Sniper's Tale," *Time* (March 14, 1994), 24.

12. Ignatieff, 21, 24.

13. Pfaff, 217.

14. Pope John Paul II, Homily at Jasna Gora, 1983.

15. Ibid.

16. Jean Bethke Elshtain, "Identity, Sovereignty, and Self-determination," in *Peacemaking*, Gerald F. Powers, ed. (Washington, D.C.: United States Catholic Conference, 1994), 97–104, at 104.

17. Elshtain, 99.

18. Elshtain, 103.

19. Miroslav Volf, "Exclusion and Embrace" *Journal of Ecumenical Studies*, vol. 29 (Spring 1992), 233–234.

20. Volf, 233.

21. Denitch, 30.

22. Denitch, 87.

23. Franjo Kuharic, "Appeal to Croatians and Muslims," reprinted in *Origins* 23 (June 3, 1993), 23.

24. Robert Schreiter, *Reconciliation* (Maryknoll, NY: Orbis, 1992), 21.

25. Schreiter, 22.

26. Schreiter, 38.

27. Schreiter, 11.

28. Schreiter, 36.

29. Ralph R. Premdas, "The Church and Ethnic Conflicts in the Third World," *The Ecumenist,* vol. 1, no. 4 (May-June 1994), 55.

30. Schreiter, 66.

31. Donald Shriver, *An Ethic for Enemies: Forgiveness in Politics* (New York: Oxford University Press, 1995), 9.

32. Federal Republic of Germany, "Restitution," quoted in Shriver, 89.

33. Shriver, 91.

34. Shriver, 99.

35. Shriver, 88.

36. Shriver, 85.

37. Shriver, 84.

Chapter Six

1. Karen Armstrong, *Jerusalem: One City, Three Faiths* (New York: Alfred A. Knopf, 1996), 400.

2. For the story of President Carter's successful mediation between Israel and Egypt, see Jimmy Carter, *Talking Peace* (New York: Dutton, 1993).

3. Quotes are taken from David Grossman's interviews of Palestinians in *The Yellow Wind* (New York: Farrar, Straus and Giroux, 1988).

4. Glenn Frankel, *Beyond the Promised Land: Jews and Arabs on the Hard Road to a New Israel* (New York: Simon and Schuster, 1994), 76. For other accounts of this period see also Thomas L. Friedman, *From Beirut to Jerusalem* (New York: Farrar, Straus and Giroux, 1989).

5. Yoram Binur, *My Enemy, My Self* (New York: Doubleday, 1989), 197.

6. Ibid., 205.

7. See Phyllis Bennis, *From Stones to Statehood: The Palestinian Uprising* (New York: Olive Branch Press, 1989).

8. Quoted in Conor Cruise O'Brien, *The Siege: The Saga of Israel and Zionism* (New York: Simon and Schuster, 1986), 359.

9. Michael Lerner, "Current Debate," *Tikkun,* vol. 15, no. 4 (July-August 2000), 27.

10. See www.peace-now.org

11. Grossman, 39, 41.

12. Armstrong, 172.

13. David K. Shipler, *Arab and Jew: Wounded Spirits in a Promised Land* (New York: Times Books, 1986), 15–16.

14. Armstrong, *Jerusalem,* 419.

Chapter Seven

1. Martin Luther King, Jr., "Where Do We Go from Here?"

2. Ibid.

3. Ibid.

4. Ibid.

5. Leonard Steinhorn and Barbara Diggs-Brown, *By the Color of Our Skin: The Illusion of Integration and the Reality of Race* (New York: Dutton, 1999), 118.

6. Ibid., 200.

7. Mirta Ojito, "Best Friends, Worlds Apart," *New York Times* (June 5, 2000), A1

8. Ibid., A17.

9. Peggy McIntosh, "White Privilege: Unpacking the Invisible Knapsack," *Peace and Freedom* (July-August 1989), 10–12.

10. Steinhorn and Diggs-Brown, 31.

11. Leonard Pitts, "Those Pesky Vestiges of Slavery," *Miami Herald* (September 9, 2000).

12. Harlon Dalton, *Racial Healing: Confronting the Fear between Blacks and Whites* (New York: Doubleday, 1995), 154.

13. Steven Mintz, editor, *African American Voices: The Life Cycle of Slavery* (St. James, NY: Brandywine Press, 1996), 101–102.

14. Benjamin DeMott, *The Trouble with Friendship: Why Americans Can't Think Straight about Race* (New York: Atlantic Monthly Press, 1995), 125.

15. Ibid.

16. Ibid., 135.

17. Ibid., 144.

18. Dalton, 156.

19. Cornel West, *Race Matters* (New York: Vintage Books, 1994), 28.

20. Melvin Van Peebles, quoted in *By the Color of Our Skin*, 136.

21. Quoted in Carl M. Cannon, ". . . Show a Little Mercy," *George* (December-January 2001), 36.

22. Albert Raboteau, *A Fire in the Bones* (Boston: Beacon Press, 1995), 52.

23. Quoted from Marilyn Richardson, *Maria Stewart: America's First Black Woman Political Writer* (Bloomington, IN: Indiana University Press, 1987), 39.

24. Martin Luther King, Jr., *Stride Toward Freedom* (New York: Harper and Row, 1958), 63.

25. "Statement by the National Committee of Negro Churchmen," in Gayraud S. Wilmore and James H. Cone, *Black Theology: A Documentary History, 1966–1979* (Maryknoll, NY: Orbis Press, 1973), 23.

26. "Statement from the Black and White Caucuses, National Conference of Churches, Conference on the Church and Urban Tensions (September 27–30, 1967)" in Wilmore and Cone, *Black Theology*, 45–46.

27. Ibid., 47.

28. James Forman, "The Black Manifesto" in Wilmore and Cone, *Black Theology*, 80–89.

29. Malcolm X, quoted in James Cone, *Martin and Malcolm and America* (Maryknoll, NY: Orbis, 1991), 166. See also *The Autobiography of Malcolm X* (New York: Grove Press, 1964), 164, 241.

30. James H. Cone, *Black Theology and Black Power* (New York: Seabury, 1969), excerpted in Wilmore and Cone, *Black Theology*, 112.

31. Ibid., 113.

32. Ibid., 118.

33. Ibid., 124.

34. Ibid., 131.

35. James H. Cone, *For My People: Black Theology and the Black Church* (Maryknoll, NY: Orbis Press, 1984), 116.

36. Beverly Daniel Tatum, "Talking about Race, Learning about Racism: The Application of Racial Identity Development Theory

in the Classroom," *Harvard Educational Review,* vol. 62, no.1 (Spring 1992), 5.

37. Ibid., 7.

38. Ibid., 18.

39. Theorists of black racial identity development describe five stages: 1) pre-reflective absorbing of the dominant culture's beliefs which disvalue black identity; 2) personal experience of racism's negative impact; 3) defense of one's racial identity against further diminishment; 4) racial self-assurance that permits the establishing of relationships across racial lines; and 5) a general sense of commitment to blacks as a group that grows to encompass concern for other groups as well. The stages of white racial identity are: 1) an initial lacking of awareness of cultural racism and race-based personal privileges; 2) recognition of racism and privilege causing shame and guilt; 3) acceptance of racism in order to be accepted by other whites unless or until one decides to move beyond this stage; 4) disavowal of racism but few alternative ways of behaving or contacts with blacks; and 5) active confronting of racism and alliances with other people combating racism.

40. Ellis Cose, *Color Blind* (New York: HarperCollins, 1997), 242.

41. The Catholic Archdiocese of Chicago has taken vigorous steps to overcome racism in society, addressing especially its own church administration, parishes, and schools. The archdiocese's Office of Racial Justice has offered workshops on Racism and Ethnic Sensitivity in over half of the 378 parishes in the archdiocese. Its Office of Catholic Schools' Racial Justice Committee works with Catholic schools to oppose racism and to attain greater racial and ethnic diversity among teachers and staff (www.archdiocese-chgo.org). On the thirty-third anniversary of the assassination of Martin Luther King, Jr., Cardinal Francis George, Archbishop of Chicago, issued a pastoral letter entitled "Dwelling in My Love: A Pastoral Letter on Racism" (April 4, 2001). The cardinal described the multiple manifestations of racism (spatial, institutional, individual, and internalized), urged all parishes to address these issues, and listed the steps that must be taken to overcome racism within parishes, schools, as well as in economic and political structures of society. He called on Catholics to uphold just housing principles and to vote for

public officials "committed to racial and systemic justice" (www.archdiocese-chgo.org/newsreleases/news 040401). A year earlier, Cardinal George joined his fellow bishops of Illinois in issuing a pastoral letter entitled "Moving beyond Racism: Learning to See with the Eyes of Christ." For information on what the Catholic Church at the national level is doing to combat racism, see the web site of the National Conference of Catholic Bishops/United States Catholic Conference Secretariat for African American Catholics (www.nccbuscc.org/saac).

42. Danny Duncan Collum, *Black and White Together: The Search for Common Ground* (Maryknoll, NY: Orbis Press, 1996), 98.

43. Dalton, *Racial Healing*, 234.

Chapter Eight

1. www.un.org/womenwatch/daw.cedaw

2. James Garbarino, *No Place to Be a Child: Growing Up in a War Zone* (Lexington, MA: Lexington Books, 1991), 14.

3. Amnesty International, "Human Rights Violations against Women in Kosovo Province" (AI Index: EUR 70/54/98, Document Series B.#1, August, 1998).

4. Slavenka Drakulic, *"S": A Novel about the Balkans* (New York: Viking, 2000).

5. Amnesty International, "Child Soldiers" (www.amnestyusa.org/children/soldiers).

6. "Domestic Violence Against Women and Girls," UNICEF, 2000.

7. Psychologists and therapists talk about the "funnel effect" in which the causes of anger are not addressed. Such anger is bottled up and explosively released, often on spouses and children. See, for example, Willard Gaylin, *The Rage Within* and Raymond Novaco, *Anger Control.*

8. Nadine Gordimer, *July's People* (New York: Viking), 1981.

9. Archdiocese of Guatemala, *Guatemala: Never Again, Recovery of Historical Memory Project,* English translation (Maryknoll, NY: Orbis Press, 1998), 83.

10. Quoted in Rita Arditti, *Searching for Life* (Berkeley: University of California Press, 1999), 35. See also Marjorie Agosin, *The*

Mothers of the Plaza de Mayo. See also www.margres.org and www.desparacidos.org.

11. Claribel Alegria, "A Writer's Commitment" in *A Map of Hope: Women's Writings on Human Rights—An International Anthology,* edited by Marjorie Agosin (New Bruswick, NJ: Rutgers University Press, 1999), 351.

12. Gerry Adams, *Free Ireland: Toward a Lasting Peace* (Dingle, Ireland: Brandon, 1885), 151.

13. Ibid., 164.

14. Sheena Duncan is quoted in Charles Villa-Vicencio, *The Spirit of Freedom,* 84. See also *Lives of Courage: Women for a New South Africa* (London: Virago Press, 1990).

15. Ibid, 207.

16. Ibid., 257.

17. Ibid., 30.

18. Kevin Bales, *Disposable People: New Slavery in the Global Economy* (Berkeley: University of California Press, 1999), 7.

19. See www.unicef.org/crc/convention

20. Rosario Castellanos, "Indian Mother" in *Another Way to Be: Selected Works of Rosario Castellanos,* Rosario Castellanos. Foreword by Edward D. Terry. University of Georgia Press, 17, 19.

21. M. Shawn Copeland, "The New Anthropological Subject at the Heart of the Mystical Body of Christ," *Proceedings of the Catholic Theological Society of America,* vol. 53 (June 1998), 25.

22. Ibid., 28.

23. Ibid., 27.

24. Ibid., 42.

25. Hattie Gossett, "World View" in Agosin, *A Map of Hope,* 352.

26. Quoted by Hillary Klein, "Women and Indigenous Autonomy" (Chiapas, Mexico: Center for Economic and Political Investigations of Community Action), n.d.

27. Copeland, "The New Anthropological Subject at the Heart of the Mystical Body of Christ," *Proceedings of the Catholic Theological Society of America,* vol. 53 (June 1998), 43.

Index